If I Had My Druthers

If I Had My Druthers

Terri Austin Chiles

iUniverse, Inc.
New York Lincoln Shanghai

If I Had My Druthers

Copyright © 2006 by Terri D. Austin

All rights reserved. No part of this book may be used or reproduced by any means, graphic, electronic, or mechanical, including photocopying, recording, taping or by any information storage retrieval system without the written permission of the publisher except in the case of brief quotations embodied in critical articles and reviews.

iUniverse books may be ordered through booksellers or by contacting:

iUniverse
2021 Pine Lake Road, Suite 100
Lincoln, NE 68512
www.iuniverse.com
1-800-Authors (1-800-288-4677)

ISBN-13: 978-0-595-39227-8 (pbk)
ISBN-13: 978-0-595-83617-8 (ebk)
ISBN-10: 0-595-39227-X (pbk)
ISBN-10: 0-595-83617-8 (ebk)

Printed in the United States of America

For Amanda

In a perfect world there would be no poverty, no racism and no illness.
In a perfect world.

Contents

Preface		xi
CHAPTER 1	The News	1
CHAPTER 2	Sweet Home Alabama	28
CHAPTER 3	The Boy Next Door	46
CHAPTER 4	The Knight in Shining Armor	53
CHAPTER 5	Newark	59
CHAPTER 6	School Days	72
CHAPTER 7	Summer Days	84
CHAPTER 8	Open Doors	92
CHAPTER 9	The Disappointment	103
CHAPTER 10	The Last	106
CHAPTER 11	The Diagnosis	111
CHAPTER 12	Christmas	118
CHAPTER 13	WalkingHome	134
CHAPTER 14	Final Days	159
CHAPTER 15	The Legacy	196
CHAPTER 16	Saving the Best for Last	210
Afterword		215

Acknowledgments

This book was a labor of love, first conceived by my mother and me when we both thought she would survive her battle with cancer. After ten years, nine months and twenty-one days, the book is finally finished. But who's counting. Writing on the train and on your laptop in bed at midnight tends to take a bit longer.

I must thank all my family and friends who have supported me along the way, too numerous to list in full: Aunt Adrienne and Aunt Yvonne (the latter of whom did not live to see the final product) both provided invaluable information about our family history; my cousin Ari, who remembers more details than anyone else in the family; Nancy Brown Jamison and all the Maude women for providing the nurturing love that women tend to give to each other; NTL where my mother's career first began to flourish; my brother Benji and sister Cathy, who have always believed in my success; my stepsisters Kathy and Barbie and their families for making me always feel like the alpha mother; my girlfriend Theresa Baker who would stop at nothing to support me; my girlfriend Angie Lorenzo, whose unwavering encouragement has lead me to believe that I could conquer the world; my dear friend Catherine Flax who actually took the time to read and edit selected parts of the manuscript despite her hectic schedule; my journalism colleagues Nick, Denene and Roy for supporting the good cause; my three children, Nicole, Christopher and Amanda, who are the light of my world and the reason I aim for the stars, however far away they may appear; and finally, my agent, editor, proof reader and husband Ben, who has put up with me through thick and thin and has read the manuscript so many times that he can recite much of it by heart, I give my utmost thanks, appreciation and never-ending love.

Preface

Two days after my mother Amanda's birth, the doctor told my grandmother that my mother would probably die. She had contracted whooping cough, a deadly illness in 1934. Two of Amanda's siblings had already died of the malady. She surprised them all with her strength and will to survive, characteristics that would later serve her well.

It was not easy being poor in the deep South. It was even more difficult being poor and African American. This is the true story of a determined black girl who survived an impoverished existence in Birmingham, Alabama with her parents and seven brothers and sisters. Her fortitude would take her on a fantastic voyage that included four marriages, five if you include the one day marriage to Walter. She traveled as far north as Canada and as far west as California. And she managed to succeed despite incredible trauma and tragedies.

Through the turmoil and confusion, she managed to raise three successful children, not to mention the fact that she opened her doors and her heart to help others less fortunate than herself. Her story will inspire you—to see the cup not half empty, but half full.

1
The News

Meeting adversity well is the source of your strength
Chinese Fortune Cookie (August 1994)

July 20, 1995, Thursday afternoon. The phone rang. I heard my secretary say, "I'm sorry, she's in a meeting right now. Can I take a message?" Then the intercom buzzed. Janie knew not to disturb me during a meeting unless it was urgent. Patience was not one of my virtues. I picked up the phone knowing that the call had something to do with my mother, or else Janie would not have interrupted. "I'm sorry to bother you," Janie said hesitantly, "but it's Larry and he needs to talk to you." I knew already that I could not bear hearing what he had to say. Larry, my mother's husband, did not call me often, and when he did, it was usually bad news, bad news about my mother's condition.

I apologized and asked my colleagues to step out of the office for a minute. I was in a meeting to discuss a claim against the company. I worked as an attorney in New York City for a large corporation. It was a very good job with an exceptionally good company. I picked up the telephone and Larry said, "Terri, your mother has taken a turn for the worse, in fact, she is dying. The doctors said it was going to be a matter of hours, maybe days, but not weeks."

For a moment, time stood still. Larry's words kept spinning around in my head, "matter of hours, maybe days, but not weeks." I inhaled slowly and deliberately but was unable to catch my breath. I tried to swallow but the lump in my throat blocked the passageway. There was a bottle of Evian water sitting on the desk in front of me, but I was too paralyzed to reach for it. I stared at the bottle and then at the wooden desk beneath it. I had never noticed the different hues of brown in the mahogany wood before now. The hues of color slowly swirled one into the other making me queasy. My styrofoam coffee cup sat half empty, typical for this time of morning. By noon, I would throw the rest of the coffee out, too cold to drink.

I brought myself back to harsh reality. Months of preparation had not prepared me for this moment. At first, I did not believe him. I sat there listening to his words, which he delivered in a bland, melancholy sort of way, like he had rehearsed these lines before. Was I the first person he called? Had he contacted my siblings, my aunts? Larry delivered the message of death because, as my mother's husband, he was theoretically closest to her at that moment in time. But back in the far recesses of my mind, I secretly thought that he felt some perverse pleasure in delivering this message to me. His voice was unwavering, reflecting pride and pleasure rather than sorrow and grief. Pride, because he was given the power to deliver this message. Pleasure, because he never liked me, and delivering such a message was sure to hurt me.

I tried to focus on my mother's condition. "Is it possible to calculate the time of death so precisely?" I asked Larry.

"No Terri, obviously it is not possible to predict exactly when someone is going to die," Larry said disdainfully. "The doctors simply said that, 'it would be a matter of hours, maybe days, but not weeks.'"

I knew from his curt response that this would be a relatively short conversation. I continued anyway. "How do the doctors know that Mama is dying? What exactly did they say? Maybe the doctors are wrong. Doctors are not always right you know."

Larry did his best to respond to my continued inquiry. Perhaps he sensed the desperation in my voice. Perhaps the tiny bit of compassion buried deep inside of him surfaced for just a moment. Perhaps not. After a slight pause and long sigh he said, "They said that her vital signs were getting weak and when that happens it would just be a matter of time."

I thought for a moment about what he had said. I debated questioning the comment about vital signs. Mama always said that I asked a lot of questions. But if her vital signs are weakening I thought, surely they have the ability to strengthen them. If her pulse is weak, then give her some more food or water or sugar or something. If she is breathing poorly, then maybe they should give her some oxygen. My logical mind was contemplating some way around this declaration of death. Something told me, however, to end the inquiry and accept his answers. The last thing in the world I wanted at this point was to end up embroiled in an argument with Larry. He was the most irascible man I had ever met, annoyed into fits of rage at the slightest provocation. I tentatively pushed the inquiry a bit further. This was, after all, my mother we were discussing.

"Can she talk?" I asked. I needed to hear for myself exactly how she was doing.

"She's really not up to it," he said, as the impatience predictably returned to his voice. "The pain medication makes her groggy."

He wasn't telling me anything I didn't already know. Mama had pain patches which were administered at certain pulse points to keep the pain at bay. She was also taking 10 milligram Vicodin tablets when the patches were not enough to reduce the pain. Both medications made her tired. It didn't matter to me if she was groggy. Groggy was better than nothing. I was sure that if Mama knew I was on the phone she would want to talk to me. But I also knew from my previous conversations with Larry that once he decided Mama was not coming to the phone, there would be no conversations with my mother that day. Unfortunately, there was not a thing I could do about it. They lived three thousand miles across the country in San Diego, California, leaving me with virtually no options if he chose to keep her away from the phone.

Larry reveled in manipulating other people's lives. He was not content unless he managed every detail of every single situation. He was the most controlling man I had ever met. Controlling and irascible, a potent combination to handle. I often wondered what my mother saw in him and why she married him in the first place.

It was obvious that I needed to travel back to San Diego as quickly as possible. I had just returned from there two weeks earlier. Mama was doing fine. Could she possibly be this sick so quickly? I was having difficulty grasping the magnitude of the whole situation. I felt strangely detached from the current circumstances, like a third person, outside of my body, observing life as it unfolded, watching events as they occurred, listening to conversations as they transpired. It had been like that often since my mother, Amanda, became ill.

I politely told Larry that I would leave on the first flight in the morning. Then I told him goodbye. I hung up the phone knowing that my life was about to change forever.

Janie, my secretary, had already closed the door to my office and sent the Company representatives on their way. I was grateful for that. I rested my forehead in my hands, elbows on the desk, rubbing my thumbs against the temples, my fingers against my hairline. For a moment my mind went completely blank. Then, all of a sudden, I wondered if Mama was in pain and whether she was coherent. Did she know that it would be "a matter of hours, maybe days, but not weeks?" Would I be able to make it from New York to San Diego in time? A swift panic rushed over me at the thought of not being present when she took her final breath. What if I don't get the chance to say goodbye? I would never forgive Larry if he caused me to miss the last opportunity to speak to my mother. My heart beat quickened and intensified, as though the muscle was about to explode out of my chest. My throat tightened and my eyes began to water. Despite my best efforts, I was unable to control the tears, the rush of emotion. I sat there, alone at my desk, sobbing uncontrollably.

Minutes later I calmed down and wondered if anyone could hear me crying through the closed door. Everyone at the office knew that my mother was dying of cancer. They also knew that it was only a matter of time before this call would come. Still, I didn't want them to know that I had lost my composure. Mama always told me, "Never let them see you sweat, and definitely don't ever let them see you cry." She knew that corporate America had little tolerance for crying women. She also knew that underneath my tough demeanor, my emotions lingered just beneath the surface, ready to erupt at the slightest provocation. If I became impatient or upset, Mama would tell me to relax and take a deep breath. She was a great believer in self control.

I tried to pull myself together. I grabbed a paper napkin from the desk drawer, left over from one of the many lunches at my desk. I dabbed my eyes on the hard substitute for a tissue, blew my nose and took three deep cleansing breaths. Snap out of it, I thought. I pushed the intercom button and asked Janie to come into the office. When I looked up, Janie was standing in front of the desk. She was only 23 or 24 years old, slender, quiet, soft spoken. She asked me if there was anything she could do for me. I told her to please get me a cup of fresh coffee (milk, no sugar) and to bring a pad for dictation. I was planning to be out of the office for the next few days, I said, and there were a number of items I needed her to handle in my absence.

Then she asked me, "Is it your mother?" I almost lost control again, but somehow I managed to restrain the tears this time. I cleared my throat and took a sip of the cold coffee. The cool liquid rolled down my dry throat, aching slightly as it passed over the lump which refused to dissipate. Just get me the damn coffee, I thought. Please, don't ask me so many questions. I was fine before she asked me that question. I hoped everyone would not be asking me questions about my mother because I didn't think I could remain composed. I pulled myself together again, more hard napkins, more deep breaths. I did not want to cry in front of Janie. If I could not remain composed in front of my own secretary, I thought, there was little hope that I would remain composed in front of everyone else.

"Yes, it's my mother, they said it was going to be a matter of hours, maybe days, but not weeks." There were those words again. I repeated them because I did not know what else to say. I repeated them because I had not yet formed my own conclusion, so those words would have to do.

"I'm sorry," Janie said. "I'm really sorry."

"Thank you," I said hesitantly. There was an awkward pregnant pause. I didn't know what else to say. Change the subject I thought. Quickly. Change the subject.

"You need to make reservations on the earliest flight in the morning to San Diego," I said abruptly.

Keep moving I thought, one step in front of the other, my mother would say.

"Leave the return date open," I told Janie, wondering when, in fact, I would return. Wondering if, in fact, Mama would still be alive when I returned. I told myself to stop thinking such morbid thoughts.

I asked Janie to check the calendar to make sure we obtained extensions on any court papers that were due within the next two weeks. I also needed to return some telephone calls. I did not want to talk to anyone right now. The thought of making conversation about insignificant issues was unpalatable. I instructed Janie to tell everyone that I would be out of the office for the next couple of weeks. Only contact me in San Diego if there is an emergency. And most importantly, I gave Janie the number where I could be reached in San Diego. She knew it by heart already.

I meditated at my desk for a few minutes before walking into my boss Steve's office to tell him the news and to inform him of my absence. I closed my eyes and cleared my mind, repeating the mantra which I had learned so many years ago in college during a transcendental meditation class. I slowly rose from my chair. I refused to lose composure in front of my boss, even though he had been exceptionally understanding throughout the entire ordeal. Not once had he objected to my frequent flights back and forth from New York to San Diego.

Steve's office was slightly bigger than mine. The Company did not spend lavishly on the working space of its attorneys. The only appreciable difference between Steve's office and mine was that he had slightly better furniture and he had curtains. I told Mama that you knew you were going somewhere at the Company when your office had curtains, the plush green ones with the matching tie back sashes.

Like most of the Company executives, Steve had an open door policy. I tapped twice on the half ajar door and peered through the opening. It seemed as though he was expecting me. I wondered if he had heard me crying, or if Janie had already told him about the call. When he looked at my face, I thought for sure that he noticed my bloodshot eyes. Never mind all that, I told myself. So what if I was crying earlier. As long as I don't break down in front of him. Another deep breath. "I just got a call from my mother's husband," I told him. I debated what to say next. I wanted him to understand both the urgency and the uncertainty of the situation. Again, Larry's words seemed to suffice. "The doctors said that my mother is dying. They said that it will only be a matter of days. I need to go see her. Everything here is under control. There are just one or two open matters which I can handle from San Diego."

It was more like a comment than a question. I was virtually certain that Steve would have no objection, particularly in light of what the doctors had said. I could tell that he was searching for the right words to say. Steve was in charge of all litigation for the Company, although ironically, he was a relatively shy, soft spoken guy. He assured me that I did not have to worry about being away from the office. Then he said, "I am really sorry Terri. Please let me know if there is anything we can do."

The lump in my throat was coming back. So were the tears. I dabbed the napkin I brought (just in case) in the corner of my eye to stop a tear from falling. I cleared my throat. "I'm o.k., I'll let you know if there is anything. Thanks Steve, I appreciate it." I told him that I planned to stay in daily contact with my secretary and that I would work remotely via fax and e-mail.

"Don't worry about it, Terri. It won't be a problem. Take as much time as you need." I forced a tiny smile of appreciation, turned around and quickly left the office, not knowing what else to say.

~ ~ ~

My mother Amanda was diagnosed with lung cancer two days after her 60th birthday in December of 1994, just seven months earlier. She didn't smoke, she didn't drink and she rarely ate red meat. Knowing these factors made it all the more difficult to accept the cancer diagnosis. Although I had made many trips back and forth between New York and San Diego, it never seemed like enough. I started feeling guilty, thinking that I should have been by her side more often. But like everyone else, I had other commitments, including two young children and a very demanding job. I had worked relentlessly for the past five years as an Assistant General Counsel at the Company. As a single mom, I could ill afford to lose ground at work. But the conflict nagged me. I should have spent more time with my mother, I thought, especially time before she became ill. I had, like most children, assumed my mother would be around forever, but forever did not last long.

I left the office very late that night, trying to make sure that nothing was left unattended. The office was empty and quiet, even the cleaning lady had come and gone. I left a pile of memos and letters for my secretary to finalize and send out the next day under my signature. My office was exceptionally clean, everything had been filed away. After I switched off the light, I turned and looked back into the small square room. The sun had set long before, leaving the room nearly pitch black. The red light on the phone was the only light in the room, except the white lights flickering from the offices across the street through my windows, windows adorned with only half drawn acrylic shades.

As I stood staring into the dark, austere office, another morbid thought crossed my mind. The next time I walk into that office, my mother would probably be dead. For a second, I thought maybe if I didn't leave, I could stop the forces of nature and she wouldn't die. Stop thinking such ridiculous things I told myself. Go home. Go home to your children. I slowly closed the door behind me, wondering just how long it would be before I returned. As it turned out, it was the last time I ever worked in that office.

~ ~ ~

When I arrived home that night, I was thoroughly exhausted. My body felt weak and drained from the day's events. The stairway up to the second floor of the three story walk-up seemed unusually long. We lived in a tiny two bedroom apartment in a pink brownstone on 75th Street between Broadway and West End Avenue in New York City. It was the only pink brownstone I had ever seen. It was pink through and through, from the outside façade to the halls in the stairwell to the walls in the rooms of the apartments. Even the bathroom was pink. The building was situated on a tree lined block with other brownstones and apartment buildings, just around the corner from Citarella's, the famous New York City fish market.

Truth be known, God sent me that apartment. Even the landlord said so. In the previous summer of 1994, I was desperately searching for an inexpensive apartment to rent in New York City and simultaneously trying to sell the house that my ex-husband, Gary, and I had purchased only four years earlier.

Gary and I met at a restaurant called Cattails on 96th Street and Broadway in New York City in March of 1984. I didn't believe in love at first sight, but when I first saw him singing up on that stage, something told me, he was the one. I knew then, at that very moment, that we would get married. I was drawn to him by a force greater than myself. Chemistry. Nature's way of preserving the species. The will of my future children creating their path to me.

I arrived at the restaurant with a male friend from law school. I was wearing tight jeans and a sweater. I was a shapely size four. When I was younger, the boys called me a "brickhouse," like the girl in the song by the Commodores. I wore very little make-up, except my signature red lipstick. My hair was long, thick and straight. When he first saw me enter the restaurant, he told his friend that he wanted to meet me. For him, it was apparently lust at first sight. In retrospect, I'm not completely sure if it was ever real love, for him, at any sight.

He was singing *Ain't No Sunshine When She's Gone,* by Bill Withers. It seemed like he was singing the song just for me, the way he kept looking in my direction. I didn't even notice his gaze gracing others in the room. All I noticed was his nicely sculptured 5'10" frame with well defined muscles, not too big, not too small. The one-quarter Cherokee Indian was evident in his reddish brown complexion, chiseled facial features and piercing dark brown eyes with thick eyebrows. He had a full head of "good" hair, dark and straight and wavy. He reminded me of my maternal grandfather, at a young age.

As he approached our table my heart pounded. "Thanks for coming to the show," he said, as he stretched his hand to take mine. I remember thinking that his hands were softer than mine, a sign to me that his family had provided well for him or that I had washed one too many dishes in my lifetime. As he moved to the next table for the next introduction, I tried hard not to let my eyes follow him. I managed to focus my eyes forward on my date, but reserved the corner to focus on Gary, the father of my future children. Later that evening he asked me for my telephone number and I obliged. The rest, as they say, is history.

In the summer of 1990, right after our first child Nicole celebrated her first birthday, we bought our dream house in the suburbs of New York City. We intended to keep the house forever, but forever did not last long.

It was a beautiful four bedroom colonial situated on a quarter of an acre on a quiet tree lined block in Westchester County, just north of New York City. In my opinion, it was the perfect house. We bought the house from the original owners who raised all three of their children there. At the time I thought, we too will raise all of our children here. We paid most of the down payment from our savings and we paid the bulk of the monthly mortgage with my income, sporadically supplemented with income from Gary, who was an aspiring singer and songwriter. His career was on the verge of success with the execution of a record deal and the release of his first album. Everything looked promising for us. We seemed like the perfect couple. But all of that changed.

In September 1992, shortly after he released his first album and nine months after our son Christopher was born, he told me he was leaving me. He swore there was not another woman.

Not long after he left us, Gary's record label declined to renew his contract for a second term. When I told Mama that he lost his record deal, she said as a matter of fact, "Well baby, God don't like ugly." I had never heard anyone use that expression, but I knew exactly what Mama meant. She often used peculiar Southern expressions to punctuate her thoughts. She learned many of them from her own mother who, like Mama, was born and raised in Birmingham, Alabama. She continued in a serious voice, "I don't quite understand why he left. He'll never find anyone as dedicated as you are. I suppose he is searching for the perfect woman. He won't find her until he finds himself." Mama was always a little philosophical, but, she was not alone in this opinion. Unfortunately, only Gary's opinion mattered and he had made his opinion abundantly clear.

Ultimately, in January 1994, when Nicole was four and Christopher was two, Gary brought the other woman from her home in California to visit his parents in New York during the Christmas holidays. Her visit with his family was a rude awakening; I finally realized that our marriage was over. I felt like I was suffocating, like I was trapped under a huge wave in the ocean, completely engulfed by water, drowning and gasping for air, but everywhere I turned there was only deep gray water. I literally had difficulty breathing. I couldn't escape from the marriage fast enough.

I filed for divorce on the very next Monday, the first Monday of January 1994. The divorce lawyer and I drafted, served and filed the papers all on the same day. On April 22, 1994, less than four months later, the divorce was final. The lawyer said that it was the fastest divorce he had ever processed. I wasn't sure if this information should make me feel elated or dejected. It certainly was not a positive reflection on the state of our marriage. The divorce would have been even faster, but Gary neglected to execute one of the documents in front of a notary, so he had to re-execute the form and return it to me by mail, adding another two weeks to the process. Who knew—we could have beaten our own record.

~ ~ ~

I was now officially a single mom, a label which defined my very existence, placing me in a category reserved for lonely people, super heroes and other extraordinary human beings struggling to save the day or to simply survive. Being a single mom affected my every action, my every move. I learned to do things on my own. I packed lightly when I took the kids on an outing to the park or to the zoo just to make sure I could carry everything on my own. I shopped frugally, to make sure that I could stretch the amount of cash until my next paycheck. I never went out. I rarely bought clothes for myself. I appreciated and actually used hand-me-down clothes from the children's cousins, especially coats and jackets. I fired the gardener and mowed the lawn myself with a borrowed lawn mower. I learned how to fix the little thing-a-ma-jig in the bowl behind the toilet when it wouldn't flush and how to unclog the toilet with a plunger when it overflowed. I killed water bugs and other multi-legged intruders silently and swiftly, even though I was more afraid of bugs and rodents than anyone I knew. I painted those parts of the house in dire need of painting, including the basement where the kids rode around on their bikes on rainy days when I did the laundry. I took very good care of the car, making sure it was regularly serviced and the oil and water were regularly checked. I did everything humanly possible to maintain stability and to remain solvent.

Initially, Gary sent money home when he could. But soon after he left, he stopped sending money altogether and the savings account slowly dwindled to nothing. Making ends meet was becoming more and more difficult. It reached a point where I could no longer single-handedly manage the mortgage on the house, along with all the other expenses. Life is a bitch, I thought.

Something had to give. Mama always said that we were in control of our own lives and destinies. "When life presents you with a problem," she said, "you have to make a decision. You may not always make the right decision, but you must make a decision just the same. You can either get knocked down and stay down, or you can get up and fight." It was as simple as that, she told me.

At the time, my choices did not seem so simple. Should I sell the house and move back to the City? Should I try to hold onto the house, no matter how impractical it seemed? Most of the debate concerned the wisdom of moving to the City before the house actually sold. The house had been on the market for the entire spring and summer and remained unsold because of buyer financing problems.

After weighing the pros and cons, I decided to sell the perfect house in the suburbs and move back to New York City by the beginning of the school year, whether or not the house had sold. I was adamant about enrolling the children in school on time, even if it meant simultaneously paying a mortgage on the house and a lease on an apartment for a few months. Nicole was entering kindergarten and Christopher was starting pre-school. I did not want to take them out of one school and transfer them to another school in the middle of the year. It had happened to me so often as a child that I wanted to avoid the same fate for my own children. I went to seven different schools between grades one and twelve. We were either moving from one city to another or we were searching for better schools.

The decision to sell the house and move back to the City was the solution to many of my problems. It would allow me to rent at a much cheaper rate so that I could get back on my feet financially. It would give me a shorter commute so that I could spend more time with my two young children, now that I was a single mom. And, it would enable me to socialize with people my age, other than parents from my children's playdates.

All I needed to do was locate an inexpensive apartment that was close to a distinguished public school like P.S. 87 in Manhattan. Private school was financially not an option. Essentially, I needed a miracle. That was my plan. Perform a miracle.

The realtor I chose was a tall slender brunette with blond highlights named Lisa. She worked for a real estate agency called I.J. Sopher which specialized in finding apartments on the upper west side of New York. She drove an old beat-up two-door stick-shift Toyota Celica, which had long ago seen its better days. The front section of the car was filled with applications, floor plans and other assorted papers. She kept a huge ring of keys in the little compartment on her right behind the stick-shift. The back of the car was filled with junk like shoes, sweaters, books, empty water bottles and candy wrappings. Considering the fact that she used the car for work, I thought she might keep it in better condition. But like the few New Yorkers who lived in the city and owned cars, it was not wise to flaunt an expensive, attractive car. Lisa was a fast talker and an even faster mover. During our two week acquaintance, we hopped in and out of her little silver Toyota more times than I could count.

I told Lisa that I needed to find a decent, inexpensive two bedroom apartment in New York City between 72nd Street and 82nd Street. If I could secure an apartment in that neighborhood, I explained, the children would have guaranteed admission into P.S. 87, the number one public school in Manhattan. After Lisa stopped chuckling, she said facetiously, "You and everyone else in New York City."

I smiled, shrugged my shoulders and said, "There must be something in my price range you can show me."

She looked at me sympathetically and said, "There is only one decent two bedroom apartment available between 72nd and 82nd Street in your price range." Having knocked on dozens of doors and responded to even more newspaper ads, I was not surprised to hear her say that.

Lisa explained that numerous qualified applicants had interviewed with the landlord to take the apartment, but he refused to select any of them, preferring instead to let the apartment remain vacant. "I'll show you the apartment," Lisa said, "but don't hold your breath, the owner is slightly eccentric." I thought to myself, what have I got to lose?

The owner of the apartment was a tall, slender man from India in his late 50's who wore traditional Indian clothing including a neatly tied turban around his head. He lived on the ground floor of the brownstone where he also taught transcendental meditation classes during the day. When I walked into the first floor of the brownstone where his office was also located, I noticed that the room was extremely clean and organized. The wall directly behind his desk was filled with books, mostly on transcendental mediation and yoga. On the opposite wall hung a picture of a peaceful looking man whose eyes followed you around the room. I concluded that the man in the picture must be some sort of religious yogi.

The rest of the walls in his office were bare and pink. His desk contained virtually no clutter, except that it was adorned with a leather trimmed desk mat and a matching pen and pencil holder. He told me his name was Professor Shah. He spoke with a very heavy Indian accent. "My business," he said in a tranquil but stern tone, "requires a calm and quiet atmosphere. No running and jumping from children and such. The floors are very thin. You can hear even the slightest noise. Of course, no smoking or drinking or loud music either."

"Of course not," I said. "As a single mom, my focus is on my children. I work during the day and take care of them at night. There is no room for partying and loud music in our schedule. I don't even own a stereo. As for the children, they are extremely well behaved," I said. "Rule number one in our house is no running and jumping allowed."

I noticed that he was watching me intensely, listening carefully to my every word and observing my every move. I wondered if he believed me. Not that I was lying, but I was stretching the truth just a bit. My focus was my children, in fact, my children were my life. I never had parties and never played loud music. I honestly did not own a stereo. I had to sell the stereo along with most of my other worldly possessions. And everyone always said that my children were the best behaved children in the world. But in reality, I knew that the children would be running and jumping in the apartment because that's what children do. It explained the genesis of rule number one, no running or jumping allowed in the house.

When the landlord told me on the spot that the apartment was mine, I thanked him profusely and then hesitantly asked him why he had selected me. I wondered why he would risk taking a single mom with two young children who would probably tear up the place, when he had the opportunity to occupy the apartment with single investment banker types. In a very serious voice, he said, "Because, my dear, God sent you to me," then he paused and added, "God sent you and your children to me." And so He did, so He did. I began to believe in miracles. So did the realtor. The miracle on 75th Street.

When we returned to the real estate office to complete the paperwork, Lisa introduced me to the other agents as the person who won over the eccentric Professor. The other agents heartily patted me on the back and gave Lisa congratulatory high fives. I heard one of them say, "So after two years we can finally take that place off the market." I had no idea what a major feat I had accomplished. Securing that apartment was the beginning of a new life for me and for my children. We moved into the little pink apartment the very next Saturday, the last Saturday in August 1994, just one month before school started.

Although I was trying hard to remain positive, the move from the house in the suburbs to the apartment in the City was a traumatic ordeal, fraught with stress and anxiety. It dawned on me that most relocations were the result of good fortune, where the family moves up in the world, leaving a smaller home to live in a bigger, better home in a nicer neighborhood. Most moves were like the theme song from *The Jeffersons*.

Well we're moving on up to the East side…we finally got a piece of the pie.

Not our move. Our move was just the opposite and it worried me. We were leaving the perfect house in the suburbs and moving to a cramped little apartment in the city. We were moving on down to the small time, we clearly lost our piece of the pie. The kids had not actually seen the apartment and I was worried that they would be deeply disappointed. What if they hated the apartment? What if they missed living in the house? What if they couldn't make the adjustment to city life?

The move from the house to the apartment was not my only problem. If death, divorce and moving are three of life's most difficult experiences, I was in the midst of experiencing all three of those events, virtually at the same time. My divorce was finalized in April 1994. My real father died of a heart attack in May 1994, a loss which affected me more than I could ever have imagined. And the move from the yet unsold house in the suburbs to the apartment in the city was in August 1994. Little did I know that the worse was yet to come.

The convergence of these events was somewhat overwhelming, even for me. My greatest concern was the fact that the house still had not sold. One evening right before the move, I called Mama for support and encouragement. We spoke often, especially during trying times. She told me, "Terri, I know this is a difficult situation, but you are one of the strongest people I know. You'll make it through this ordeal and emerge even stronger." That very night, after that very conversation, I splurged and ordered Chinese food. I ate the food, cleaned the dishes, cracked open one of the three fortune cookies in the bag and read the following words, "Meeting adversity well is the source of your strength." I smiled, shook my head in sheer disbelief at the coincidence of the message and tucked the little piece of paper away in my wallet. I kept the fortune, to remind me of what Mama said, to remind me of my strength, to remind me that no matter what happens in life, you gotta' do what you gotta' do.

~ ~ ~

August 22, 1994. Card from Mama.

Dear Terri,

'It's difficult to hold on sometimes—but someday beyond our tears and all the world's wrongs—beyond the clouds and all we can see and touch—there will be love, compassion and justice...and we shall understand.' By Flavia

...and I love you very much!

Mama

The telephone call and card from my mother were all I needed to lift my spirits and motivate me to focus. Mama suggested that I ease the transition to the apartment by making it comfortable and filling it with familiar items.

I strategically planned the days preceding the move so that the children would spend time elsewhere, giving me an opportunity to get organized. Being organized was second nature to me. Both my mother and grandmother, my two strongest role models, were bastions of organization and cleanliness. As fate would have it, the children's father was in New York City on business and available to watch them for the weekend. He spent most of his time working and living in Los Angeles, California with his girlfriend, and the remainder of his time in the New York area staying with friends and family.

The move was scheduled for 9:00 a.m. on the last Saturday morning in August. I took a personal day from work on Friday to finish packing the house and to prepare the apartment for the move.

The apartment was designed in the shape of the letter "T." When you entered the apartment, you entered into the hallway at the top of the T which faced 75th Street. All the walls in the apartment were painted pink, except the kitchen walls which were paneled with fake wood. Situated on the top left hand side of the T was my bedroom, which was barely long enough to fit my queen sized bed and my dresser.

My entire closet consisted of one four foot bar and one four foot shelf overhead. That was the extent of it. I put some of my extra clothes that didn't fit into the closet in a small storage trunk. I intended to put the trunk at the end of the bed, but the room was not nearly big enough. The trunk ended up in the hallway, along with everything else that didn't fit into the tiny rooms of the little pink apartment.

The children's room, which was located adjacent to my room on the top right hand side of the T, was even smaller than my room. It was even smaller than my old dormitory room at Columbia Law School on 116th Street. It could not even accommodate Christopher's crib and Nicole's tiny bed. I ended up selling those items, along with most of my other furniture and worldly possessions that wouldn't fit into the tiny rooms of the little pink apartment. What I couldn't sell I gave away. What I couldn't give away, I threw out. The kids ended up sleeping in hand-me-down bunk beds. Life is a major bitch, I thought.

The rest of the apartment was a long hallway forming the leg of the T. Real estate advertisements would describe the design as a railroad apartment or a "floor-through" where the entire apartment was connected by a long narrow hallway stretching from one end of the apartment to the other. The design was a common schema in "pre-war" buildings erected in New York City before World War II. The kitchen was on the left side of the long narrow hallway and the living room and bathroom were at the end of the hallway.

The kitchen was not really a kitchen at all, except if you lived in New York City. It was really a small hole in the wall with appliances. In New York City, real estate agents were allowed to classify a hole in the wall with appliances as a kitchen. There was no room in the kitchen for a table or chair, it was stand-up room only. I had to buy a new kitchen table, the kind that folded up when not in use. It was a bit ironic that although I had to sell all of my existing furniture, there I was buying new furniture to fit into the little pink apartment.

I found a table just the right size at a Workbench store around the corner from the apartment. One good thing about living in New York City was that everything you ever needed was right around the corner. I placed the little wooden table up against the wall of the long pink hallway and kept it folded during the day. Every morning and every evening I unfolded and refolded that little wooden table. If I didn't fold the table back, you could not pass through the hallway, unless you held your breath and narrowly squeezed around the table into the kitchen and back out into the hallway again. Or slide under the table, as the kids were prone to do.

There were only two chairs at the table. Nicole and Chris would eat together while I fussed around in the kitchen, inquiring about their day. They ate mostly cereal or waffles for breakfast, spaghetti, chicken or hot dogs for dinner. I was not an elaborate cook—to say the least. I kept it simple with one ingredient entrees. Fortunately, the children liked my cooking, not that they had much choice in the matter or a basis for comparison. For snack they ate celery with peanut butter or bananas with peanut butter or graham crackers with peanut butter. We soon became massive consumers of peanut butter. I figured that peanut butter was the perfect food. It was filling, nutritious, cheap and delicious. We were on a very tight budget. Cookies and chips became luxury items, too much money, not enough nutritional value.

I would eat only after the kids ate. My dinner, which usually consisted of a salad or a Lean Cuisine or a bowl of cereal or soup, rarely took more than ten minutes to eat. Without even trying, I lost five pounds. My five foot (almost) four inch frame now weighed 112, the least I had ever weighed.

The living room of the little pink apartment faced the backyard. We were very lucky. The backyard was filled with grass and tall maple trees. Most backyards in New York City were filed with concrete. Sometimes at night, after the kids fell asleep, I would pour myself a glass of Kendall Jackson Chardonnay, snuggle on the couch with Raquel (our cat) and listen to the sounds of light music on the little boom box Mama sent me after learning that I had to sell my stereo. When she sent the boom box, she told me not to mention it to her husband Larry because he wouldn't understand why she spent the money. I held my tongue.

As I sat thumbing through paperwork, I would watch the leaves of the tall maple trees sway back and forth in the wind. Maybe not all of life is a bitch, I thought. Things could be worse. I had no idea.

~ ~ ~

Friday morning before the move, the first task was to clean the apartment from top to bottom. When we were young children, Mother Dear, my maternal grandmother, always told us that cleanliness was next to Godliness. We called our grandmother "Mother Dear" which is a Southern term of affection for the alpha mother of the family. We pronounced it, "Muh'Dea."

I often wondered if Mother Dear meant God didn't like dirty little children who lived in dirty old houses. I wondered too, if that was why Mama gave us baths every single day, no matter what, as if the soap and water washed away the dirt and germs, along with any evil spirits we may have encountered that day, right down the drain.

In any case, I debated hiring a cleaning person to clean the apartment, but I figured I could do a better job for much less. Expenses were a constant factor in my decision making process. I swept and scrubbed the floors. I dusted and wiped the woodwork and cabinets. I disinfected the sinks, toilet and tub. The little pink apartment may be small and simple, but at least it was going to be clean, next to Godly, should my grandmother turn out to be right.

After I finished cleaning the apartment, I looked around and realized that there was no play area for the kids. There was, however, a small walk-in closet situated off of the living room. It seemed an odd place to put a closet, but it would suit my needs perfectly. If I converted the closet into a playroom, then the kids would have a place to play, in full view of the living room where I spent most of my time.

The conversion of the walk-in closet into the new playroom took a little effort. First, I removed the poles from the sides of the closet, painted a rainbow on the back wall and laid down plush pink carpet, all by hand. My experience from handling small jobs around the house had served me well. I put the children's toy chest on one side of the closet and a tiny wooden table with two chairs on the other side. This was now their playroom, a shadow of the 20' by 15' playroom which preceded it in first house. I prayed that the kids would like the apartment, especially the playroom. I hoped that they would not be too disappointed.

On Saturday morning, the day of the move, Gary picked the children up from the house in Westchester minutes before the moving van arrived at 9:00 a.m. He pulled the car up to the front of the house and blew the horn five times in a familiar pattern, "beep, beep be beep beep." As always, he left off the last two beats. The kids recognized the sound of the horn and ran to the window. When they saw that it was their father, they ran down the stairs shouting, "Daddy's here, daddy's here." They always got so excited when he came to see them.

I walked the children to the car and hugged and kissed them a little longer than usual. They waived goodbye, blowing air kisses to me and to the big perfect house through the back window of the car until the car turned around the corner and disappeared from site. It dawned on me that this would be the last time the children would ever see the house in Westchester. I wiped the tears which had clouded my vision of the vanishing car, took a deep breath and turned back towards the house to complete the move, alone.

The "For Sale" sign was still prominently displayed in front of the house, sticking up out of the grass like a flashing beacon, announcing to the world that we had to leave, forced out because we could not handle the bank payments. It was embarrassing. After five straight deals failed to close because of buyer financing problems, I was beginning to think that the house would never sell. The perfect house that was once my dream house had become the biggest burden of my life.

At noon on the day of the move, I loaded the car with Raquel, our cat, my only plant and two suitcases of essential toiletries and clothing for me and the children for a week. I let the movers take everything else. I arrived at the apartment before the movers and quickly unloaded the car. When I walked into the apartment, like Mama suggested, I staked my territory by placing the plant on the window sill. It was my only plant, a sturdy philodendron which my mother gave me and which her mother had given her a decade earlier. It was the only plant I ever owned that survived. It obviously meant a lot to me because it once belonged to my mother and grandmother. It was also something familiar to brighten up an unfamiliar place.

I carefully placed the philodendron on the window sill in the living room facing the back yard. It blended in nicely with the green leaves of the tall maple trees located in the backyard. The plant made the apartment feel more like home, not exactly like our house in Westchester, but a little more like home. I thought about buying more plants to fill the window sill, but decided I should probably not push my luck.

My strategy was to unpack the children's room and the bathroom first. I figured we could settle into the apartment and at least the kids would be situated. First I unpacked the suitcases for the three of us. Then I unpacked the sheets, towels, soap and toilet paper which I had clearly marked in a box labeled: "Bathroom: Important, Unpack First."

I wanted everything to be just right when Gary returned the children to me. In fact, I had hoped he could keep them overnight so that I had a little more time to prepare the place, but he was staying with friends in the City and was unable to keep them. Just as well. I missed them anyway. I dreaded the thought of staying alone in the apartment on the first night. I couldn't even find our cat Raquel. Somehow she had managed to escape from her container and was lost in the apartment or even worse, somewhere in New York City. I set up her litter box in the bathroom and her food and water in the kitchen, hoping that she would eventually appear if she smelled her food and her kitty litter. I looked everywhere for her, under the beds, in the cabinets, in empty boxes. I stopped every now and then to listen for her cry, to no avail. The thought of telling the kids that I lost Raquel somewhere in the vastness of New York City was unbearable. Thank God she finally reappeared the next day after all the commotion settled. She had been hiding the whole time under the radiator behind a wooden panel in the living room. She emerged shaking and crying as though her entire world had been turned upside down. I knew exactly how she felt.

After the movers left, I looked around the apartment, it was packed wall to wall with boxes. I had my work cut out for me, it was too depressing for words. There was no space to walk anywhere in the apartment, except one small path leading from the entry door down the long hallway into the living room. I didn't know where to start. I climbed over boxes and made my way to the bed in my room. The movers even put boxes on top of the beds. I shoved some of the boxes over and rested on a small clear space on the bed and began to cry. I closed my eyes for a second and minutes later I was drifting off to sleep. As my mind and body slowly succumbed to slumber, I thought, life is a major bitch, can't nobody tell me any different.

I awoke to the sound of a truck backfiring outside my bedroom window. Get up, Terri, it's 5:00 p.m. Gary will be back with the children in no time, I told myself. For two straight hours I moved boxes, unpacked boxes and threw out boxes. Many of the boxes could not be unpacked because there was no place to put the contents. Most of the kitchen boxes would remain forever unpacked; there was simply no room in the kitchen cabinets for champagne glasses and fancy china. I carefully placed the boxes of champagne glasses and fancy china in the hallway, along with everything else that didn't fit in the tiny rooms of the little pink apartment.

Gary returned with the children around 7:00 p.m., it was almost dark outside. There was a street light directly outside my bedroom window which switched on just before they arrived, pouring bright florescent light through the naked window straight into my bedroom. I'll need to get heavy drapes or a thick shade to block that, I thought, hoping that Gary would not notice the intrusive glaring beam filling the room. When the door bell rang, my heart skipped a beat. I hastily wiped my grimy hands on the side of my blue jeans and held them out in front of me for a quick inspection. They were shaking uncontrollably. I noticed also that every nail was broken and nearly all of the polish had vanished, leaving tiny red spots in the middle of each nail. Not only was I anxious about the children's reaction to the apartment, but it dawned on me that I had not eaten since early morning. At some point while the movers were unloading the truck into the apartment, I managed to run to a deli around the corner and buy a toasted bagel with butter and diet Snapple. It was obviously not enough to sustain me for the long and grueling day.

I buzzed the intercom to let Gary and the children into the building and then ran to the bathroom to wash my hands and throw some water on my face before they reached the apartment door at the top of the stairs. I glanced in the mirror, dreading the image I would likely find there. Fortunately, God had blessed me with decent looks. I had my mother's almond shaped brown eyes, her aptly shaped nose and her signature full lips. Unfortunately, I looked a mess, not a stitch of make-up, not even my trademark red lipstick which I never went without. Make the most of what you have Mama always said. But, it was too late to throw some make-up on now. The little bit of style my hair held that morning had long ago melted away in the heat of the day. I quickly took the scrungie out, readjusted the pony tail and put the scrungie back in my hair. We may be divorced, but I still wanted to look presentable. Seconds later the kids were knocking at the apartment door. "Mommy, Mommy, it's us, open up," Nicole said.

Then I heard Christopher say, "It's us Mommy, let us in, let us in."

"I'm coming, I'm coming. Hold your horses," I said. I sounded like my mother; she used to always say that. It's funny how that happens. You watch your mother over the course of the years and slowly but surely you begin to acquire her ways and mannerisms. Slowly but surely, without even trying, you adopt her morals and values. Slowly but surely, before you know it, you become your mother. As far as I was concerned, that was a blessing.

No sooner had I opened the door, the kids ran through the apartment like flashes of lightening, one after the other. Gary stood in the doorway and said calmly, "O.k., you got them from here."

"Yeah, yeah, I'm good, thanks," I said, trying hard to act nonchalant.

"O.k., so I'll give you a call tomorrow and let you know what time I'll be by to pick them up."

"Bye daddy, see you tomorrow," Nicole said.

"Bye daddy, see you tomorrow," Chris said. "What time are you coming to get us daddy?" Chris always wanted to know what time you were coming or what time you were going. Both of the children were accustomed to their father traveling back and forth because he spent a good deal of his time on the road or in California. But Chris insisted upon knowing exact times of arrival and departure.

"I don't know baby, but I'll call you tomorrow. I love you guys. Be good," Gary said. And with that, he turned, walked back down the stairs and disappeared into the warm summer night.

The kids immediately found their room. It was the only room that was not entirely filled with boxes. They were sitting on the bottom bunk bed looking around at the bare pink walls of the four cornered room. I crawled up on the bed to lie down next to them. I was too tall to sit upright on the bottom bunk. "So, what do you think? Do you like the apartment?" I asked.

Nicole said, "It's great Mommy, it's all pink, I love it."

Chris echoed, "Yeah Mommy, I love it too."

I thought how lucky I was to have such great kids. It's like they knew how hard I was trying to make this difficult transition not so difficult. Then, out of the blue, Nicole said, "Mommy, I love the little pink playroom with the rainbow, it's so cute, it's just right."

I looked at Nicole and chills ran up and down my spine. She was only five years old. I wondered how she always knew just the right thing to say. Despite my best efforts to remain cheerful, I could not control myself. My throat tightened and my eyes began to water. When Nicole said that she loved the playroom, I thought about something Mama used to say to us when we were children. She told us, "I'm so lucky you guys chose me to be your mother." I never completely understood what she meant, until then. My mother believed that parents didn't simply have children. Instead, she believed that before children were born, they knowingly selected their parents. Nicole and Christopher selected me because they knew that we needed each other.

"Oh sweetie," I said, "I am so lucky that you chose me to be your mother," repeating what my mother had so often said to me. I hugged them both long and hard, until they started to squirm loose. Nicole asked me why I was crying. Chris asked me if I was all right. "I couldn't be better I said. As long as I have you guys, I couldn't be better."

The house in Westchester finally sold (albeit at a deficit) in November 1994, seven months after the divorce, six months after my father's death and four months after the move to the little pink apartment. The children were already enrolled in P.S. 87, the number one elementary school in Manhattan. Another month and financially I would not have been able to pull it off.

We sold the house to a young couple with a newborn baby. As I sat alone across the table from the couple signing the closing documents on behalf of myself and my ex-husband, I felt envious, envious of the life their family would share in our house. Despite my feelings of envy, I considered the sale of the house in Westchester another miracle. It felt as though the waters of the Red Sea had just parted, providing me with a path to freedom and independence.

Free at last, free at last. Thank God Almighty, I'm free at last.

~ ~ ~

July 20, 1995, Thursday evening. When I arrived at the top of the stairs that evening, after the ominous phone call from Larry about my mother's tenuous condition, the door to the little pink apartment flung open before I could take the key out of my purse. The kids always heard me coming up the stairs and asked Cynthia, our babysitter, to open the door before I had a chance to open it myself. It was as though they sensed the time I was coming home. Everyday after school they ate snacks, did homework and watched cartoons. At a certain point they began to listen intently for my footsteps up the two flights of stairs. Then, when they heard my footsteps reach the landing on the second floor, they raced to the door dragging Cynthia behind. Christopher, who was three and could not yet pronounce her name, called her "Thin-the-a."

"Thin-the-a, Thin-the-a, hurry, hurry, come open the door, Mommy is here, Mommy is here, come open the door," Christopher shouted, repeating every phrase, just in case Cynthia had suddenly gone deaf. Cynthia dried her hands from the dishwater and obligingly opened the door for the children to greet me. Christopher ran into my arms and Nicole grabbed my leg. Cynthia continued to hold the door open with one hand and took my briefcase with the other hand, allowing me to greet the kids. She sensed my exhaustion and did not complain about my lateness. Fortunately for me, she never complained. I considered myself very lucky indeed, Cynthia was a rare find.

Cynthia began working for me in January 1995, one month after Christopher's third birthday and one month after Mama's cancer diagnosis. I always measured time around my children's ages and accomplishments. After Mama's diagnosis, I began to measure time around the cancer; four months before the cancer…one month after the cancer. The diagnosis was an uninvited bookmark in all our lives, literally changing the way we viewed life itself. Before the cancer, all was right with the world. After the cancer, nothing was right, it was all wrong. Skies were perpetually gray. Sunsets lost their magic, just another day vanishing beyond the horizon. Rainbows faded before they ever formed, the splendor of their colors lost upon my dwindling awareness. I wondered if things would ever be the same again.

As dismal as it was, finding Cynthia was a miracle. If locating the apartment on 75th Street was the first miracle and selling the house was the second, then finding Cynthia was clearly the third miracle. When we moved to the City, my old babysitter was not able to make the transition. The search for a new caretaker was daunting to say the least. Finding the right caretaker for your children is crucial. Trust is essential. I hired and fired five successive caretakers in a matter of months for reasons ranging from unauthorized excessive use of the telephone to reading pornographic magazines on the job. Cynthia worked in the after school program at P.S. 87 and saw the help wanted advertisement I posted in the lobby of the school. It was Mama's idea to post the sign. It turned out to be a very good idea indeed.

During the interview process, the children instantly fell in love with her. It was a match made in heaven. My instincts told me that divine intervention had sent Cynthia to me and to my children. In retrospect, her arrival was clearly in preparation for that which I was about to face.

~ ~ ~

When I managed my way into the apartment, after the ominous call from Larry, I quietly told Cynthia that I would be traveling again for a few days, back to San Diego. She agreed to sleep over in the apartment and watch the children 24/7 until I returned home. I didn't have the heart to tell Nicole and Chris that I was leaving again for San Diego. They hated it when I traveled, for any reason, for any length of time. They both cried uncontrollably, first one and then the other. If I tried to explain that Mommy had to go on a business trip to pay for the food we ate, they declared that they wouldn't eat so much food. If I told them that I had to go back to San Diego to visit my ailing mother, they would ask to come with me. No explanation was ever good enough to appease them. They fretted from the moment they knew until the moment I walked back through the door.

To ease their fears, I tried to limit my travel. But the cancer changed everything. It forced us to make choices. Choices between leaving our children behind or not visiting our sick mother. Since the diagnosis in December, my siblings and I took turns visiting Mama so that one of us would be with her at all times if possible. With such an arrangement, it was not possible to limit my travel. I desperately wanted to bring the children with me, but seeing their grandmother in this condition was not an option.

I consciously delayed telling Nicole and Christopher about trips until it was absolutely necessary. The delay decreased their fret time. So this trip, as with all the other trips, I waited until the last minute to tell them. I always told them the truth. Mama said it was essential to tell your children the truth, even if the truth was painful. She never sneaked out of the house or lied about how long she would be gone like some parents. Her theory was that children grew up more secure if they knew when you were leaving and when you were coming back. "Tell your children the truth and they will always trust you," she said. To tell a lie in our house, even a little white lie, was a major transgression.

That night, after the ominous phone call from Larry, after the kids had taken their baths and gone to bed, I ate my chicken and pasta Lean Cuisine, poured myself a glass of wine and set it out on the tiny kitchen counter for later. Once the dishes were cleaned, the house was straight, the toys were put away and the kids were sound asleep, I walked back to the tiny kitchen, sipped down the entire glass of wine in one motion and placed the lone glass in the sink. I stared at the glass for a second and debated whether or not to wash it. I decided against it, thinking that such behavior was surely borderline obsessive compulsive, either that or a single mom thing. That thing where you must do everything now or your world will surely fall apart. Go to bed Terri, go to bed now before the entire night slips away. I turned out all the lights in the apartment, made sure the door was locked and walked back into the kid's room to check on them one more time.

The children looked so sweet and innocent lying in their bunk beds in tiny bundles. I decided to sleep in their room that night to savor the time with them for as long as possible, first with Christopher on his bed below and then with Nicole on her bed above. I put my face up close to Christopher's face so that I could feel his warm sweet breath. I kissed his fat cheeks a couple of times until his little hand reflexively brushed my mouth away and then rested on my face. I didn't bother to remove it. It felt so right.

I still had not told them I was leaving for San Diego. In the morning, I thought, I will tell them in the morning at breakfast, before we walk to school. That way, I can explain it to them again along the way to school. It was not easy being a single mother. No matter what you did, it was never quite good enough.

~ ~ ~

July 21, 1995, Friday morning. I woke up at 4:30 a.m. in the morning with a splitting headache and a sore neck from sleeping in a cramped position all night in Nicole's bed. I carefully climbed down from the top bunk bed and gingerly placed my feet on the cool wooden floor. I regretted not sleeping in my own bed or putting the children in my bed in the first place. Then I remembered that I put the kids in their own beds so they would not suspect anything out of the ordinary. If I let them sleep with me, they might realize I was going out of town again.

It was still dark outside and I longed to go back to sleep. But my adrenaline was running high and my mind was racing. I might as well take advantage of the time and pack my bags, I thought. I walked into the kitchen and turned on the light to make a pot of coffee. This was New York City and I half expected to see a roach or two scurrying under the cabinets. But the roaches were hard pressed to find any tidbits in our little apartment. The mixture of boric acid powder and powdered sugar that I placed in a little bowl under the sink did not help their cause either. The solution worked wonders to kill roaches. It was a little trick I learned when I was in law school on 116th Street. The roaches ate the sweet sugar mixed with the poison powder, crawled back through the holes in the wall and died a slow, probably painful death. It didn't seem quite right, but in the war of me against the world, all was fair. You gotta' do what you gotta' do.

I traveled with very little luggage, so it only took a few minutes to pack. I remembered to pack a sweater. It was a lesson Mama taught me. She figured that no matter where you traveled, you may need a sweater in the evening when there was a chill in the air or in an air conditioned restaurant when the vent was right over your table. Make it either black or white, she said, so that it will match any outfit you are wearing. I packed my black sweater for this trip.

I occupied my remaining time with an extra long shower. The bathroom of the pink apartment was the best room in the entire apartment. It was huge by New York standards. We spent a lot of time in the bathroom, taking long showers and even longer baths, getting dressed and undressed, doing make-up, sitting and reading or playing with toys. I even carpeted the bathroom floor with thick pink carpet so that the kids could sit and play while I dressed in the mornings.

On this morning, I let the hot water run over my face and slender frame for a good fifteen minutes, long after the soap, germs and evil spirits had rinsed away down the drain. I stared at the water as it ran down my stomach, sculptured from two hundred daily crunches. The water ran past my legs, sculptured from three mile daily runs. Stomach and legs that had not felt the comfort and warmth of intermingling body parts for a very long time.

By the time Nicole and Christopher awoke, I was already dressed and packed. I got them dressed and sat them down at the kitchen table for breakfast. As I wiped the kitchen countertops clean, I debated how to tell them I was leaving for San Diego. When they were nearly finished eating their waffles, I mustered the courage to say, "Listen you guys, Mommy has to go to San Diego to see Dah again. She is very sick this time. The doctors said she might even go to heaven soon."

All the grandchildren called my mother Dah. The oldest grandchild, my sister's son Isaiah, started the tradition when he was two years old. He heard everyone else calling my mother Amanda, but he could only pronounce the last syllable, Dah. No one ever corrected him and soon we all started to call my mother Dah. The name stuck.

As I predicted, Nicole and Chris simultaneously began to whine and cry when I told them I was leaving. I gently admonished them to stop fretting and to finish eating their waffles so we could head out to school, as if rushing them through breakfast might make them change their focus. "I'll be back in no time flat," I told them cheerfully, as I placed their backpacks on their little backs.

"But Mommy, why can't we go with you this time to see Dah?" Nicole asked again as we walked the three and a half blocks to summer camp at P.S. 87. "If Dah is that sick, Nicole continued, we should go see her too." Her logic had not escaped me.

"I want to go too," chimed Christopher from his little umbrella stroller in his squeaky little three year old voice. "Why can't we go too?" he demanded to know.

We strolled toward the school yard at a slightly slower pace than usual. I intentionally left the apartment a little earlier that morning so that we could linger and talk before the 8:30 bell rang dismissing the parents from the school yard. The sun was shining through a perfectly clear blue sky. I noticed other mothers walking their children to school making small talk about eating their lunches and playing nicely with the other children. I wished our conversation could have been as light and casual.

When we arrived at the schoolyard, I strolled over to a quiet spot to talk. Even though I had anticipated the children's questions and had thought long and hard about a response, I was at a loss for words. The desperate looks on their little angelic faces made it even more difficult to say anything at all. "I know it's hard to understand," I began, "but I have to go see Dah by myself this time. You guys saw her in April and she was walking and talking and doing fine. Remember when we were all playing down on the beach? She can't do those things now. She may not even be able to wake up again when I get there. I want you to remember all the good times you had when Dah was healthy. That's what Dah would want too. I promise to come back as soon as I can, I promise. What if I call you guys as soon as you get back home today, o.k.? How does that sound?"

Just then the 8:30 bell rang and it was time to go. Hugs and kisses and then more hugs and kisses. One tissue to dry the tears, another to wipe the noses. A promise of a gift, a promise of a call. And then they were gone. They, like me, now had to deal with our separation in the best way they knew how. Just keep moving, Mama would say, one step in front of the other. I watched my feet move, one and then the other, out of the school yard, and onto the street. When I reached the curb, my right hand instinctively went up to hail a yellow cab to the airport for the next flight to San Diego. "Go up Central Park West to 125th Street," I authoritatively told the driver, "there will be less traffic that way." In typical New York fashion, the driver didn't respond to my suggestion. Instead, he silently flipped on his meter and sped up Central Park West to 125th Street.

I was taking the next flight to San Diego to see my dying mother, who had traveled far and wide since her humble origins in Birmingham, Alabama. I prayed that the Lord would allow me reach her on time.

2

Sweet Home Alabama

To be born and raised in Birmingham, Alabama is a distinction not many can profess, though it is one I have often claimed, even if only half true. It is completely true for my mother and her twelve siblings who could honestly declare the city their home. I was merely raised in this great city.

There is something magical about Birmingham with its rolling hills, rocky mountains and red soil, soil so red that after it rains the muddy water looks like thick streams of blood flowing down the mountainside. The aftermath of the lingering air smells fresh and wet and thick, just like the bloody muddy ground below it. The reds and browns of the earth beneath the contrasting blues and blacks of the sky and rocky mountains are simply breathtaking.

Sweet home Alabama/Where the skies are so blue/Sweet home Alabama/Lord I'm coming home to you.

At the turn of the century, Birmingham, Alabama was a typical southern industrial town. The primary industry was steel manufacturing. The majority of the male workforce was employed by steel companies. One of the largest steel manufacturers was a company named U.S. Steel located on the outskirts of Birmingham in a small town named Fairfield. Granddaddy, my mother's father, worked at U.S. Steel from the mid 1930s through the mid 1960s. For thirty years, he poured his muscle and sweat into the backbreaking work of lifting and hauling heavy steel beams. Granddaddy said the work was good and steady, especially for a Southern black man with barely a high school education. So he didn't complain. In any event, that wasn't his style. He was the tall silent type, not one to make waves in the often stormy sea of life.

It was not easy making a way for your family as a black man in Birmingham, Alabama. At the time, it was the most segregated city in the nation. The members of the Ku Klux Klan drove unmasked in police cars by day and marched masked on foot by night. The hidden enemy from within. Blacks were not allowed to attend the same schools, eat at the same restaurants or drink from the same water fountains as their white counterparts. That was the law. Defiance often resulted in harassment, imprisonment or the ultimate sacrifice, death. Granddaddy did his best to ensure that he and his family walked the proverbial straight and narrow path and avoided any contact with the law. Walk tall, but not too tall. Chin up but not too far.

Sweet Home Alabama/Where the Skies are so blue/Sweet Home Alabama/Lord I'm coming Home to You.

Granddaddy, who everyone called Willie, was the oldest of four siblings. He was the only sibling who did not know his father. His sister Amanda knew her father's last name was Lark. His sister Lillie Belle and brother Jimmie had the same father whose last name was Givan. But no one knew the name of Granddaddy's father, except of course Granddaddy's mother Jean. And she chose to remain silent on the issue.

Suffice it to say there were many rumors regarding how Willie's mother, Jean, managed to bear four children from three different men. In those days, such predicaments were somewhat unusual, to say the least. Jean's situation was a constant source of heartbreak to her mother, my great great grandmother, Amanda Jones.

The greatest hullabaloo surrounded the circumstances of Willie's birth and the identity of Willie's father. It was the source of many debates which continue to this day. Some say Willie's father was a white politician who was ashamed to be associated with a Negro family. Others say that Willie's father was old man Jentry who owned the local corner store. Jentry, who was also white, allegedly took advantage of Jean, who was notoriously beautiful, and abandoned her when she became pregnant knowing he could get away with it. No one would dare question the word of a Caucasian proprietor against that of a poor little black girl.

Granddaddy's version of the story of his father suited him best. He used to say that his father was a tall handsome American Indian who passed through Birmingham, Alabama on his way to great adventures in far away places. The handsome Indian fell in love with great grandma Jean, made passionate love to her, conceived a baby with her and then suddenly, as unexpectedly as his arrival, departed in pursuit of his next great conquest. This explanation, of course, would explain Granddaddy's long straight hair and his deep red complexion.

One thing was for certain, Granddaddy did not have a last name. Theoretically, he could have assumed the last name Jones from his mother Jean and his grandmother Amanda. But taking their last name would have been an admission that he did not know the identity of his father. To remedy the situation, when he started grade school and the teachers asked him his name, he made up the name Fouther. At first, the teachers did not understand what Granddaddy was saying. So he distinctly spelled the name out for them, "I said Fouther, F-O-U-T-H-E-R, Fouther, that's my last name." The teachers did not question him any further and his mother Jean never objected to the use of the name.

It seemed odd that Granddaddy would concoct such an unusual name. But when you pause to consider it, Fouther is a combination of the words father and mother. Perhaps subconsciously, Granddaddy was making a statement that his father, although missing, and his mother, albeit promiscuous, were both embodied in his last name and indeed, his very being. Either that, or Granddaddy simply could not think of something better. Either way, four generations of children, grandchildren and great grandchildren now bear the Fouther name.

Willie would eventually meet and marry Annie Mae. Annie Mae had just one sister named Velna Childers. Velna, like her sister Annie Mae, would ultimately have eight children.

Willie and Annie Mae Fouther of Birmingham, Alabama had thirteen children, although only eight of them survived to adulthood. The oldest was Marshall, who was Annie Mae's son from a prior relationship. Mother Dear, never talked about Marshall's father or the circumstances surrounding Marshall's birth. It was as though he was somehow immaculately conceived out of nowhere. Once, only once, I overheard the word "rape" whispered in connection with his name during a conversation not intended for young ears. I drew my own conclusions with no evidence to support them. If there were other conversations about Marshall's Immaculate Conception, they were vigilantly kept out of range of listening children and meddling interlopers.

The next five children of Willie and Annie Mae Fouther never made it through infancy. Two of them died in Mother Dear's arms as she unsuccessfully tried to nurse them back to health from the whooping cough. In those days, there was not much one could do for serious bacterial infections like whooping cough, except use a combination of home remedies, which Mother Dear relentlessly tried. The doctor told her to use herbs, steam baths and menthol poultices, but unfortunately the remedies were ineffective. The babies kept coughing until they began to foam at the mouth and eventually stopped breathing. Three other babies died during childbirth.

The next seven births for Willie and Annie Mae Fouther produced healthy children, although ironically, all eight children (including Marshall) caught whooping cough at the same time only days after Amanda was born. Knowing how deadly whooping cough could be, Mother Dear was worried that she would not be able to save her children. She was determined, however, not to lose another child to the fatal illness.

The doctor examined all eight of the children and initially thought Amanda was too young and fragile to survive the rigors of the illness. Again, Mother Dear frantically used a combination of home remedies. But this time, she was assisted by her next door neighbor, Mrs. Thomas. While Granddaddy paced back and forth on the back porch smoking his unfiltered Camel cigarettes and drinking his straight whiskey, Mother Dear and Mrs. Thomas gave the children steam baths, menthol poultices and plenty of fluids to flush the illness away, including lots of chamomile tea. Mrs. Thomas was a strong believer in chamomile tea. She said it was, "good for what ails you."

Mother Dear and Mrs. Thomas toiled day and night for nearly a week tending to the children. When one stopped coughing, one or two more would start up again. The two women moved methodically back and forth from one child to the next giving them steam baths and chamomile tea. There was a great deal of attention given to baby Amanda because she was only days old and her immune system was not developed. The rest of the children were two years and older and had a fighting chance to beat the illness. Amanda was kept segregated from all the rest, to decrease the risk of re-infection. Miraculously, Amanda survived her bout of whooping cough. As it turned out, all eight children survived, Marshall, Willie

Jr., Robert, Samuel, the twins James (Bubba) and Yvonne, Adrienne and Amanda.

By the time Amanda was born, Mother Dear's life revolved around feeding, dressing, changing, nursing, teaching and otherwise i-n-g-ing her eight children. While Willie toiled all day at the steel factory, Annie Mae toiled all day and night at the baby factory. Steel and babies. Babies and steel. The identities of Willie and Annie Mae Fouther were lost between the great divide of unyielding cold metal plates and vulnerable warm bundles of joy. It was difficult for one of them to relate to the woes and worries of the other. After awhile, like so many married couples, they stopped trying.

Despite their heroic efforts to make a way for themselves, Willie and Annie Mae Fouther were dirt poor. Dirt poor is worse than plain poor, although it is better than homelessness. When you are plain poor, you have a roof over your head, clothes on your back and food on the table. When you are dirt poor, the roof over your head leaks, the tattered clothing falls off your back and on some nights, there is no food on the table. When you are dirt poor, your tiny front yard, like the front yard of all the neighbors, is filled with dirt—hence the name dirt poor. Maintaining a manicured grass lawn is only a priority for the filthy rich, not the dirty poor.

Truth be told, Willie and Annie Mae Fouther's dirt poor house on 4th Avenue, did not constitute a house at all. It was actually a shack, or more precisely, the left side of a shack in a row of identical two-sided shacks. There were three steps on each side of the small front porch leading to two doors, one on the right to enter the neighbor's house (Mrs. Thomas) and one to the left to enter the Fouther house. The shared front yard was filled with dirt and rocks. Not even dandelions managed to grow through the dry lifeless soil. The small shack had a living room, two bedrooms, a kitchen and one bathroom to accommodate two adults and eight children.

All of the children slept in one bedroom while Granddaddy and Mother Dear slept in the other. If one of the children wanted privacy for any reason, he or she had to sleep on the living room sofa. In the South, couches were called sofas, lunch was called dinner, dinner was called supper, soda was called pop, and so on and so forth. Southerners have their own distinctive vernacular.

The sleeping situation was somewhat overbearing at times. Mother Dear said that the house was too crowded for the children's sake. Granddaddy said that they had to make do with what they had. The children knew enough not to say anything at all.

Like their neighbors with identical homes, Willie and Annie Mae could not afford the luxury of gas heat or air conditioning. In the summertime, when temperatures sometimes soared to 103°F, the doors and windows of the house were opened wide and fans were strategically placed for maximum air circulation. In the winter, a large pot belly furnace located in the middle of the living room heated all five rooms. When temperatures sometimes reached the freezing point, the children dragged their pillows and blankets and gathered around the front of the big pot belly of the furnace, each vying for a spot close to the furnace, those left on the outside of the heap relying on the body heat of the others for warmth. Mother Dear said that the house was too cold for the children's sake. Granddaddy said they had to make do. The children didn't say anything at all.

Granddaddy took comfort in the age old conventional Southern Comfort, the bottle. He was a heavy drinker and an even heavier smoker. He drank straight whiskey with no ice and smoked two to three packs of unfiltered Camel cigarettes a day. He drank and smoked so much that when all the children finally moved out of the house, Mother Dear told Granddaddy that he had to sleep in the second bedroom if he wanted to "carry on with all his foolishness." For as long as I can remember, Mother Dear slept in the main bedroom in the front of the house while Granddaddy was relegated to the small bedroom in the back of the house. Granddaddy was not even allowed to keep his clothes in Mother Dear's room because, "they stank," plain and simple.

Like so many Southern black woman, Mother Dear turned to the church for comfort and consolation. Her sanctuary was Sardis Baptist Church located at the top of a hill on a corner of 4th Avenue. There were 24 steep stairs leading to the entry of the church. Considering all of the old women climbing those stairs every Sunday, the church should have renovated the entrance to eliminate the long climb. Mother Dear climbed those stairs at a pace slower than molasses going uphill on a winter day. Her legs were perpetually swollen and she moved like an old brontosaurus, even when she wasn't climbing stairs. But she wasn't missing church for "nothin' in the world."

Sunday was her day to sing and pray and socialize with all her other old, church-going girlfriends. She got her hair done on Saturday, wrapped it up Saturday night so that it would stay fresh for Sunday morning and got up at the crack of dawn on Sunday to start getting ready for the 10:00 o'clock service. First she took a long bubble bath, being careful not to wet her hair. Then she placed her towel on the toilet and sat there drying her body, one body part at a time. After all the water was dried, she slathered cocoa butter from the tip of her toes all the way up to the top of her neck. It took her forever to slather the cocoa butter over every nook and cranny of her body, except her face. The only lotion to touch her face was Oil of Olay. She swore by it. Then, she dressed in her Sunday best with a matching hat and strutted down the street proud as a peacock in bloom.

Oh Happy Day/Oh Happy Day/When Jesus was/When Jesus was/He took our sins away/Oh Happy Day.

When church services concluded, it was a time for socializing. Socializing occurred in the vestibules of the church and often carried over into the nearby homes. Dressed in their best Sunday clothes, women and children gathered to share gossip and games. When company came to visit, it was customary in the South to offer them something to drink. You offered them either iced tea or lemonade. Water was an acceptable alternative, but it usually meant that you really didn't want to be bothered with the company in the first place. It could also mean that you were too poor to offer anything else but water. If you were a polite and respectful visitor, you accepted only water, unless you were well acquainted with your host, in which case it was all right to drink up their beverages, always mindful that you never wanted to, "wear out your welcome." Soda pop, which was considered a luxury item, was never seen in our refrigerator and therefore was never offered. We drank it only on rare occasions, like when we went out to a restaurant, which was never. It was an exceptional treat indeed when we went visiting and were allowed to drink soda pop.

At first Marshall and his stepfather Willie did not get along because Marshall was jealous that his mother married Willie. They were constantly at each others throats arguing about everything from Marshall getting up and going to school on time to Marshall coming home and going to bed on time. Eventually, the relationship between Willie and Marshall improved with the addition of seven more children. There simply was not enough time to bicker over inconsequential minutia. They saved their energy for the bigger brawls like earning your keep and staying out of trouble with the law.

In his early life, Marshall earned a living from professional boxing in the local gymnasium. It was a common way for Southern black men to make money back then. It was also an avenue to release pent up frustration. Marshall trained religiously and quickly developed a reputation in the local gym for being rough and tough. His reputation rapidly spread outside of the gym. Because of his physical stature and tough demeanor, Marshall became the protector of the family, especially the girls. If a boy tried to get too close to one of his sisters, Marshall appeared out of nowhere like the superhero who shows up just in the nick of time to annihilate the bad guy, sometimes with far too much force.

Once, when Amanda was dating this boy, he tried to force himself upon her. Amanda was 17 and very much a virgin. Back then, good girls remained virgins until they were married. Mama was a good girl. The boy was no more than 22 or 23, a ripe young age, neither worldly nor wise.

When the boy grabbed Mama's arms to hold her back from fighting off his advances, he felt a hard sudden tap on his right shoulder. As he turned around to see who tapped him, his face met Uncle Marshall's right fist, then his left fist, then another right to the head, then another left fist to the gut. After a while, it was difficult to see who or what was hitting him, the blood blocking his vision, the dizziness draining his energy. After a while, the boy fell to the ground and stopped moving. After a while, Marshall backed away and stopped hitting him.

Amanda ran home right after the first punch was thrown, following the instructions of her older brother Marshall to the letter. There was no arguing or rationalizing with brother Marshall when he was in a rage. He didn't hear anything anyway. He was like a wild animal in a hunt with only one objective. Annihilate the enemy, kill the beast, overpower the prey. In any event, Amanda did not want to witness the violence, violence which was out of her control, violence which was unstoppable once begun.

Mama never saw the boy again. He never showed his face again in the neighborhood. Rumor had it that he was beaten senseless, beaten so badly that he could not talk straight, beaten so badly that he had to be institutionalized. Marshall had broken the law. He had assaulted and battered another human being. He had strayed far and wide from Granddaddy's straight and narrow, but it didn't matter. This was black on black crime. The police couldn't care less. One less n _ _ _ _ _ to contend with.

Marshall went on to marry three times, first to a woman named Betty, then Celestine and then Elizabeth ("Liz"). Marshall and Liz had one son named Cedric. Cedric was the love of Marshall's life and eventually the cause of his death. Cedric was always in trouble with the law. His father had to bail him out of jail for possession of drugs on more than one occasion. At one point when Cedric was in high school, he missed so many classes that his father was not sure whether he would graduate. Marshall called his sister younger Yvonne, who was a school teacher, and asked her to make some inquiries to the school to determine whether Cedric was going to graduate and, if not, how to remedy the situation. He figured that Sister Yvonne could pull some strings if necessary because of her academic credentials. Aunt Yvonne made the appropriate inquiries and determined that Cedric was indeed going to graduate, provided he successfully completed his final exams, a feat he narrowly accomplished. Although Marshall was relieved to hear such news, the entire ordeal took its toll on Marshall. He lost countless nights of sleep and the constant aggravation elevated his blood pressure and ultimately took its toll on his heart.

Marshall eventually died of a massive heart attack while cutting the grass in his front yard. His wife Liz claimed that she rushed him to the hospital, but by the time they arrived it was too late to save him, he had already slipped into a coma. Apparently, there was some discrepancy in the record between the time of the 9-1-1 call and the time of initial heart attack.

Aunt Yvonne blamed Liz for not getting her brother to the hospital quickly enough. Once Marshall was admitted to the hospital, Liz called Yvonne and told her that Marshall had a heart attack and, "It doesn't look good." Yvonne took the next flight from Birmingham to Chicago, steadfastly praying for a miracle the entire trip. When she arrived at the hospital parking lot, she found Marshall's son, Cedric, walking aimlessly around in circles talking to himself. As she approached him, he looked up at her. When their eyes met, she knew all that she needed to know. Marshall, the oldest brother and the protector of the Fouther family, was dead.

Uncle Billie (Willie Jr.) lived in Chicago with his second wife and six children. He was Granddaddy's and Mother Dear's first born son together. His first wife died in 1984 at the age of 49 of a brain tumor. After she died, he married a much younger woman. Uncle Billie was a kind man with a gentle heart, although financial success always seemed to elude him and his family. They settled in the inner city of Chicago on the proverbial wrong side of the tracks. It was a struggle just to keep food on the table. To complicate matters, one of his daughters had epilepsy and lived her entire life in a government subsidized nursing home. The rest of the children eventually married and moved away from home.

Robert was the third son. Like his father before him, he was a notorious drinker and smoker. Like his father before him, he was tall, handsome and proud. He looked just like Granddaddy, only a shade or two lighter. Unlike Granddaddy, Uncle Robert was a notorious hustler and was considered a lady's man. His good looks and reputation preceded him everywhere. He eventually settled down in California. Robert's first marriage was to a woman named Ellen. Robert and Ellen had two children, Elizabeth (Liz) and Bobby. Liz had one daughter named Nia. Nia and her mother Liz were complete opposites. Liz was 5'5" and thin as a rail. Nia was much heavier and towered over her mother. To see them together, it was difficult to believe that the mother birthed the daughter. Robert's second marriage was to an attractive woman named Ruby. Robert and Ruby had one son named Michael. Uncle Robert died of lung cancer not long after Michael was born. Ruby and Michael reside in California.

Uncle Samuel was the fourth son of Willie and Annie Mae Fouther. He was an enterprising young man, which had its advantages and disadvantages. Once, when Uncle Samuel was 15, he and Uncle Billy decided to go over to the Bush Hill section of Birmingham, Alabama, which was a whites only part of town. They went there for the sole purpose of mowing lawns for a little pocket change. After asking permission, they proceeded to mow one woman's lawn. When they were finished, the woman refused to pay them. Uncle Billy and Uncle Samuel left disillusioned but without incident.

Later that evening, the police appeared at the front door of the Fouther household. They demanded to question the two boys. The white woman from the Bush Hill section of town called the police claiming that Uncle Billy and Uncle Samuel attempted to rob her. One of the boys was in the shower, but that did not stop the police. They forced the boys to appear, one in night clothes, the other dripping wet with a towel wrapped around his waist. If Mother Dear had not made a phone call to a white lawyer she knew, the boys would have been taken to the police station and subject to interrogation by the police. Fortunately, the white attorney vouched for the family and the boys were set free.

Uncle Samuel later married a woman named Joyce. They had one son named Sammy. Joyce thought the Fouther family was overbearing. After Uncle Sammy died of a massive heart attack, Joyce took little Sammy away to Minnesota. That was the last time anyone in the Fouther family ever laid eyes on little Sammy.

James (Bubba) was the youngest of the boys, he was also Aunt Yvonne's twin brother. He was the first of the eight siblings to die. He died of a massive heart attack in December 1973. When Uncle Bubba died, the Fouther family was devastated, but no one was as distraught as Aunt Yvonne. The death of her twin brother completely overwhelmed her. She never completely recovered from the loss. Months after his death, she caught herself dialing his number, thinking he was still alive. She felt his presence in her world, especially at night when she dreamed. Yvonne had long conversations with Bubba in her dreams, conversations about vital subjects which troubled her at the time. She communicated with him in this way for years.

They say that twins, even fraternal twins, are deeply affected by the loss of one another. Years later, when my mother was first diagnosed with cancer, Aunt Yvonne told me that Uncle Bubba came to her in a dream. During the dream, he told Aunt Yvonne that it was not yet time for Amanda to leave our world and join him in heaven. The message from Bubba reassured Yvonne beyond belief.

Later, when she tried to communicate with him again about Amanda's fate, he would not come to her. She interpreted his silence as an ominous sign of things to come.

Uncle Bubba was married to Celesta. They had James Jr. and Valerie. James is married to Angelle and has a daughter named Danielle. James became a well respected minister in a Southern Baptist church in Miami, Florida. Little did anyone know, that James would become the official minister to preside over the funerals of his Aunts and Uncles who died much too young in rapid succession.

The three Fouther girls were the last of thirteen births to Willie and Annie Mae. Yvonne, Adrienne and Amanda. They were all blessed with beauty and brains. Yvonne was the oldest and acted much like the little mother of the Fouther household. Being the first girl after so many boys, Yvonne's birth order dictated that she help Mother Dear take care of the family. She grew up quickly around her brothers and learned early on how to take care of herself. She was independent and free spirited. She enjoyed school, but looked forward to dating boys and getting out of the house, away from Granddaddy's tight grip. Because Yvonne was the first girl, Granddaddy was strict and overprotective. He set early curfews and often forbade her to go to dances or clubs. Granddaddy's strictness with Yvonne was the source of constant bickering and perpetual punishments. Yvonne rebelled by lying about where she was going and staying out beyond her curfew. Before long, Yvonne found herself pregnant. When Granddaddy discovered she was pregnant, he was furious. There were many, "I told you so's" and "I don't care's" shouted between the two of them. Mother Dear's patient wisdom intervened with many, "let it be's." As fate invariably unfolded, Yvonne gave birth out of wedlock to the very first grandchild, Andre, who everyone called Butch. She later married Bernard Green, although Bernard was not Andre's father. Yvonne and Bernard never had children together, which ultimately was probably best for everyone.

In 1950, having children out of wedlock was simply scandalous. The situation was a source of great conflict and tension between Yvonne and Granddaddy. He berated Yvonne about her predicament and blamed her for not heeding his advice. Yvonne sought refuge in Bernard, who was tall and handsome. Unfortunately, he was a notorious lady's man. He cheated on Yvonne from the very beginning of the marriage. He came and left with little or no explanation, often for days at a time. There was very little Yvonne could do. She felt trapped because of her situation.

Yvonne discovered that Bernard was traveling back and forth on the weekends between Birmingham and Atlanta. One of her friends told her that Bernard was seeing a woman in Atlanta. Although her mind was in denial, her heart suspected her friend was telling the truth. She tracked him down at a hotel in Atlanta and confronted him with the information she had learned. He did not deny that he had been cheating. He was not even sorry. The woman later showed up with a bottle of booze when Yvonne answered the door. She told the woman, "Not tonight honey." The woman was shocked and left, never to return. Unfortunately, there were many others who did return.

Bernard spent weeks at a time away in Atlanta, often without even feigning an excuse. Yvonne became increasingly lonely and depressed. One day, Yvonne ran into a childhood friend named Cag who she had not seen in years. They began sharing life stories over coffee at a nearby diner. Cag was kind and gentle and supportive. He told Yvonne that she was the most beautiful woman he had ever known. He asked her to run away with him to Nashville with her son Andre. For several weeks, Yvonne seriously considered his proposal. Then, one day out of the blue, she finally agreed to run away with him. On that very day, as she was preparing to leave her husband Bernard for good, she heard the key to the front door of her house open. She walked through the living room towards the front door and there stood Bernard, as big as day. He told her he was back, back for good. He took her into their bedroom and made love to her all night.

Yvonne interpreted Bernard's return as a sign from God to stay in the marriage. She called Cag the next day and told him she could not go away with him. Her plans had changed. Bernard was home and this time he was home for good. Everything was going to be different now, Yvonne told Cag. Broken hearted and depressed, Cag left for Nashville without Yvonne. She never saw nor heard from him again. Weeks later Bernard began disappearing again, first for hours, then for days at a time. Although Yvonne was initially depressed by Bernard's recurring infidelities, she picked herself up and continued to function, this time without any expectations of love from anyone else. She decided that her survival depended upon her own capabilities and her own self esteem.

Uncle Bernard did not make matters any easier for Yvonne. He spent lavishly on the women who kept him company. He also developed an insatiable habit for gambling. At one point, Bernard failed to pay the mortgage on the house for three consecutive months and Aunt Yvonne returned home from teaching one day to find an eviction notice nailed onto the front door of their house. For weeks, until she managed to straighten out the situation, Yvonne had nightmares of being evicted and returning to the four room shack on 4th Avenue where she spent much of her childhood. The dream was one that recurred from time to time whenever Yvonne was stressed or anxious. After she nearly lost the house,

Aunt Yvonne decided to keep her money in a separate bank account, barring all access to Bernard who, according to Aunt Yvonne, had "clearly lost his goddamn mind."

Adrienne, the second daughter born to Willie and Annie Mae Fouther, married a real estate entrepreneur who was ten years her senior, Afton Michael Lee. Adrienne and Afton had three children named Ari, Michael and Adrianne. As young children, Ari and I were inseparable. Although we are now miles apart, she and I remain close today.

Aunt Adrienne and Uncle Afton raised their three children in the Homewood section of Birmingham, Alabama. Uncle Afton's family owned a good deal of property in the Homewood area, which he and his father leased and managed. The family was considered fairly affluent in the community. They lived on top of a hill in the nicest house in the neighborhood. The house was a large white three bedroom, two bathroom ranch with a patio overlooking the backyard and a porch overlooking the front yard. Uncle Afton made sure that the flowers and shrubs in the yard were neatly trimmed and the grass was evenly cut. He kept the house stocked with essential supplies like paper goods and canned goods. If a roll of toilet paper or paper towels was empty, there was plenty more where that came from, stocked on the shelves above the washer and dryer or in the kitchen cabinets above and below the counters or in the wood shed next to the house. Long before the supplies dwindled to nothing, Uncle Afton would go down the hill to the corner grocery store which he owned and operated with his father and replenish his supply.

Uncle Afton's grocery store (called A & A) was a small store located on a prominent corner in Homewood, Alabama. Afton Senior, Uncle Afton's father, managed the store. In October, 1989, Afton Senior was at the store behind the counter waiting on customers, like any other day. Two young men came into the store and lingered behind the aisles until all of the other shoppers were gone. When the store was empty, the boys demanded the cash from the register. Afton Senior surely knew what was coming next, but he was trapped and defenseless. According to later testimony, he offered no resistance. Indeed, he begged for his life. But the two boys calmly walked up to Afton Senior, emptied the cash register and then, for no apparent reason, bashed him repeatedly over the head with an iron pipe until he fell to the floor and stopped moving. Then they dragged his limp body to the meat freezer, leaving him for dead.

When they called Uncle Afton to come to the store, he found his father lying semi-conscious in a pool of blood, barely alive. They had beaten him so badly that his head was indented on one side. He was pronounced dead several hours later at the hospital. During the criminal trial which followed, the jury learned that the two boys were gang members who were told to rob and kill a prominent member of the community as a right of passage into the gang. After a short deliberation, the twelve member jury convicted the boys of first degree premeditated murder. The Judge sentenced each of the boys to life imprisonment. Every year when the boys are eligible for parole, a family member goes down to testify against the release of the prisoners. To this day, those two boys remain in prison for the ruthless murder of Afton Senior.

A loving father and grandfather and a cherished member of the community was brutally murdered to prove a senseless point. Uncle Afton was especially devastated over the murder of his father. He blamed himself for not being at the store when the murder took place. He had recurring nightmares about the incident, imagining the worst as his father helplessly endured his fate. After the murder, Uncle Afton's typically fast pace slowed down considerably. The pep in his step was no longer discernable. He joked and teased less frequently. Truth be told, Uncle Afton was never quite the same after the murder of his father. He died unexpectedly from a pulmonary embolism after a routine hip fracture less than five years later.

~ ~ ~

Amanda was born on December 17, 1934. Willie and Annie Mae knew she was special. They knew she would be their last. They named her Amanda, after her great grandmother, Amanda Jones. The name means worthy of love.

Amanda nearly died during the deadly bout of whooping cough that all eight siblings contracted when she was born. But Mother Dear refused to let her die. When Mother Dear and Mrs. Thomas (the next door neighbor) were tending to the sick children, Mother Dear made sure that she personally kept a close vigil on Amanda. The baby was either at her nipple or on her shoulder at all times. Mother Dear prayed that the Lord would spare her baby, the last baby Willie and Annie Mae Fouther would ever birth. In his infinite wisdom, God spared the fragile infant. Amanda was destined to make her mark on this world, a lasting and deep impression.

From the minute she was born, people were astonished by Amanda's beauty. Her dark brown eyes were the shape of large almonds which captivated observers with a look like she had been here before, the look of an old soul. Her perfectly shaped lips were plump and cherry red. If you didn't know better, you would think that she was wearing lipstick and lipstick liner. Her dark hair was thick and wavy, like Granddaddy's hair. It would eventually grow down her back until it reached her tiny waist. Her complexion was perfect, a light golden brown, neither too dark nor too light.

Southern blacks were notoriously preoccupied with the color of skin. If you were too dark, invariably it meant that you were ugly and stupid. If you were too light, you were probably the object of envy and hate. If you were Mama's complexion, you could probably avoid being called either "darkie" or "high yellow."

When Mother Dear took Amanda out for a stroll, complete strangers would stop to admire her beauty. It was as though there were no other words to speak once you saw Amanda, her looks simply captivated everyone. Amanda would later learn how to make her good looks work to her advantage, though she never let them serve as a substitute for hard work or a good education. She would later tell me that you had to use the gifts God gave you, whatever those gift may be.

As the youngest of eight children growing up in the Fouther household, Amanda soon became the center of attention. She not only charmed complete strangers, but she fascinated her brothers and sisters as well. Sister Yvonne, in particular, was completely captivated by her youngest sister. The attention previously directed towards Aunt Adrienne, was now lavished upon Amanda. Yvonne cared for Amanda like she was her own personal baby doll. She changed her diapers, dressed her every morning, combed her hair and fed her. When Adrienne tried to reclaim Yvonne's attention, Yvonne said she was too busy taking care of Amanda to play silly games. Adrienne soon realized that she would have to learn new ways to entertain herself.

Amanda's beauty did not always work to her advantage. The other girls in her class were scandalously jealous of her looks. It didn't matter that Amanda was poor just like everyone else, with struggling parents trying to make ends meet. The other girls talked about her behind her back, they refused to pick her for their team in gym and worst of all, they picked fights with her. More often than not, Amanda would ignore the teasing and jaunting, even when it became slightly physical. Usually, she could avoid an altercation all together because one of her five brothers would miraculously show up and intervene, stopping would-be offenders in their tracks. While her looks cost her many friendships, Amanda developed even closer bonds with her siblings, especially her sisters Yvonne and Adrienne. When you saw one of the Fouther girls, you generally saw all three.

On one occasion when Amanda was in eighth grade attending Holy Family Middle School, one of her classmates decided to pick a fight. This time, not one of her brothers managed to miraculously appear at the school yard. Her sisters Yvonne and Adrienne were held in abeyance by a group of girls pushing and shoving them out of the way. Amanda was forced to resort to her own devices.

She had witnessed enough fights to know that kicking was an effective way to inflict injury while maintaining a safe distance. She also knew from watching her brothers box, that punching someone right in the middle of the solar plexus would cause the person to double over. As she mentally prepared to battle her opponent, the last thought crossing her mind was to avoid oncoming slaps to the face where sharpened nails were sure to cause lasting damage. Amanda raised her right leg and kicked the girl in the stomach. Before she could react, Amanda punched her directly in the solar plexus. The girl doubled over and then fell to her knees. The fight was over in a matter of seconds. The Fouther girls glanced one at the other and calmly left the school yard, leaving astonished faces and gaping mouths behind them. To her sisters' surprise, Amanda won the fight, fair and square. Amanda soon developed a reputation as a force to be reckoned. Years later, my cousin Ari and I would encounter similar altercations at the same school.

As my mother matured into a beautiful young woman, numerous men were attracted to her beauty. She was pursued and approached on a regular basis. Although it seems unfathomable, my mother Amanda was married five times (including a one day marriage to a man named Walter). It may seem like an exorbitant number of marriages, but it never seemed so to me. In my mind, there was a perfectly good explanation for each marriage and each divorce to Walter, Arthur, Gene and Bob. Alas, I do not understand why she decided to marry Larry.

I didn't know about Walter until I was an adult. My cousin Ari and I were talking once about men and marriage and she let the secret slip out. "Auntie LaLa (my mother's nickname, the origin of which is unknown) married Walter before she married your father Arthur," she said.

"Who the hell was Walter and what ever happened to him," I demanded to know. My cousin Ari informed me that Mama and Walter fell in love, but the hasty elopement was annulled days after the ceremony. According to my mother, who I immediately accosted for details, the marriage was never consummated; they never even slept under the same roof. Mama later explained that Walter, who was tall, dark and handsome, wanted Mama to be his stay-at-home wife, cooking and cleaning, barefoot and pregnant. They got into a huge argument on the night of their wedding and Mama commandingly stormed out of the room and ran home to Mother Dear and Granddaddy. Mother Dear wasted no time seeking an annulment the next day.

Mama had other ideas beyond birthing babies, cooking and cleaning her way through life, totally dependant upon a man. Like all young girls, she wanted to get married and raise a family. But she knew that there was more to life than just catering to her husband. During the 1930s and 1940s, there were not many career options for women, especially if you were poor and black. White women could aspire to become nurses and teachers. Black women who wanted to work were limited to cooking, cleaning and babysitting for wealthier white families. Slavery may have officially ended in the South, but the slave mentality was severe and pervasive.

None of that phased Mama. Her dream was to become a nurse to help the sick and infirmed, like her World War I heroine, Florence Nightingale. So marriage would have to wait. Mama was destined to become more than just a wife and mother, she thought. She was going to establish her own identity. She was going to make a difference. Marrying Walter was a mistake she was not afraid to admit. In her opinion, it was better to remedy the situation sooner than later. Sometimes her decisions were impulsive and sometimes they were wrong, but they were always her decisions, guided by her heart. "Follow your heart," Mama said, "it will eventually lead you to the right place."

So Mama followed her heart. After the marriage to Walter was annulled, she boldly announced that she was going to college. Of course, Mother Dear and Granddaddy had no money to send any of their eight children to college, but that did not stop Mama. As the family listened in amazement, Mama told them how she intended to enter a beauty contest and win enough money to attend college and become a nurse. She would use her God given strengths to accomplish her goals and dreams. During the 1950s, the schools in Alabama were all completely segregated. This meant that Mama not only needed money for tuition, but she also needed enough money to travel out of state to attend a school that was willing to accept blacks. This was no small hurdle. No one in the Fouther family had ever before attempted to go to college because of the tremendous social and economic barriers facing black families. Mama was undaunted, even naïve about the road ahead.

She left home the day of the contest, bags packed, performances rehearsed, prayers recited, ready to go. Before the competition, the family took a picture of Mama posing in the bathing suit she had selected for the contest. Curvaceous and enthusiastic, she is smiling her classic smile, a grand infectious smile that lights up the room and mesmerizes her audience. Her right arm is raised slightly above her right shoulder; her left arm is extended in front of her to the left. She is posed as if to say, "Ready or not world, here I come." The actual inscription on the lower left hand side of the picture has faded slightly, but it is her handwriting and it reads: "We're Ready. Amanda Fouther."

The beauty pageant was sponsored by a private black fraternal organization known as the Shriners. It was the black version of the Elks, a popular white fraternal organization. At the time, blacks were not allowed to enter the nationally sponsored Miss America Pageant. So the Shriners raised money to sponsor their own beauty pageant to send poor disadvantaged black children to college. Mama sang for the talent portion of the contest and she succinctly articulated her hopes and dreams for the monologue section. To the astonishment of friends and family, Amanda won both the city wide competition and the state wide competition. The family was ecstatic as they cried tears of joy. Amanda Anastasia Fouther, the youngest of thirteen children born to Willie and Annie Mae Fouther, was the Shriner's 1953 beauty contest winner for the State of Alabama. She became an overnight local celebrity. She was well on her way to making her mark on the world.

The Shriners gave Amanda a four year scholarship to attend nursing school in Cleveland, Ohio. After a little research, Mama discovered that it was not uncommon for desegregated schools of one state to finance some of the expenses for minority students who had to travel out of state to attend school. When the school learned that Mama's entire four year tuition was secured, it gladly paid for her travel and housing expenses. Mother Dear praised God for the blessings He bestowed upon her daughter and she praised her daughter for her persistent efforts. According to Mother Dear, the Lord helps those who help themselves. Praise the Lord.

Before Amanda left for Cleveland, another young man wooed her and convinced her that she would be better off moving to Ohio as a married woman with a husband to protect her from the harsh realities of the world, to support her dreams and aspirations and to provide a safe loving environment. That man was my father. Arthur Benjamin Tiddle, Jr., the proverbial boy next door who didn't drink, who didn't smoke and who would never cheat on his wife. And according to Mother Dear, it didn't hurt that he was so light skinned he could easily pass for white. Mother Dear's own experiences as a dark skinned Negro woman led her to the conclusion that life would be less difficult as a light skinned Negro. If you didn't know better, you would have thought that my father was white. For most of my childhood years, I thought just that.

3
The Boy Next Door

I always thought that he left us. As it turns out, it was she who left him. From the very beginning, the relationship lacked passion. My mother married Arthur because he convinced her that it was the right thing to do at the right time in her life, a time when she was venturing out on her own. Arthur was thrilled when Amanda agreed to be his wife. After all, he was marrying the winner of a national beauty contest. Arthur adored Amanda, he showered her with constant attention and he craved the same from her.

A few weeks after Arthur and Amanda were married, Amanda discovered that she was pregnant. The doctor calculated that she probably conceived on her wedding night. It was the first time my mother had ever had sex. Nine months later Mama gave birth to my older brother Benji on June 14, 1956. My auspicious birth occurred 16 months later on October 25, 1957. My sister Cathy was born 13 months later on November 3, 1958. The family teased my father claiming that all you had to do was look at Mama and she would get pregnant. After my sister Cathy's birth, Arthur thought twice before looking at Mama.

Although Arthur adored my mother, it was far more difficult for him to accept the fact that his children needed as much attention as he did, if not more. Arthur was in the military and traveled frequently for weeks at a time. He often relegated the childcare to Amanda. When he returned home, the reunions were awkward at best. He spent most of his time vying for Amanda's attention instead of forging a bond with his children. It was difficult for him to show affection to his children. During one of their discussions regarding the matter, Arthur actually admitted to my mother that children were not a part of his original plan. Plan or no plan, Amanda's children meant the world to her and that was obvious to anyone who knew her.

It wasn't long before Mama began to feel that the marriage was not right. She felt that she was trapped and that it would never be right. Leaving Arthur would be one of the most difficult decisions she ever made. Back then, divorce was not as commonplace as it is today. Mama was only 26 years old with three children aged two, three and four. My sister Cathy was barely potty trained.

Arthur was stationed on a military base near Cleveland. The week after Mama graduated from nursing school, she was scheduled to interview for a local nursing position. Instead, she packed all of our belongings and took her three children on the next flight back to Birmingham, Alabama, leaving behind all those things that would not fit into a suit case, including her husband Arthur. She told no one about her plans, not even her parents and siblings.

Ironically, her two sisters Yvonne and Adrienne had planned a surprise visit to Cleveland the very day Amanda packed up and left for Birmingham. When Aunt Yvonne and Aunt Adrienne arrived at our house in Cleveland, no one was home. They contacted Arthur at the military base and he rushed home to a deserted house, with no wife and no children. In an effort to locate Amanda, Aunt Yvonne called Mother Dear.

Much to everyone's surprise, Mama had returned home to Birmingham to live with Mother Dear and Granddaddy. Despite Arthur's humiliation over the situation, he pleaded with Amanda to return.

Ain't to proud to beg, sweet darling/Please don't leave me girl/Ain't to proud to plead-eed, baby baby/Please don't leave me girl.

Alas, Arthur's beautiful bride and three young children were gone for good. For a number of years, even after the divorce was final, Arthur continued to hope and pray that one day Mama would return. She never did.

Life at home with Granddaddy and Mother Dear was not easy. Living with your parents while trying to raise three young children was awkward at best. Mother Dear and Granddaddy attempted to impose their own rules and regulations in their own house. Amanda was more lenient with raising children, but felt like she was imposing upon Granddaddy and Mother Dear in a tenuous situation which would not remain stable for long.

Amanda looked desperately for a decent paying job that would enable her to move into her own place. Eventually, she landed a menial job at a small hospital working as a nurse's assistant, but it was barely enough to support herself, much less three dependent children. No one in the South was willing to hire a black woman for the position of a full time registered nurse, even with a fancy nursing certificate from a reputable school in Ohio. She prayed that leaving Cleveland and her husband had been the right decision.

Mama soon realized that her nursing degree was not enough formal education to accomplish her ultimate goal of financial independence, at least not for a black woman. She had to be better than her white counterparts to be taken seriously. Discouraged but not downtrodden, she set her sights on obtaining a bachelor's degree from Tuskeegee University, only two hours away from Birmingham by car. The short commute allowed my mother to maintain a watchful eye over her three children and to monitor the caretaking skills of Granddaddy and Mother Dear, who were strict and not always savvy about the latest child rearing techniques.

Once, when my sister Cathy and I caught a bad flu, Mother Dear tried to administer medication to us. Cathy refused to take the nasty smelling liquid. She held her lips tight and shook her head back and forth defiantly. Granddaddy watched incredulously, shaking his head all the while, as Mother Dear futilely tried to force the spoon down Cathy's throat, "for her own good." Eventually, Mother Dear gave up and shook her head claiming, "Lord knows I just want to help you feel better chil'."

Then she turned the spoon on me. Like my sister Cathy, I had no desire to take the nasty smelling liquid which Mother Dear said was castor oil. To prepare myself for the unpleasant taste I was about to experience, I thought about the Mary Poppins song my mother used to sing to us.

Just a spoon full of sugar helps the medicine go down/The medicine go down/Just a spoon full of sugar helps the medicine go down/In the most delightful way.

I held my breath, opened my mouth and dutifully took two full tablespoons of the nasty smelling liquid. Mother Dear patiently told Cathy, "Now see, yo' sister is gonna' be feeling much better soon because she took her medicine like a good girl." Cathy was unfazed.

Nothing could have been further from the truth. Shortly after I swallowed the nasty medicine, I began to have severe stomach cramps and nausea. Mother Dear called Mama in Tuskegee who panicked over the phone, but had the wherewithal to ask Mother Dear to read the label on the bottle. The label said "turpentine," not castor oil at all. My mother shouted, "Oh my God Mother, turpentine could kill her. Get off the phone right now and take her to the emergency room immediately!"

My mother met us at the hospital. Fortunately, I ended up throwing up the offending liquid before the doctors needed to pump my stomach, saving me from an even more painful experience. Mother Dear was beside herself, crying that she almost killed her granddaughter. She kept repeating, "Lord, help me. I nearly killed the po' chil'. Lord, please forgive me." The Good Lord saw fit to help Mother Dear in her time of need and saved me from the throngs of death. My sister Cathy was relieved that I would recover, but seemed even more grateful that she had held her ground. After all, had she taken the nasty potion, she too would have had a near death experience. My mother was mortified. She wondered whether she had made the right decision to leave her children with her parents, who mistakenly administered poisonous turpentine to one of her children.

After the turpentine incident, we began spending more and more time in Tuskegee living in the dormitory with Mama. She had numerous female colleagues who took turns babysitting us. The babysitting schedule rotated around everyone's class schedules. The kids in the dormitory even had a pet pig who we kept in a fenced yard behind the building. The students adopted Charlie the pig from a local farmer who had plans to slaughter the runt. The students all took turns feeding Charlie, who was one of the cleanest pigs I have ever seen. Dormitory life was great. It felt like one big happy communal family.

It was special living with Mama in the dormitory, like she couldn't bear being separated from us. We slept four to a bed, two one way and two the other. We were still all under the age of five, so school was not exactly an issue. But Mama made sure that we studied our numbers and learned the alphabet. She read stories to us every night. Dr. Seuss was our favorite. *Green Eggs and Ham. The Cat in the Hat.* Life was good.

After the divorce, our real father came to visit us once or twice a year at Easter and Christmas until September 1962, when my mother married for the second time (third including Walter). She married a handsome young air force pilot named Gene Collins. Shortly after the marriage to Gene, our real father stopped visiting us. We soon began calling Gene "daddy" because we were so young and because he was so kind to us. This meant that when our real father came to visit we had to make a distinction between him and Gene. We decided to call our real father Daddy Tiddle, a name that struck him like a dagger. We tried not to call him by any name at all to ease the pain, but he knew that his role was slowly diminishing. Daddy Tiddle's Christmas and Easter visits were fraught with tension and anxiety. It was an exciting time of year when family gathered to celebrate over food and drink, but Daddy Tiddle's arrival was always awkward.

During the Christmas visits, Daddy Tiddle made sure that he brought gifts for each of us. For reasons beyond my comprehension, he always brought me and my sister long thick house coats with flower and heart designs. We knew right away when we saw the long flat bow-less boxes wrapped in thin department store Christmas paper that the contents contained another housecoat. We whispered softly to each other, making sure no could overhear our whispers, "How much you wanna' bet that it's another dumb housecoat?" In retrospect, he probably had no idea what little girls dreamed of for Christmas. He approached us cautiously, leaned over and kissed us with his full wet lips and handed us our gifts. I dreaded having to kiss him. I barely knew this man and yet I was expected to affectionately greet him. I politely obliged because my mother would not have it any other way. But as far as I was concerned, right or wrong, he left my mother alone with three children. I didn't think I owed him much more than a quick hello and a peck on the cheek.

I was five years old when Mama married Gene and when Daddy Tiddle stopped visiting us altogether. I would not see my real father again until I was a 23 years old. The brief visit occurred in 1980 when I was attending law school at Columbia University in New York. I had traveled to a Black Law Students convention in Los Angeles for the weekend. Daddy Tiddle drove two hours from his home in Diamond Bar, California to see me. I stood on the front porch of the house where I was staying and watched him pull his car into the driveway. I saw him take a handkerchief out of his breast pocket and dab his eyes and nose as he climbed out of his car. He was older and heavier, but looked much like the man I had remembered. His hands trembled slightly as they reached for mine, so did his lips, as they forced a nervous little smile. He kept saying that I looked just like my mother. He said that he could not get over the resemblance. This, of course, was the greatest compliment he could have given me. After all, my mother had won the title of Miss Alabama in the Shriners' beauty pageant contest. Personally, I thought she was the most beautiful woman in the world.

We sat and talked for about two hours. I offered him something to drink, like a good Southern host. He would accept only water, like a good Southern guest, barely sipping the glass as we spoke, all the while staring straight at me. His unyielding gaze made me uncomfortable, but I understood his need to take it all in, to stare at me for as long as he could. Daddy Tiddle told me that he was very proud of me and that I had matured into a beautiful young woman. Before he left, he kissed me on the cheek with his full wet lips. It reminded me of the kisses I anxiously anticipated when I was a young girl. He asked me to please keep in touch with him, like my brother and sister had done. I told him I would. I never did.

The next time I saw him was May of 1994. He was wearing an attractive dark suit with a starched white shirt and red tie. His hands were laid neatly across his chest. His eyes were closed shut and caked with make-up. His full red lips did not seem quite so full. The coffin where he had lain was white and fluffy on the inside, smooth and wooden on the outside. He died of a massive heart attack after suffering for many years with high blood pressure and a weak heart. He looked small and fragile and, oddly enough, he looked darker than I had recalled.

My father had married a sweet unassuming Caucasian woman named Deanna. They had three young sons who looked like younger versions of my brother. It was strange seeing them, like looking into a mirror and seeing your own reflection. I wondered what it would have been like growing up with three more brothers.

Daddy Tiddle's second family genuinely welcomed Cathy, Benji and me. Deanna, the wife, asked us to join her and the boys in the family section at the funeral. She even included us in the memorial program. I felt guilty for never contacting them, guilty for thinking negative thoughts about Daddy Tiddle, guilty for never getting to know my father.

After the chapel service, the mourners piled outside one by one toward burial grounds to pay their final respects to my father. Yes, he was my father. I realized it then. It was a beautiful clear and sunny California day. A cool breeze was blowing from the coastal direction. There were a dozen men dressed in full military gear gathered around the newly unearthed plot. These uniformed strangers with the most powerful of bonds, gave my father a twenty one gun salute for a life dedicated to serving his country.

I was overcome with emotion and guilt. My father was lying before me and I never so much as wrote him a post card. I never allowed my stepfathers to serve as real fathers and I never allowed my real father to enter my world. Now it was too late to change any of that.

4

The Knight in Shining Armor

He seemed to appear one day from out of nowhere, but obviously he and Mama had been dating long before Benji, Cathy and I met him. The passion between them was undeniable. It was evident in their eyes, it was apparent in his touch. He was handsome beyond belief, just like her. He was 6' tall and well built, with light brown skin and wavy hair.

The day he came for us, he stood on the doorstep, like a tall knight in shining armor. We were living with Mother Dear and Granddaddy, but I knew enough to know that Mama wanted to live on her own. I also knew enough to know that the man she chose would have to love her children. It was as though Gene had come to rescue Mama, just like in the movies or storybook tales of Cinderella and Sleeping Beauty, only our story had children instead of mice or little men.

Mama never let on that she was dating. There were times in the evening when she would shower and change into something soft and pretty. She would comb her long hair into a bun, put on a little lipstick and spray on a little perfume. As I watched her prepare, I was in awe of her sheer beauty.

When she was ready to leave for the evening, she would tell us how long she would be gone, but not necessarily where she was going. More often than not, if we asked her where she was going, she would simply say, "I'm going to see a man about a dog."

We didn't know exactly what she meant by that comment. What man was she going to see? Were we really getting a dog? Why did she always come back home without a dog? Did other parents go see men about getting dogs? We wondered about the mysterious man with the dog for years until one day Mama stopped mentioning him. Just like that, he vanished into thin air, without a trace, never to be heard from again.

It was around that same time when Gene entered our lives. It was the summer of 1962. I was turning five years old. Like every other summer in Birmingham, it was hot, sweltering hot. Gene walked into our little house and sat down on the living room sofa, cool as a cucumber on ice. We didn't have multiple air conditioners like some of our neighbors, but Mother Dear strategically placed little fans around the house to create a cool breeze from the one air conditioner we owned. Mama brought Gene a tall cold glass of Mother Dear's sweet iced tea.

Mother Dear made the best iced tea I ever tasted. She mixed just the right amount of Lipton tea with hot water and heaps of Dominos sugar. Back then, Lipton was the tea manufacturer of choice. Celestial Seasonings had yet to make its mark on the market. The trick was to bring the water to a light boil, take it off the flame before it was too hot, let it sit for just a minute and then add the tea and sugar. Mother Dear scooped out the bags of tea when just enough flavor had seeped from the bags, not too much, not too little. She stirred the tea and the sugar directly into the pot of hot water on the stove and let the concoction sit to cool before pouring it into a clear glass pitcher and then placing it on the top shelf in the fridge to chill through and through.

I watched Mama bring him the tall glass of iced tea which made clinking sounds from the swirling ice hitting the sides of the glass. He watched her too. It was nice the way he watched her. I could tell that he admired her, that he appreciated her beauty. She looked like one of those sophisticated fashion models from a magazine. She wore dark slacks with straight legs and a cotton button-down shirt which hung just over the top of the waistband of her pants. Her shoulder length hair was straight and pulled back with a long black sash.

At one point during the visit, Mama sat my brother, sister and I down for a talk. She told us that she and Gene had fallen in love and gotten married. He was going to be our new father, although we still had our old father. She explained that the five of us were moving to Newark, New Jersey, a place far, far away from our beloved Birmingham. We were going to drive there in Gene's brand new car. In response to our concerns about leaving Mother Dear and Granddaddy, she said that it would not be so bad because we would come back to visit them every summer. Wow, I thought. We are going on some great adventure! Bigger than *The Cat in the Hat* or *Oh The Places You'll Go* or anything else Dr. Seuss could think up.

When it was time to go, Gene helped Mama with all of our bags. He loaded them carefully into the trunk of his big blue Chevrolet. I had never seen such a pretty car. It had a white roof and white trim with long tips on either side of the back which looked like wings. Gene was my mother's knight in shinning armor and the blue Chevy was his chariot. He was a complete gentleman. He treated Mama with such respect. Every time she walked next to him, he would place his hand at the small of her back, as if to guide her or hold her up. I wondered if he would care for us in the same way. I tried to be very good so that he would like us too. In preparation for the road trip, Gene placed a wooden board between the front and back seat of the car. Then Mama spread out thick blankets and pillows on top of the board and car seat. "This is where you guys will sleep when you get tired," she told us. "We have a long trip ahead of us."

Gene drove us all the way from Mother Dear's house in Birmingham, Alabama to our new house in Newark, New Jersey. It took nearly a week. We must have made a million stops along the way. We were moving to Newark because Gene had family nearby and because Mama got a nursing job at Beth Israel Hospital in neighboring New York City.

Mama warned us that there would be no horseplay in the car. She was serious about that. Mama had a way about showing us her displeasure that was incontrovertible. She would raise her right eyebrow into a large arch over her eye and glare at the offending child. We called it the "evil eye." Heaven help you if you were the direct recipient of the evil eye. She didn't use it often, but when she did, it commanded an immediate response from all three of us. The evil eye meant so many things, but mostly it meant, "You better stop whatever you are doing immediately because when I get you home you are going to be sorry you ever even thought about doing what you are doing."

So we played quietly together in the back seat. First we played the typical car games where you tried to find certain letters or numbers on a license plate, or "I Spy," where you tried to find certain objects before they disappeared out of sight. Then, when we tired of that, Mama started singing songs like *A Hundred Bottles of Beer on the Wall* or *Old MacDonald Had a Farm*, or any other song with simple repetition and multiple verses to occupy the time.

When we ran out of games to play and songs to sing, Mama would tell us, "Put your head down. Put your head down and close your eyes." We knew then that it was time for a nap. We never argued or talked back to Mama. We might argue with each other, but never with Mama. As I lay there falling asleep in the car, I remember hoping we had made a good impression on Gene. It was important to make a good impression on our mother's new husband, our new dad. I wasn't sure why our first dad left, but I knew that I desperately wanted this dad to stay.

Years later, after Mama and Gene divorced, I received a letter from him. It was written shortly after an emotional reunion preceded by a nine year hiatus.

February 11, 1982

My Dearest Terri,

I am at work, just returned from lunch and not in a particularly energetic work mood. I've just finished cutting your picture to fit my wallet, having shown it to several of my co-workers. There were comments like, "Who is she?" ("My daughter, of course"); "God, she's beautiful!?" ("You're damn right—fantastically beautiful!!!")

Hey, Sunday is St. Valentine's Day. Will you be my Valentine?

Terri, I've been on a high since last Saturday. Let me take a few minutes to tell you what seeing you meant to me.

It was the fulfillment of a nine year dream—well, 1/3 of that dream anyway, I've wanted so desperately over the years to see you, Benji and Cathy. Thinking often of how you have grown into adulthood, wondering where "your heads are"—and generally, how your lives were developing. I cannot, at this time make any comparisons between my visions and reality concerning Benji and Cathy because I have not seen them. I truly hope that someday, I'll be so fortunate. Meanwhile I can relate to some perceptions as they relate to you.

First, I was very touched when Pauline [Gene's sister] relayed your message some months ago. The fact you hadn't forgotten me and still considered me your Daddy created a feeling I cannot describe. You see, I always felt I had four children. I always felt that my blood and genes were as much a part of you three as it is with Glenda [Gene's daughter from his first wife].

All this reminds me again of something else and I want to tell you. It has been said that sometimes people don't learn certain lessons until it is too late. That has been my lot. It wasn't until I had lost you all did I finally realize what a dummy I had been. I came to regret not adopting you and giving you another brother and/or sister. I was so wrapped up in my own fears of how to better provide for you all and how I could make something better of my work career. Of course, there are additional reasons why I lost your Mother. To what extent the above may have been a factor, I don't know, but they are factors that are significant to me.

These admissions are also a part of the mixed feelings I was experiencing while on my way to see you. On one hand, I was feeling great excitement, on the other, I knew the sight of you would open me, open my consciousness to all I've tried to suppress over the years. Somewhat successfully because I did not want to confront the pain. Then it happened. The absolute joy in seeing and holding you. The anguish I felt during those hours together. The mind numbing distraction because you were not only Terri, but Cathy and Benji and your Mother as well. Still, I was absorbed in you. I wanted to re-discover you. I did. I like what I saw and what I heard. I remember my Aunt Peal asking if I was okay. My response was yes but I lied. I lied because I was re-living the years I'd spent with you all. I lied because I didn't want anyone else to share those all too few hours with us.

Did the intensity of my gazing upon you, the strong embrace discomfort you? I hope not for that was not my intention. Those acts were expressions of my love for you, the warmth and comfort I felt, the multitude of thoughts racing wildly through my mind.

I am so proud of you! Happy. Sad because I have not shared these years with you. I admire your perseverance and determination to become what you seek. I have no fear that you won't become successful in your career. More importantly, I <u>know</u> you will be successful as a loving, caring and sharing human being. Those attributes, for me, are the greatest ones an individual can ascribe to. I sensed the wonderful foundation you're building on, Terri. Let no one or anything re-case you.

Dear Terri, now that I've found you I would not want to lose you again. I want only to watch as you proceed through life. And as it unfolds, for you to know I love you so very, very much. And to know you'll always be able to find me if the need arises—no matter the time span or distance.

All my love, forever

Gene

I never saw Gene again after that. I graduated in 1983 from graduate school and life became hectic, juggling the demands of adulthood. Once I married and had two children of my own, life became even more hectic, bordering frenzied. My husband, Gary, was always on the road leaving the demands of raising a family upon my shoulders. Then, once I became a single mom, there was no time for anything else.

In late 1996, Gene was diagnosed with cancer. In early 1997, he and I talked one last time about my visiting him in Potsdam in the spring, when the weather warmed up a bit. I planned to drive there with the children the first weekend in May. Nicole and Christopher were excited by the prospect of meeting their step grandfather. Gene told me that he could not wait to meet them.

Gene died the first week of May. I drove to Potsdam that weekend as planned. Except instead of rekindling my relationship with my stepfather, I attended his funeral.

He never met my children.

5
Newark

Druthers (drutherz) pl.n. *Informal.* A choice or preference: if I had my druthers. Alteration of the phrase I would rather. (Webster's Dictionary)

Days after we left our beloved home in Birmingham, Alabama, we arrived in Newark, New Jersey, exhausted, excited and oblivious to the challenges we faced ahead. The year was 1962. Newark, New Jersey was a stark awakening for all of us. Mama had grown accustomed to the warmth and safety of her mother's house. Even though it was not large or expensive, our house in Birmingham, Alabama was safe and comfortable. The same could not be said about Newark, New Jersey or about our house on 201 Dewey Street. Newark was dark and dank and dirty. It seemed as though the sky was always blocked, perhaps by the tall buildings, I wasn't quite sure. There was little or no grass and barely any trees on the narrow concrete streets. The streets were filled with strange looking people we didn't know, strangers we truthfully did not want to know. No one smiled or said hello. They made us feel like we were visitors from another planet. In my humble little opinion, Newark, New Jersey was a far cry from our beloved Birmingham, Alabama.

Our house on 201 Dewey Street, was a three family house with each apartment stacked one on top of the other, separated by flights of connecting stairs in the hallway. We were not allowed to play on the stairs in the hallway. It wasn't the danger of falling down the stairs, but the unknown element of strangers lingering in the halls. Mama never worried about strangers lingering in Birmingham. Our apartment was on the second floor, sandwiched between the first floor apartment and the third floor apartment. We could hear every move from our upstairs neighbors, even though we were repeatedly cautioned to avoid disturbing our downstairs neighbors. The apartment had two bedrooms, a living room, a dining room, a kitchen overlooking the tiny back yard, one small den overlooking the street and one bathroom off of the main hallway.

Our apartment building was practically attached to the house on the right. The woman next door, Beatrice, was Mama's best friend. Beatrice was married to Buddy. They had three children, Hope, Jonathan and the baby Sherrie. We played with all three of them. To the left of our house was a driveway and then a vacant lot separating it from the store on the corner which faced Lyons Avenue. Lyons Avenue was a major thoroughfare in Newark with a great deal of traffic. Because of the traffic and the unknown element of dangerous people, we were not allowed to go past the corner of Dewey Street and Lyons Avenue. Crossing Lyons Avenue was strictly forbidden.

We were allowed, however, to go to the candy store which was situated directly on the corner of Dewey Street on this side of Lyons Avenue. Mr. Bea owned the candy store. Mr. Bea was a big fat black man. He was about 5'11", 260 pounds, brown skinned with a short afro. We all thought he must be eating some of the candy after we left the store because he was so big and fat. Everyday after school, all of the neighborhood children would converge upon "Mr. Bea's."

"We're going with Hope and Jonathan to Mr. Bea's," we would scream running out of the door.

Mr. Bea displayed all kinds of candy throughout the store stacked behind glass counters and piled up on wooden shelves behind the counter, Good and Plenty, Ju Ju beans, M&Ms, Hershey's chocolate, Wrigley's gum and my favorite, Almond Joy. I always felt like a nut. There was one cash register in the corner of Mr. Bea's store which rang loudly after every sale. Mr. Bea made lots of money. Everybody knew that Mr. Bea made lots of money.

One day we came home from school and there were police cars and an ambulance parked with flashing lights outside of Mr. Bea's store. We all ran up to the corner to see what the commotion was all about. Something told me, before we even reached the corner, that something terrible had happened to Mr. Bea. The ambulance attendants were taking a man out on a stretcher. There was a white sheet pulled over the man's head. I heard one of the adults whisper that the man was dead. Someone else said that the dead man was Mr. Bea and that he had been repeatedly stabbed to death.

I couldn't believe what I was hearing. I knew Mr. Bea. He was kind and gentle. Sometimes, when I didn't have enough change, he would give me an Almond Joy with a wave of his hand meaning, don't worry about it, you're a good customer, a good kid. What monster could have stabbed and killed him in cold blood? Did I know the person who killed him? Was he ever in the store at the same time I had been in the store? Mama tried to answer my incessant questions. She realized that this was our first encounter with the death of someone we knew. She explained that bad things sometimes happen to good people. She said that Mr. Bea was in a better place now, where no one could hurt him.

Then she said, "Listen sweetheart, if I had my druthers, there would be no violence and no sickness in the world. There would be food and clothing for everyone. We would all love each other and help one another. But the world is not like that. In his infinite wisdom, God decided to allow both the good and the bad in the world. That way, we will always appreciate the good."

I tried hard to understand.

Mama then proceeded to limit the permissible parameters of our outdoor play to the back yard, the front stoop, and the next door neighbors' house, where we played with Hope, Jonathan and the baby Sherrie.

When we first moved in next door, Sherrie had not yet been born. By the age of four, she had become the most beautiful little girl I had ever met, so sweet and so tiny. Her hair was long and curly and when her mother pulled it back, it made little ringlets down her back. Pony tail for one, pig tails for two. Sherrie was the apple of her family's eye. Her parents doted over her and her older brother and sister spoiled her. All the older girls in the neighborhood played with her like she was a little doll.

One day Sherrie was outside playing hopscotch with us and she said she didn't feel well. She went upstairs to lie down and rest. Her mother told my mother that Sherrie was lethargic and unresponsive. Because my mother was a nurse, she realized that severe lethargy was an indicator of something serious. My mother told her best friend Beatrice to take Sherrie to the emergency room for tests. Sherrie's parents admitted her into the hospital that evening. Her family went everyday to see her, hoping that she would get better. Two weeks later they came home from the hospital without Sherrie. The doctors said that Sherrie died from acute leukemia, a type of cancer. The family was overwhelmed with grief. The neighborhood was in a state of shock. I was confused and beyond consolation.

The death of Mr. Bea was horrible enough. But Sherrie's death was unbearable. Once more Mama tried to explain that sometimes bad things happen to good people and that Sherrie was at peace now. But I wasn't buying it this time. Sherrie was a sweet little girl. She never hurt anybody. Life was not fair. And what's more, this illness they call cancer was downright evil. If I had my druthers, there would be no such thing as cancer.

~ ~ ~

Eventually, after the deaths of Mr. Bea and little Sherrie, life in Newark went back to normal. Like the broken leg that eventually mends, time does, at least to some extent, heal all wounds, allowing you to function, enabling you move on. But the scar remains, re-opened by the slightest provocation, playing hopscotch, eating an Almond Joy.

Mama used to say that scars, both the physical and the emotional kind, gave life perspective and marked the events in your life. She told me not to be so concerned about my scars, that I should embrace them as symbols of battles conquered. She was right about one thing. Memories of day to day life often fade. But the traumatic events, for better or worse, seem to shape our lives, build the foundations of our character.

I remember once when I was around seven or eight years old, I was riding on the front handle bar of a friend's bicycle. He was older and generally thought to be responsible, until he took me flying down a steep hill. When we hit a bump in the road, I flew over the front of the bicycle onto the cement pavement and busted my left knee wide open. He helped me off of the ground and rode me back home. When we reached my house, he rang the door bell and then quickly rode off on his bike, disappearing down the hill and out of sight.

My mother was furious that my friend had been so reckless. Though it was difficult to tell, I knew that her anger was not directed at me. As she rushed me into the bathroom, she shook her head and mumbled something about the boy knowing better and only fools taking such chances. She told me I was not allowed to ride his bike or anyone else's bike, for that matter, ever again, for the rest of my life. She would buy me my "own damn bike," and teach me how to ride it safely. Through my tears of pain I nodded and smiled gingerly. Her nursing instincts automatically kicked into high gear. After thoroughly rinsing my knee, she ran a tub of warm water and knelt next to the tub while I soaked. She rubbed my back to soothe me, I squeezed her hand to ease the pain.

As I sat in the warm water, I looked at my knee. The whole top layer was gone. I wondered if my skin was laying in the middle of the road somewhere. I remember thinking that it would leave a huge scar. It did. But when I look at the scar, I only remember how loving and caring Mama was when she tended to my knee that day. I barely remember the pain from the fall at all. The arrival of the new bike several weeks later didn't hurt either.

It was the same way when I got my hand slammed in the front door of the big blue Chevy. We were coming back from Christmas shopping and everyone was in a really good mood. Benji, Cathy and I were running to get into the front seat of the car, though I called it first, so it was my privilege for the ride home. Mama shooed us into the car out of the cold and in her rush, slammed the door closed on my right hand. I could barely open my mouth to scream, but the look of anguish on my face said it all. My mother threw down her packages, yanked opened the door and leaned over to inspect the injury. There were no broken bones and the skin remained intact, but my index and middle fingers were already swollen from the impact and throbbing with pain. I eventually lost the nail on my middle finger. Mama asked a friendly bystander to look for some ice and the next thing I remember I was sitting in the big blue Chevy with the heat blasting, eating vanilla ice cream on a sugar cone with my injured finger sitting in a second scoop of vanilla ice cream. Again, I barely remember the pain, but I will never forget how Mama made the earth move to set things right for me.

We did not have a lot of money back then. In fact, by government standards we were considered poor, hovering just above the poverty line. Poor, but not dirt poor. However, my siblings and I did not actually know that we were poor. We had a roof over our heads and food on the table. Our parents went to work every morning and we went to school everyday. We had no complaints. We thought everyone lived as we did.

Being poor meant that we had to find ways to be frugal. To help make ends meet, we either wore hand-me-down clothes from our cousins or my mother made us hand sewn outfits, like many black women from the South. It was like cooking food from scratch instead of the box. That's just the way it was done. Unlike our friends in private school, it was very rare that we bought new clothes, unless it was Christmas or someone's birthday. Unlike our friends in private school, we were proud to wear the clothes our mother made for us. Mama even made matching outfits for me and my sister which fit our skinny frames much better than most store bought clothes.

Mama did all her sewing on this big white Singer sewing machine. It was her pride and joy. She sat at the helm of the enormous contraption in the evenings, with her left arm raised at the wheel and her right hand guiding the material, while her right foot pressed the floor pedal to make the needle shoot vigorously up and down. She looked like an enchanted princess weaving magical threads from her precious golden material, material which served as the foundation for our fall wardrobe.

One late summer day, Mama told Benji to take out the trash. It was one of his routine chores and least favorite activities. Without fuss or fanfare, he went through the apartment, tying and collecting all of the large black bags. In addition to throwing away the garbage, he accidentally threw out three bags of material which Mama intended to use to sew our new fall clothes.

Few things upset Mama. She had long ago learned to take life in stride. But when Benji threw out all of her material, material she had planned to use to make our clothes for the upcoming school year, we thought the world had temporarily stopped turning on its axis. She asked him how could he do such a thing, how was it possible to mistake bags of cloth for bags of garbage? She frantically told him to go outside and look to see if they had come to take the garbage away. It was too late. The bags were long gone. She pondered the possibility that maybe they would open the bags, see the cloth, realize that someone had made a terrible mistake and return the bags to their rightful owner. No such thing happened.

"Do you know how much that material cost? I can't believe you threw out all of my material," she walked back and forth repeating.

Of course, Benji had no idea how much the material cost, although he quickly concluded that it must have been extremely valuable, at least a million dollars judging from Mama's extreme reaction. Mama finally calmed down, poured herself a gin and tonic and tried to put the matter in perspective. None of us realized the importance of that material. It represented my mother's never ending efforts to make ends meet. It was literally and figuratively the clothes off of our backs. Suffice it to say, we did not have new clothes for school that year. Mama never completely forgot about the misplaced material. She mentioned it from time to time, years after the fact, as though somehow, the mere mention of the far away fabric might bring it back.

No matter how upset my mother became, her love did not waiver. We never doubted her devotion. Like the fiercely dedicated mother lion, loving and protecting us was the essence of her existence.

The richest family in our neighborhood was the Lee family. They were Chinese, the only non-African American family on the block. They had two sons our age named Calvin and Jo-Jo. From the outside, their house looked like all the other three story walk-ups on the block, but the inside of their apartment was filled with all kinds of good stuff. For one thing, they had the only color television set on the block. When the Batman series aired on Thursday night, all of the neighborhood children were allowed to come and watch the show on the Lee's 32 inch color console television set. It was like going to a movie theatre.

We were not allowed into the rest of the house, but the living room alone had more ornaments and knick-knacks than our entire apartment. My curiosity about the existence of other possible treasures in the rest of the house prompted me to ask about using the restroom. Mr. Lee politely told me no. We were allowed into their living room for thirty minutes on Thursday evening to watch Batman. No more and no less. The terms of the deal did not entail going to the bathroom. According to Mr. Lee, we could do that in our own house. Who wants to see your old junky house anyway, I thought.

Being poor did not keep us from being robbed one day on our way back from church. I don't think Mama ever got over the irony of the situation. No sooner had we finished thanking God for the wonderful blessings bestowed upon us, when a fellow human being randomly selected us and tried to take it all away. Even as a young child, I remember feeling violated.

Mama had just pulled the blue Chevy into a parking spot across the street from the Dunkin' Donuts shop. He must have watched her pull into the parking spot. She turned around and said with a big smile, "You guys were so good in church today, I am going to get you some donuts. How about some glaze and some chocolate?"

We could hardly contain our excitement.

"O.k.," she said. "Sit tight and I will be back in a second."

The police later confirmed that the perpetrator had been watching my mother's every move. No sooner had she exited the car and crossed the street, the front passenger door opened and a man got into the car. The three of us sat frozen in the back seat of the car, not knowing what to do. We had been taught not to talk to strangers and never to get into a stranger's car, but we did not know what to do if a complete stranger got into our car. This was a circumstance that even my mother had not anticipated. Our resolve was about to be tested. The man turned around and asked, "Where is your mother?"

I was sitting in the middle of the back seat and I stared at his face, memorizing his features. He was a dark skinned black man with a short afro and a clean shaven face with razor bumps. He noticed that I was staring at him and he quickly turned his head around to face forward. Looking straight ahead, he repeated his question, "I said, where is your mother?"

"She's in the store and she's coming right back," I said as forcefully as an eight year old girl could say. My brother elbowed me as hard as he could, a signal to remind me that we are not supposed to talk to strangers. I sat back and said nothing further.

The man exited the car as quietly and swiftly as he had entered. Just then, Mama walked out of the Dunkin' Donuts shop holding the bag of donuts. She saw a man walking down the street, not knowing that he had just been in our car. She crossed the street towards the car with a big beautiful smile on her face. Her smile quickly faded as she opened the door and saw the looks on our faces. I hated that anything was able to take her smile away.

Cathy was softly sobbing in the corner of the car as I leaned over the middle of the front seat anxiously waiting to tell my version of the story. Benji sat quietly, prepared to give his version of the incident when asked. As it turned out, the man stole Mama's pocketbook which she left behind in the front seat of the car when she ran into the store with ten dollars to get the donuts. The purse, which was made of fabric that matched her shoes, contained very little money and only two credit cards, one Visa and one Sears. The police later found the purse in a garbage can in a nearby alley. It was completely empty. The man took everything, including our personal information and any feeling of security we may have once harbored. We did not go back to church for a long while after that. I figured it was because Mama was mad at God for letting such a terrible thing happen to us.

In reality, things could have been much worse had we stayed in Birmingham. It was around this same time that the now notorious bombing occurred at the Sixteenth Street Baptist Church in Birmingham, Alabama, killing four little black girls, Denise McNair, who was 11, and Cynthia Wesley, Addie Mae Collins and

Carole Robertson, who were all 14. Early Sunday morning on September 15, 1963, the girls were in the basement of the church preparing for a Sunday school choir performance when the bomb exploded. Members of the Ku Klux Klan had placed the bomb under the stairs of the church the night before. The intensity of the bomb was so severe that it ripped the limbs from the bodies of the girls who were found underneath the rubble. Dozens of others in the church were seriously injured. Parked cars caught on fire and windows in nearby homes were shattered.

The death of the four little black girls marked the beginning of widespread unrest among the black community and widespread support in the white community for the end of segregation and the beginning of equality for black people. The cowardly actions of the Ku Klux Klan in the bombing of the church were horrifying by any standards. It left a deep scar on the face of America, one that society desperately wanted to heal.

Local FBI agents recommended that at least four suspects, Robert Edward Chambliss, Herman Frank Cash, Thomas Blanton Jr. and Bobby Frank Cherry be charged with the bombing. However, FBI Director J. Edgar Hoover blocked the prosecution of the suspects stating that the possibility of winning a conviction was remote. The case was closed. It was later determined that Hoover had blocked evidence that prosecutors could have used to bring charges against the suspects, all active members of the Klan.

In 1971, Alabama Attorney General Bill Baxley reopened the case. Ultimately, in November 1977, Robert Edward Chambliss was convicted of murder in connection with the bombing and sentenced to life in prison. Chambliss died of natural causes at the age of 81 in October 1985, without ever publicly admitting any role in the bombing. In 1994, Herman Frank Cash died before a case could be established against him. In May 2001, 38 years after the bombing, Thomas Blanton Jr. was convicted of murder at the age of 62 and sentenced to life in prison. One year later, Bobby Frank Cherry was finally convicted and sentenced to life in prison, after his former wife testified that he admitted to planting the bomb. He died in prison at the age of 74 in Montgomery, Alabama.

The deaths of the four innocent black girls galvanized the civil rights movement, much like the death of Emmett Till had done eight years earlier. Like the death of the four girls, Emmett's murder was unspeakable, yet the news of his murder rang out all over the world and continues to echo throughout history.

Emmett Louis Till was born on July 25, 1941, in Chicago's Cook County Hospital to Louis and Mamie Till. At the age of 14, he was a handsome boy filled with curiosity and a zest for life. There are two pictures of Emmett that will remain indelibly etched in the minds of people everywhere. The first picture shows a well dressed boy with chubby checks and an innocent smile. He looked like a little cherub. The second picture shows his badly beaten and unrecognizable body. His mother Mamie allowed the body to be photographed so that people could witness the brutality of his murder.

Mamie Till adored Emmett, her only child. Not long after Emmett's mother and father were divorced, his father, Louis Till, was killed during World War II. At the time, Mamie was not told any details about her ex-husband's death. The United States army did, however, return Louis Till's belongings to Mamie, including a ring inscribed with his initials, LT.

In August of 1955, Mamie sent Emmett to Mississippi to visit his great Uncle, Moses Wright. The day before his departure, Mamie gave Emmett the ring once owned by his father and inscribed with the initials LT. The ring would serve as the principal source of identification for Emmett's otherwise unidentifiable body. Mamie Till took her son Emmett to the 63rd Street station in Chicago on August 20, 1955, to catch the southbound train to Money, Mississippi. It would be the last time she saw her son alive.

On August 24th, Emmett and a group of seven black boys and one black girl went to Bryant's Grocery Store for soda and candy to cool off after a long day of picking cotton in the hot sun. Bryant's Grocery was owned by a white couple, Roy and Carolyn Bryant. Their clientele was mostly black sharecroppers and their children. Emmett went into the store to buy bubble gum. Some of the kids outside the store would later say that they heard Emmett whistle at Carolyn Bryant.

Four days later on August 28th at 2:30 a.m. in the morning, Roy Bryant and his half brother J. W. Milam, kidnapped Emmett Till from the safety of his Uncle Moses' home. They later describe brutally beating him, taking him to the edge of the Tallahatchie River, shooting him in the head, fastening a large metal fan used for ginning cotton to his neck with barbed wire, and pushing the body into the river. His crime was allegedly whistling at Carolyn Bryant, a white woman.

The next day, Bryant and Milam were arrested on kidnapping charges in LeFlore County in connection with Emmett's disappearance. They were jailed in Greenwood, Mississippi and held without bond. On August 31st, Emmett's partially decomposed corpse was pulled from Mississippi's Tallahatchie River. Moses Wright was able to identify the body from the ring with the initials L.T. Mississippi Governor Hugh White ordered local officials to "fully prosecute" Bryant and Milam in the Till case.

When Mamie Till arrived at the Illinois Central Terminal in Chicago to receive Emmett's casket on September 2nd, she was surrounded by family and photographers who took her photo collapsing in grief at the sight of the casket. The body was first taken to the A. A. Rayner & Sons Funeral Home and then to Chicago's Roberts Temple Church of God for viewing and funeral services. Mamie decided to have an open casket funeral so that thousands of Chicagoans could witness Emmett's brutally beaten body. *Jet* magazine, the nationwide black magazine owned by Chicago-based Johnson Publications, published photographs of Till's mutilated corpse, shocking and outraging African Americans from coast to coast.

On September 6th, the same day Emmett was buried, a grand jury in Mississippi indicted Milam and Bryant for the kidnapping and murder of Emmett Till. They both pleaded innocent to the charges. The trial began on September 19th in Tallahatchie County. Four days later an all white jury fully acquitted Milam and Bryant of murdering Emmett Till. The jury deliberation took only 67 minutes. One juror told a reporter that they wouldn't have taken so long if they hadn't stopped to drink pop.

Some scars take longer to heal than others.

~ ~ ~

It was a sunny Saturday morning. The year was 1964. I was a slender seven year old little girl with long pig tails hanging down my back. Pony tail for one, pig tails for two. When my mother let my hair out, everyone said that I looked like a young Indian princess. My nickname was "Princess." It made me feel special. It was a time when we played hopscotch, jump rope and marbles on the sidewalk and stickball down the middle of the street. We were still living in Newark, New Jersey, on 201 Dewey Street, in the three story walk-up. The sun was shining brightly onto the enclosed porch which doubled as my brother's room, making it warm and cozy.

We were watching the Bugs Bunny Show. Road Runner was speeding across the screen exclaiming "beep beep" every time he escaped or avoided the coyote's lair. It was my all time favorite cartoon. I loved the way Road Runner always got away, without violence, without any effort. He was so smart.

I was sprawled out across the couch facing the television, still in my pajamas. My stepfather's 18 year old nephew, was watching cartoons with me. He had been living with us for the past few months while he attended a local college in Newark. As always, my mother did not hesitate to open her house when my stepfather Gene asked for the favor. It was a good will gesture to help my cousin manage his college expenses. Free room and board would allow him to spend the little money he had on tuition and books. In exchange, he could help around the house with chores. The arrangement would last until he landed a part time job to pay for his own expenses.

My cousin was sprawled out across the couch behind me, as he had often done before. But this time I noticed that he was a little closer than before. My sister Cathy and brother Benji were playing elsewhere. There was no one else in the room. My cousin started talking to me about the Road Runner. "Isn't he incredible? How do you think he always manages to get away?" As he spoke to me, he eased his hand under my shirt and began rubbing gently back and forth across my back. I did not move, I did not speak. The massage felt good. I continued to stare straight ahead at the Road Runner and the Coyote. He slowly moved his hand from my back to my stomach, rubbing gently back and forth. I did not move. I did not speak. He was my cousin. He would never do anything to hurt me, I thought.

Then he slowly moved his hand down my stomach underneath my pajamas, under my panties, between my legs where he began to gently rub up and down. I could feel his body behind mine. I could tell that his thing was getting hard. I knew that this should not be happening. No one had ever touched me there before, except my mother when I learned to wipe. I remember Mama telling me that no one was ever supposed to touch me there. I knew it was wrong, but by then I was paralyzed in a moment of time, mesmerized by the touch of his hand, by the images on the screen. Unlike the Road Runner, I was not smart enough to escape his lair.

"Don't move. I am not finished. If you tell anyone about this, I am going to kill you and whoever you tell." I don't remember what happened after that. I don't remember my mother bursting into the room. I don't remember her hitting my cousin, screaming and yelling at the top of her lungs that she was going to kill him. Her motherly instincts took over and she was determined to protect her daughter. She picked up a chair and threw it at him. She took some of his clothes and other possessions and threw them out of the window two stories below. She tried to push him out of the window. If my stepfather Gene had not come into the room and restrained her, she would have killed my cousin.

My cousin was not allowed back into our house ever again. He was not allowed to attend any of the family functions which we attended. I suppressed the entire event, never recalling that my mother had intervened. My mind remembered only that I had been violated and that I was not supposed to tell a soul. For many years after the incident I thought he would kill me or anyone I told.

Road Runner, the Coyote's after you/Road Runner, if he catches you you're through.

It was not until I interviewed my mother for this book that I learned she had walked into the room and witnessed his assault. She told me that we met with a counselor to discuss the event and to process the ordeal properly. To this day, I do not recall those sessions. In my mind, that day remained a dirty little secret, between me and him.

Some scars take longer to heal.

6
School Days

Cathy, Benji and I grew up thinking that everyone went to school all of their lives. We thought this because Mama was always going to school. Even when she was working, she was taking part-time classes from nearby universities. Education was the ticket out of poverty, the incontrovertible path to success. Mama's objective was to provide her children with a good life and, according to Mama, the good life was only obtainable through a good education. During even the most difficult times, my mother made sure we had a roof over our heads, clothes on our backs, food on the table and a good education. Education would be our salvation.

Until she could afford to put us into private school, Mama sent us to Catholic school. In Newark, New Jersey, the only alternative to the horrendous public schools were the horrendous Catholic schools, which provided a better education but were horrendous just the same. They were horrendous because the nuns would hit you with extra long rulers for no apparent reason, especially the boys, most of whom, according to the nuns, were condemned to eternal damnation.

The fact that we were not Catholic did not faze my mother. In order to gain entrance into Catholic school, she converted us from Southern Baptist to inner-city Catholic, practically overnight. One Sunday we were dancing in the aisles singing gospel songs, the next Sunday we were kneeling in the pews praying for forgiveness of our sins.

We all have our reasons to believe/We all need to learn a thing or two/We all need something to cling to/So we did. (Alanis Morriset)

Initially, my mother thought that Catholic school would be a safe haven for us. We were very obedient children, so she assumed we would not become the object of corporal punishment or abject humiliation. That notion was quickly dispelled. The nuns were more like prison guards than teachers and they frightened us to death. They spent most of the day disciplining students for minor infractions instead of teaching meaningful lessons.

We spent a significant portion of everyday kneeling and praying, which obviously did not enhance our academic achievements. Praying was serious business in Catholic school. We were not allowed to lean back on the benches to relax our back or to relieve the pressure on our knees. If you were caught leaning back, the nuns would walk by and smack you on the backside with the extra long rulers they carried.

The nuns also went out of their way to discourage creativity and independent thinking. Once, in second grade, I drew a picture of a house with a tree in the front yard and the sun in the sky and a little stick family of five standing outside of the house. I was proud of the drawing and could barely wait my turn to show it to the teacher when I was finished. I raised my hand as the teacher walked around observing all of our drawings. She stopped, looked at the picture and casually said, "Well, it is clear that you will never become an artist." One small comment, eleven little words. I was crushed. An entire dream vanquished forever in the span of twenty seconds. The power of teaching.

The humiliation was sometimes more severe. Once, one of the boys in the class raised his hand to go to the bathroom. Sister Elizabeth, our teacher, told him to put his hand down. Instead, he said out loud, "But I have to go to the bathroom and pee."

Well, you would have thought that the poor child used profanity. Sister Elizabeth told the boy to stand up. When he did, she proceeded to beat his legs, at which point he proceeded to pee down his legs onto her ruler. This only managed to completely infuriate Sister Elizabeth, who yanked him by the arm and escorted him to the Principal's office, leaving a trail of yellow pee behind.

Meanwhile, I was so nervous and upset by the whole situation that I sat frozen behind my little desk squeezing my legs together. I squeezed my legs together so tightly that it caused an orgasm. At the time, I had no idea what had happened. But I figured it must have been something very, very bad; bad enough to condemn me to eternal damnation along with the rest of the really bad black children.

It didn't take long for Mama to realize that the Catholic school system might indeed do more harm than good. She had an occasion to witness the arbitrary cruelty herself when she dropped me off early to go back stage for a second grade school play. My costume called for short bobby socks. I didn't have short bobby socks; Mama usually folded our socks down if the weather was too hot. That way, we could use the socks for all seasons. From the other end of the hall, in front of all the children, one of the nuns said, "Miss Terri, I see you are, once again, not properly prepared for the day. You were specifically instructed to wear bobby socks. I don't understand why you people can't follow simple instructions."

Well, you would have thought that the nun used profanity. Mama, who had lingered behind to watch me walk down the hall in the outfit she had lovingly put together for me, walked straight past me over to the nun. In a calm deliberate voice, she told the nun, "If you ever embarrass or humiliate my daughter like that again, I will personally see to it that you never teach in another school for the rest of your natural born life."

Well, you would have thought that Mama used profanity. She left us all speechless, especially the nun. After uttering her proclamation, Mama abruptly turned away from the nun, held her chin up high, strutted back to me, leaned over, kissed my check and without skipping a beat she said, "Break a leg baby, remember I love you more than anything in the world."

I smiled and said, "I love you more."

It was one of those endearing exchanges we said to each other, like, "Who loves you baby?" To which we responded, "You do Mama." We had a million of them. We were never short on expressing our feelings for each other. This time, it meant even more than usual.

I gave the performance of my life that day. I never felt more confident. At the end of that school year, we left the Catholic school system, forever. Not a minute too soon.

By the time I entered third grade, Mama had saved enough money for us to attend private school, well at least two of us. My sister and I interviewed at all of the elite private schools in the area. We were the only black faces in the hallowed halls of all the establishments we visited. Mama got us all dressed up and took us from one school to the next in the big blue Chevy to interview with the principals of half a dozen schools. I was petrified. Everyone looked so mean and so smart...and so white, not at all like our neighbors in Newark or Birmingham.

Most of the administrators at most of the schools kept us waiting in the halls. When they finally met with us, they glossed over my mother's questions and rushed through the interviews. In fact, most of the administrators and teachers at these schools did not even bother talking to me and my sister. When they bothered to direct the inquiry to our attention, the questions were so difficult to answer that my sister and I did not stand a chance. When this occurred, Mama would intervene on our behalf commenting, "Well, the girls have not been exposed to period artwork. It would be difficult, therefore, for them to tell you their favorite 18th century painter."

No matter how uncomfortable the interview, Mama always told us that we did a great job and that it would be the school's loss if we ended up at another establishment. After the most difficult interviews, I remember thinking, "Who wants to come to your mean old school anyway?"

Mama ultimately chose an all girls school in Summit, New Jersey named Kent Place. Of all the schools in all the towns we visited, the people there seemed the nicest to me. They smiled real smiles. They acted like they really wanted us to come.

And so it came to pass that Cathy and I would attend Kent Place while my brother Benji would remain in the public school system to fend for himself. There just wasn't enough money to place all three of us in private school at the same time. Benji didn't complain, but we all knew that if Mama had her druthers, Benji would also be attending some fancy private school. Instead, he was left behind in a system where learning to fend off drugs and gangs was far more important than any lesson he could be taught in the classroom. It turned out to be the single most important decision my mother could ever have made for me. It set the course for a life of learning and an ambition to be the best that I could be.

Kent Place was situated in Summit, New Jersey, an upscale neighborhood with large estates surrounded by towering maple trees and flowery grassy fields. It was a stark contrast from our home in Newark, New Jersey, which was surrounded by identical row houses and concrete sidewalks. My sister and I traveled an hour each way back and forth between Newark and Summit. At first, Mama drove us back and forth to school each day. But soon, the demands of her nursing job at Beth Israel Hospital required another solution. The solution was public transit, the bus.

The thought of putting her seven and eight year old girls alone on a colossal public bus frightened my mother. She introduced us to every bus driver on the route and told them our stop, in case we forgot which one it was. She rode on the bus with us for a few days. Then she let us go alone—or so we thought. She actually followed the bus for weeks thereafter to ensure that we got off at the right stop. It was her way of teaching us independence without completely letting go. Finally, when she was confident in our ability to handle the situation alone, she let us travel unsupervised. It was a big step for my mother. The difficulty of letting go was compounded with guilt for not being able to personally escort us back and forth to school. Such was the price of being a working mother, especially a working black mother who was either the sole or the primary wage earner.

Although we appreciated the opportunity to attend such an elite establishment, it was intimidating to say the least. We were the only black girls enrolled at the school and we felt like everyone from the other girls, to the teachers, to the principal was watching our every move. We were enrolled at Kent Place from 1965 to 1968 during my third, fourth and fifth grades. I learned a great deal during those three years, including multiplication and long division, not to mention confidence and pride.

The class work and the homework were far more challenging than the work in the Catholic schools we previously attended, but the teachers and students were encouraging. They took the extra time to teach us lessons which we had never been taught in Catholic school, like tricks to add in your head or to memorize the times table. They made the process fun by playing speed games. For instance, I had always added double digits the traditional way where you write down one number on top, the second number on the bottom, draw a line, add the right column and then add the left column to get your final answer. At Kent Place, the girls were doing all of this in their head by using shortcuts. When they added 52 and 46, they knew that 50 plus 40 was 90 and that 2 plus 6 was 8. It was a simple process for them to get to 98 without even picking up a pencil. It didn't take long for me to catch on; I could barely control my enthusiasm which was captured in a candid class shot. The enthusiasm in the classroom was contagious. The other girls were just as excited when I won a round of speed math.

Every evening after the long bus ride home, we usually had two to three hours of homework to complete. Mama was good enough to let us play outside with our neighborhood friends as soon as we got home, then eat dinner, then do our homework. She thought that it was important to relax at the end of a grueling day and to maintain relationships with our friends. She was right.

My best friend, however, was not from the neighborhood at all. On the first day of school at Kent Place, a girl named Jackie Roser came up and introduced herself to me. We immediately became best friends. She was different from all the other girls who were a little afraid to talk to us at first. She sat with me at lunch and next to me in class. She was the only friend who ever asked me to sleep over at her house, just for the fun of it.

Jackie's house was the biggest house I had ever seen in my entire life. I didn't know that people in real life actually lived like that. Going to Jackie's house was like being in a movie or going on a great adventure. The house was situated on several acres of land just outside of Summit, New Jersey. There was a stable with actual horses and a big lake in the back surrounded by a forest of plush evergreen and tall maple trees.

The house itself was made of brick and stone. It had huge columns in the front with wide double entry doors. The entry foyer was marble with a spiral wooden staircase leading to the second floor of bedrooms and bathrooms. The spiral stairway had oriental carpet running up the middle of the stairs, leaving the exposed wood on the sides. There were seven bedrooms and nearly all of them had separate bathrooms. Jackie's house had more bathrooms than our apartment had rooms. I ran from room to room and wing to wing, just because it was there. Jackie's parents didn't care if we ran around the house, a stark contrast from our house where we were not allowed to run around for fear of disturbing the upstairs or the downstairs neighbors.

Jackie's bedroom looked like the bedroom of a princess. The moment I laid eyes on that bedroom, I said that I would have one just like it when I grew up and got my own house. There were two beds in her room, one for Jackie and a second matching bed just for guests. The thought of an extra bed for guests was mind boggling to me. The curtains, rugs and bed linens were all color coordinated shades of pastels. Each bed had fluffy thick pillows and comforters which we pulled high over our heads because Jackie liked to sleep with the windows wide open, even in the middle of winter. In our apartment, we did not open the windows in the middle of the winter. The concept of letting the heat escape through the windows was foreign to me.

Meal time was an elaborate ordeal at Jackie's house. Everyone had to "freshen-up" before sitting down at the table. Often times that meant a change of clothing. The French Country dining room table was extensively set with matching china and shiny silverware. There was lots of silverware, most of which I had no idea how to use. There was more food and more courses than I had ever seen. The housekeeper kept bringing one course after another, first a broth, then a salad, then the main course, then the dessert. The main course often included unique meats and side dishes, like lamb with au gratin potatoes and green peas with miniature pearl onions or veal and shoe string potatoes with steamed baby carrots and miniature acorn squash. And there were real desserts, like blueberry pie with fresh (not in a spray can) whipped cream or chocolate mousse cake with blackberry sauce carefully spread into a design on the plate. Dinner at Jackie's house was an elaborate ordeal.

When I sat down at the table, I just copied whatever Jackie did. If she picked up the outside fork, I picked up the outside fork. If she drank from her water glass, I drank from my water glass. When she was finished eating, I was finished eating. And that's the way dinner went at Jackie's house.

At our house, we just washed our hands and all sat down at the kitchen table to eat. The thought of changing our clothes just to eat dinner did not occur to anyone. We never ate in our dining room because it was always being used for other purposes. The dining room and the living room were adjacent to each other, neither being large enough to constitute a decent sized room alone. But together, the rooms provided an all purpose place to do everything from homework projects to sewing projects.

When we sat down to eat, Mama would have already brought the food from the stove to the table. There was no such thing as multiple courses being served at different times. Everyone ate everything at the same time on the same plate. The daily menu was usually baked chicken or pan fried fish, rice or potatoes, a vegetable and sliced white bread. Back then, no one knew the virtues of seven grain bread or the shortcomings of bleached white bread. Dinner rolls were reserved for special occasions like Christmas or Thanksgiving. We used one fork and shared the butter knife. Steak knives were reserved for Mama and Gene. The only dessert was leftover candy we had stashed from our visit to Mr. Bea's candy store. It was discretely eaten shortly after leaving the dinner table. And that's the way dinner went at our house.

We left Kent Place when I finished fifth grade. Jackie and I lost touch. I missed the whole experience, the challenging atmosphere of the school, the dreamlike adventure of life with my best friend Jackie. At the time, I didn't know exactly why we left, but I knew enough to know that money was a factor. Despite his best efforts, my stepfather Gene had not found a decent paying job in Newark. It was difficult for a black man with no formal education to get a good job. His only training had been in the air force. As it turns out, the money my mother made as a nurse at Beth Israel Hospital was not enough to carry the full load, a load made even heavier with private school.

But money wasn't the only reason we left Kent Place and ultimately moved from Newark. Mama and Gene were considering a move because Newark was becoming more and more dangerous. Committing to another expensive year at Kent Place was not an option when such a drastic move was being contemplated.

There were ominous signs of the impending danger on the streets of Newark. I noticed the little things at first, wrinkled brows of anxiety, hushed conversations between the adults that ceased when children entered the room. The parents on our block began to call us inside a little earlier than normal. They watched us more regularly from open windows and told us to stay within eyesight. Front doors were immediately locked, almost before you could get inside. Other people in the neighborhood walked at faster paces and looked over their shoulders as they passed. Stores began to close and lock up early. Sometimes shopkeepers locked their doors even during the day and only let people into the store one at a time, after fully assessing the character of each potential customer.

And then it happened. The year was 1968. On that 4th day of April, all the neighborhood children were at the doctor's office for our annual physicals and vaccinations. There were about eight of us playing with the toys in the waiting room, along with some of the mothers who were gossiping about whatever mothers of ten year olds gossip about. All of a sudden, one of the fathers burst into the waiting room and shouted, "King's been shot, King's been shot."

I didn't know who this King person was, but I could tell from the reaction in the waiting room that he was someone very important. At first I thought that perhaps he was a prominent King from a far away land. But all the parents reacted as though they knew him.

My mother snatched up the four or five kids she was responsible for that day and threw us into the back seat of the big blue Chevy. Back then, no one wore seat belts and you could squeeze half a dozen small kids into the back seat of a big car. Other than the Chinese family with the big screen t.v., we were the only people on the block who owned a car. Mama shoved us into the Chevy and told us to sit still and be quiet. If you hadn't received your annual booster shot or peed in a cup by that point, you were cleared to go anyway. As she drove down Lyons Avenue, she switched the radio back and forth on the dial to catch the latest breaking news. She kept saying to herself, "Please God, don't let him die. Please God, don't let him die."

I kept asking her, "Don't let who die Mama? Who is going to die?" She just kept shushing me.

As we drove down Lyons Avenue, everyone on the street looked agitated. People were literally running down the block screaming and shouting. They looked as upset as my mother. I assumed that they had all heard the terrible news about this man King who had been shot. Mama finally turned around to face the back seat and told us, "Martin Luther King was shot today. They still haven't said if he survived the attack. It doesn't sound good. It doesn't sound good at all."

Then I asked what I thought was an innocent enough question, "Who is Martin Luther King?"

Well, you would have thought that I had used profanity. Mama started yelling something about how could we not know who Martin Luther King was, had we not been paying attention to anything going on in the real world, what good was an excellent education if we were ignorant about the world around us? A series of rhetorical questions I knew better than to try and answer.

When we got home from the doctor's office, Mama and Gene turned on the television set and solemnly sat down to watch the inevitable unfolding of events. I saw Walter Cronkite's solemn face. I heard his reassuring voice, which was not so reassuring that night. Everything was in slow motion.

Mama and Gene did not generally drink alcohol during the week, but that night Gene filled two small glasses and set them down on the coffee table in front of the living room sofa. Gene handed Mama one of the glasses of clinking ice and clear liquid. I knew from the size of the glass and the color of the liquid that it was a gin and tonic, their drink of choice. They watched the news for most of the evening, glued to the television set in shock.

Walter Cronkite said that Martin Luther King was senselessly gunned down while standing on a hotel balcony in Memphis, Tennessee. He was in Memphis to lead a protest to help sanitation workers obtain higher wages and better working conditions.

The reports said that the shot was from a lone sniper, that no one else had been injured. It was later determined that the shooter was James Earl Ray. Ray was ultimately sentenced to 99 years in the Tennessee State Penitentiary. There were reports of riots and widespread looting in Harlem, Watts and Newark. President Johnson declared a State of Emergency and ordered the National Armed Guard to patrol the streets and to control the chaos. Stores were ordered to lock up by dusk and citywide curfews were imposed after sundown.

Before my mother tucked us into bed that night, she patiently told us all about Martin Luther King. She said that he was a great man, a man of peace. She said that without his leadership, black people would not have a clear direction. She feared that whatever strides America had made with race relations might be compromised now. She feared the violence that might erupt now that the voice of reason was silenced.

When we began to express our concerns, she told us to remain positive and not to worry about the situation. We could pray and when we got older we could try to make a difference in the world, like Martin Luther King had made a difference. Things would eventually all work out. She would keep us safe.

As it turns out, keeping us safe meant getting the hell out of Newark. For the weeks and months following King's death, however, we were stuck there. During that period, Mama decided to wait for us at the bus stop when we came home from school to personally escort us home. I saw the soldiers on our block carrying huge machine guns with their hands placed in the ready position. The soldiers frightened me, their guns scared me even more. I knew that the soldiers were there to protect us, but I was not sure if the soldiers knew that we were the good guys. Frankly, I wasn't quite sure who the bad guys were. It seemed to me that this was a war against all black people. Everyone was suspect. I had heard about innocent children being accidentally shot. God willing, we would not become one of those statistics. To minimize the risk factor, Mama made sure to smile and speak to the soldiers. Maybe they won't shoot you if they like you. But the soldiers never spoke back to us. When I dared to lift my eyes from the sidewalk, I smiled meekly too, like my mother, just in case.

At night, when I closed my eyes to sleep, I heard the gun shots outside my window and I wondered just how close the shots really were. Did the bullets we heard actually hit and kill someone we knew? Could a stray bullet hit and kill us? I kept my head down and pulled the covers as high as I could, leaving just the tip of my nose exposed so that I could breath. I said the Serenity Prayer to myself, "God grant me the serenity to accept the things I can not change, the courage to change the things I can and the wisdom to know the difference." I decided that this was the time to accept the things I could not change. Later, I thought, when I get bigger, I would change the things I could, make a difference, like Martin Luther King had made a difference.

We left 201 Dewey Street and Newark, New Jersey not long after the riots of 1968. In the interim, Mama pulled us out of Kent Place and my brother out of public school, and sent us to a boarding school in the country for six months so that she and Gene could "regroup." The name of the boarding school was School of the Arts. It was located on a 40 acre farm in Northern New Jersey.

I met my first boyfriend at School of the Arts. I was eleven, he was twelve. His name was Terry too, only he spelled his name with a "y" instead of an "i." Terry had sickle-cell anemia. He was thin as a rail and was always sick. He was kind and sweet and completely infatuated with me. He told me that I was the most beautiful girl in the world. He picked me fresh flowers from the garden and helped me with my chores. Each of the students was given a specific chore like plucking the corn, milking the cows or cleaning the kitchen. The older students joked that the school was running the farm with free child labor and getting paid tuition to boot. My primary chore was going downstairs to the dark, dank, spooky basement to bring up the beets or turnips for dinner. Terry held the flashlight for me as I gathered the vegetables in my basket. We had our first and only kiss in the dark, dank, spooky basement. It took him months to gather the courage to approach me. The kiss was uneventful, but I will never forget it.

My brother, sister and I left School of the Arts after six months in the middle of my sixth grade. I never saw Terry again after that. Many years later, I learned that he died during a sickle cell crisis at the age of 17, two months before graduating from twelfth grade. I felt really guilty for having lost contact with him. He once told me that he hoped he would not die a virgin. I wondered if his dream ever came true.

All in all, I attended seven different schools between first and twelfth grade: St. Charles and St Peters in Newark for first and second grades (to avoid public schools); Kent Place in Summit, New Jersey for third, fourth and fifth grades (for a good private school education); the first half of sixth grade at School of the Arts in New Jersey (to regroup after the 1968 Newark riots); the second half of sixth grade at Wilkenson Elementary School in Birmingham, Alabama (to continue regrouping after the 1968 Newark riots); seventh, eighth, ninth and half of tenth grade in Potsdam, New York (where we sought permanent refuge from the violence in Newark); and finally, the second half of tenth, eleventh and twelfth grades at Fayetteville-Manlius Senior High School outside of Syracuse, New York (to follow Mama's graduate studies at Syracuse University). Our moves were frequent and swift, always in search of a better education, always in pursuit of a better life.

Mama believed that education was the key to success. Even though she worked all her life, first as a Registered Nurse, then as a psychologist, she continued her pursuit of higher education well into her adult life. If getting a good education was that important to Mama, I planned to make it a priority in my life as well. My mother was very proud of me when I became an attorney and began practicing law in New York City. Her pride motivated me to tell all sorts of far fetched stories about the sights and sounds of New York and the demands of law school. We'd all sit around the kitchen table, laughing at my exaggerated portrayal of every day life. I once told my family that my dormitory room was so small that there was only room enough for me, the bed, the dresser, my trunk, and the family of cockroaches who shared the room with me.

"You're not leaving food in the room, are you?" Mama asked seriously, trying to determine the source of the problem.

"No, I wouldn't dare leave food in the room," I said. "But the roaches don't need food. They survive off of the exhaust fumes from the buses 16 stories below." The comment was not very funny, but it didn't matter. They all laughed anyway.

7
Summer Days

Even though we moved miles away from our beloved Birmingham, when I was five, we never strayed far. Every summer, until I turned twelve, Mama took us back to stay with Granddaddy and Mother Dear. Sometimes she would stay, but more often she would leave us in Birmingham for the entire summer. She and Gene would return to Newark, New Jersey and do whatever it is parents do when their children are away for the summer. Mama came in and out of our world like an angel arriving to help us at our most crucial moments. We missed her terribly when she was gone, but we knew she would always be there when we needed her.

We loved going back to the familiar South, with its slow peculiar ways. It was much better than summer camp in our opinion. We were anxious to see our family and old friends, and to hang out at Uncle Afton's grocery store. It was like coming home again.

Mother Dear was more like a mother than a grandmother to me and my siblings. She cooked for us when we were hungry and nursed us back to health when we were sick, in spite of the near death turpentine incident. Her big fat arms engulfed us with love and protected us from the world. They greeted us when we came home, comforted us when we were sad and rocked us when we were sick.

By this point in their lives, Granddaddy and Mother Dear were living on 11th Court West, a far cry from their first dirt poor house on 4th Avenue. The rectangle shaped kitchen on 11th Court West was not particularly big, but it was spacious enough to hold Mother Dear's vast collection of pots, pans and utensils. The little window over the kitchen sink held a variety of pink and purple African violets, always in bloom. Although the window was small, the sunlight spread through the entire kitchen making it warm and bright. When it became too hot in the kitchen, Mother Dear would move the garbage can aside and crack open the back door sending a warm breeze throughout the small two bedroom house.

Mother Dear was the best cook on the face of the earth. She made everything from scratch, like sautéed okra with corn, onions and tomatoes or honey glazed baked ham with apples and clove garnish. She baked even better than she cooked. We regularly feasted on fresh baked breads, cakes and pies. When we waltzed into the kitchen and asked what she was baking, she would tell us, "Ya'll get out from under me now so I can cook."

Even after being shooed out of the kitchen, we knew from the sweet smells and the ingredients spread out on the countertop that she was working on a special German chocolate cake or a triple deck coconut cake or a juicy peach cobbler. As Mother Dear grew older, her mobility slowed down a bit. Instead of standing over the counter mixing and rolling, she would line up all the ingredients and utensils on the kitchen table and pull up a chair to sit and do her work. The results were the same, but it would take her much longer, making the anticipation almost unbearable.

For as long as I can remember, my grandparents slept in separate rooms. I actually thought that all married couples slept in separate rooms. Because Granddaddy was relegated to the back bedroom, we interacted less often with him. But he didn't mind being segregated off on his own. In fact, he relished the isolation.

When he wasn't sitting on the edge of his wooden twin bed smoking an unfiltered Camel cigarette, he sat in the front yard watching us play or watching the cars go by, in his metal green rocking chair, with the widest metal green back ever, casually smoking his cigarettes, sometimes letting the ashes pile up on the end of the butt until it reached his middle and index fingers and he had to flick it out into the yard, narrowly escaping singed fingertips.

During these early visiting years, Benji, Cathy and I used to play outside with our cousins or the kids in the neighborhood. We were not allowed to play in our back yard where Mother Dear maintained her vegetable garden. Meticulously kept tall vines of tomatoes, stalks of corn, potatoes, yellow squash, cucumbers, parsley and mint, a venerable cornucopia of delectable treats waiting to be plucked for our consumption. And all for the price of the seeds plus Mother Dear's back and knees, constituting the tax and tip. Running feet and stray balls were strictly forbidden anywhere near Mother Dear's garden, lest you suffer the fury of Mother Dear's wrath, which was not nearly as frightful as Granddaddy's wrath. We could ill afford crushed tomatoes or mashed potatoes in the garden, before they had a chance to grace our plates, unless we thought money grew on trees, which we all knew better, because if it did, "We'd sho 'nuf be growin' it in the garden," according to Mother Dear.

The only place we were allowed to play was in our front yard or in the next door neighbor's front yard. That was the extent of our permissible gallivanting. It didn't matter. Our front yard was plenty fine. For one reason, there was a huge weeping willow tree in our front yard. In my eyes, the tree was practically 1000 feet high and at least 100 feet wide. The majestic creation was a living testament to God's awesome power. The trunk was gigantic with large branches spiraling up toward the sky into smaller, thinner branches holding long narrow leaves that swayed back and forth, dancing to the music of the wind.

Sitting out in the yard in his metal green rocking chair, Granddaddy would occasionally pause long enough to notice us climbing the weeping willow tree. Since the great willow was in our front yard, Granddaddy was the enforcer of how much climbing was allowed on her magnificent old branches. He'd shout at his grandchildren, or any of the kids in the neighborhood, "Ya'll need to watch yo' selves climbin' dat tree. One of these days you gonna' fall out and break yo' neck," he would yell with a heavy Southern drawl. "Dat tree wasn't meant for all yo' climbin'. Mind you don't break one of dem branches neetha'." It wasn't exactly clear which limbs he was more concerned about, ours or the tree's.

Occasionally, if we were lucky, we were allowed to go all the way to the neighborhood candy store to buy a soda pop or a popsicle or a box of fake cigarettes made out of chewing gum. To get to the candy store, we had to cross over a ditch and then a street. Not even a busy street or a wide street. Then we had to walk down the block, around the corner and then up half another block. From her bedroom window, Mother Dear watched us walk across the ditch and then the street, until we turned into little specks and disappeared up the block. One would think we were crossing the Daytona 500 speedway with all the rules we were given for crossing the street to and from the candy store. We all crossed together holding hands, after looking both ways and back again, walking not running, crossing at the corner not in the middle. Those were the rules. If you broke those rules, you were not ever allowed to go to the candy store again, not for the rest of your natural born life. Needless to say, we all followed the rules, religiously.

    The walk back from the candy store was always twice as long as the walk, skip, walk even faster but don't run, walk to the candy store. During the walk back, my big brother Benji would carefully open the candy or soda pop or popsicle, discard the wrappings in the paper bag provided by the store clerk and hand us our treats. We waited patiently, knowing we had no other choice with Brother Ben. It was either wait patiently or forego your treat. Whichever one of us selected the fake cigarette chewing gum would dole out one or two to the rest. We had to share. Another rule. Then we would walk down the street, blowing pretend smoke into pretend smoke rings which were broken up in mid air by one of the other pretend smokers. All this was before the Surgeon General determined that smoking, even for pretend, was bad for your health.

    If we stopped playing long enough to listen to Granddaddy's stories, the sweet smell of tobacco and Old Spice would rise up and tickle our noses, sending warm chills from the top of our head to the tip of our toes. Granddaddy's smell. Smokey. Sweet. Comforting. Granddaddy's look. Cleanshaven. Tall. Dark. Handsome. I loved my Granddaddy, even when he was invariably yelling at us about one thing or the other.

    Although Mother Dear relegated Granddaddy to his own room in the back of the house, she still had certain standards she imposed upon him. He had to shower and shave daily. No scraggly old smelly n_ _ _ _ _s in her house. The "N" word was the only bad word I ever heard her utter and it was a rare utterance indeed, reserved for very small audiences, usually Granddaddy.

    There were numerous forbidden utterances in Mother Dear's house. It was a given that all curse words were taboo, including the common four letter words, h-e-l-l and d-a-m-n, except in church where the minister made reference to the place where you were sent for eternal damnation. I cringed every time the Minister, a law abiding, God fearing man, used words like "hell" and "damn." If we used those words, we would literally have our mouths washed out with soap, a fully lathered fresh new bar of Ivory soap. Mother Dear would say, "Go wash that chile's mouth out with soap," but my mother never had the heart. If she wanted it done, Mother Dear would have to do it herself. I never had my mouth washed out with soap. I either refrained from the offensive behavior in the first place, or was never caught in the act. I learned early how to play the game.

In addition to curse words, other quite normal words were also forbidden in Mother Dear's house. We were not allowed, for example, to use the word "hate" because it was too strong an emotion. "You should not hate anybody," Mother Dear said. "Even if people are unkind to you, turn the other check and forgive them, never hate them."

Likewise, we could not say, "I swear," because that meant you were swearing to God thereby using the Lord's name in vain, a breach of one of the Ten Commandments. Essentially, Mother Dear figured that you were calling on God to reinforce whatever you were talking about in the first place, which could not be that important and certainly not a good enough reason to call on the Lord for help. This was a particularly difficult phrase for us to refrain from uttering because young children could not trust the veracity of each other's comments unless, of course, you swore to God. "Pick me, pick me, I'll give you the rest of my Jolly Ranchers, I swear to God."

We were also not allowed to say "by the way," "hey you," "shut-up," "liar" and a whole host of other words and phrases. The explanations for these prohibitions have escaped me, but I am certain they had something to do with God or one of the Ten Commandments.

Growing up in the South essentially meant that you were expected to be seen and not heard. We were constantly admonished that we should be quiet, polite and respectful. When we addressed an adult, we were expected to say, "Yes mam," or Yes sir." It was a different life style, as much a reflection on parental preferences as cultural mores and values.

In hindsight, it is remarkable how Mother Dear and Granddaddy raised all their children in such small houses. The house on 11th Court West was by far the nicest and the biggest. It had a big yard which wrapped all around the front, right side and back of the house. There was a driveway on the left side of the house, split in half to share evenly with the neighbors. There were four other houses to the left of 205 11th Court West. We spent time in and out of all of them.

Cheryl Ann and her family lived in the first house to the left of our house. Many people from the South were christened with two first names. In fact, my mother intended to give me a boy's name like Bobby Jo until she fell in love with a nurse named Terri who assisted with my birth in the hospital. I am grateful she came up with the alternate name, though she lost touch with my namesake not long after she checked out of the hospital.

Cheryl Ann was light brown with large breasts for an eleven year old girl. Mother Dear used to say she was "fast." She was the first girl on the block to get a training bra. She flirted with all the boys in the neighborhood, including the boys who said they liked me and who I told, "I like you back." My mutual interest in these boys never stopped them from flirting with Cheryl Ann.

Tele lived one house to the left of Cheryl Ann. Tele was a nickname. For what exactly I don't know. Tele was the antithesis of Cheryl Ann. She was dark as midnight with short "nappy hair" and flat as a board. She compensated for these apparent deficiencies by talking a mile a minute and staying in everybody's business.

During the 50's and 60's in the South, it was considered an advantage to be light skinned with long straight hair. It meant that you had descended from a higher class of people, namely, white people. These features could also work against you if people thought you were too light or your hair was too long, in which case all the other girls hated your guts.

Granddaddy was always very strict with me and Cathy. We feared coming into the house when we were late. If we dared miss the curfew at dusk, Granddaddy would make us go outside and tear off a switch from the weeping willow tree in the front yard, bring it back to him and stand there while he whipped our bare legs.

My brother Benji routinely came home late and never got a "whuppin'." We resented the disparity in treatment. We complained to Mama over the phone, but she was all too familiar with Granddaddy's philosophy. He believed that you must be stricter when raising girls because girls did not know how to take care of themselves. Presumably, boys were born knowing how to defend themselves better than girls.

A strict philosophy of child rearing did not bode well with Cathy, who was very strong willed if not downright stubborn.

Mother Dear made vegetables for dinner every night. I learned early on that the trick to pleasing your elders was to take the path of least resistance, so I ate my vegetables. Unlike me, my sister Cathy never ate her vegetables, which became a constant source of conflict with Mother Dear and Granddaddy. Every night after I climbed into the bed with my sister, I would whisper softly to her, "Cathy, just eat your vegetables, they really aren't so bad. You are going to keep getting punishments if you don't eat your vegetables. It's better for you to just eat them." At the very young age of four or five, I thought I had learned the secret to life. Listen to your elders, always eat your vegetables and you shall be rewarded. If you refuse to listen or if you fail to eat your vegetables, you shall be punished. It was as simple as that, or so I thought.

Cathy either never understood the lesson, or she did not care. She simply told me, "They can't make me eat them." She was right about that. They never made her eat her vegetables. But she sure missed out on a lot of chocolate cake and ice cream when they sent her to bed early without dessert.

Punishments, especially those of a physical nature, were barbaric rituals, but quite common in the South among the black households where disobedience was rarely tolerated. We were very obedient little girls with little need for corporal punishment. Besides, I always thought that Granddaddy was wrong no matter how much he beat us. At times, I argued so persuasively that I managed to convince him that none of us deserved to be punished. One day, in a moment of weakness Granddaddy told me, "Girl, you ought to be a lawyer 'cause you can argue your way out of anything." Consequently, the idea of being a lawyer was planted early in life and it grew into reality as I advanced from one phase of development to the next.

When I argued my way out of punishments with Mama, she could hardly control the smile that inevitably crept onto her face. When I saw that smile forming, I knew my job was nearly done. One more assurance that the offense was not intentional, one more promise that it would never happen again and freedom was in the bag.

Granddaddy stayed fairly active until the very end of his life. One day he contracted bronchitis, went to the hospital and never returned. Sometime thereafter, Mother Dear's health began to deteriorate. It began slowly at first; her legs being the first part of her body to turn against her. She began to use a cane, then a walker, until finally she could barely walk at all. Then sometime in 1982, she developed a benign brain tumor. Because of her fear of surgery, she refused to have the tumor removed. Initially, the tumor was unobtrusive, but as it grew, it began to block certain brain functions, like her perception and her speech. She lived alone at 11th Court West until she could no longer take care of herself. Aunt Adrienne and Aunt Yvonne, who were the only children living in close proximity, regularly visited to keep a close vigil over her.

For a time, when I was 17, Mother Dear even came to live with us. Mama showed me how to help Mother Dear in and out of the bathtub to take her daily bath. One day when Mother Dear was getting out of the bathtub, her foot slipped and I had to quickly lean over to catch her. I strained my lower back in the process, but saved her from a devastating fall. I think about Mother Dear from time to time when my lower back aches.

Eventually, Mama, Aunt Adrienne and Aunt Yvonne decided to put Mother Dear in a nursing home. It was a painful decision, but the constant attention was draining on everyone. Ay least, they reasoned, the nursing home provided Mother Dear with around the clock attention and enabled the family to visit her at any time.

I rarely saw Mother Dear after she was admitted to the nursing home. Time and distance made it difficult to visit. Not long before she died, Mother Dear asked to see me, the way sick people sometimes do. I flew back to Birmingham on short notice to be by her side. For two days straight I sat next to her, talking and trying to comfort her in her time of need. She didn't seem to recognize me, she barely opened her eyes. I told my cousin Ari that I should have visited more often so that Mother Dear would have recognized me. As we rose to leave the room on the last day of my visit, Mother Dear lifted her arm in my direction and said in a weak voice, "Terri, don't forget to wear your boots, it's cold up there chile'."

I looked at my cousin Ari whose expression said, "See I told you that she recognized you." I walked back to Mother Dear's side, held her hand, holding back the tears. After all that, she knew exactly who I was.

When I got back to New York, I bought those winter boots, just in time for an unexpected winter blizzard. Mother Dear died two months later.

8
Open Doors

My mother's first career choice as a Registered Nurse tending to the sick exemplified her giving nature. When that wasn't enough, she opened our house to share with those less fortunate.

Charlsie was the first to share our home in Birmingham. She was a light-skinned black girl with long thick hair down to her waist. She was from a family of nine girls, enough children for a baseball team.

When Charlsie got married and moved away with Ralph, my brother and sister and I baked a little cake with one of those little Suzie Homemaker toys. It was a real oven and it baked real cakes. We didn't have any icing, so we substituted the icing with toothpaste. It looked great, or so we thought. Charlsie said the cake was so beautiful that she didn't want to eat it. She kindly suggested that we save the cake from an untimely demise and freeze it for all eternity. She made us feel like it was her one and only wedding cake. We carefully placed the tiny cake in a corner of my mother's freezer and there it sat for years. I don't know how many years exactly. Mama was careful not to throw it away. At some point, of course, we forgot about that cake and I assume Mama eventually threw it out. But it was there for as long as I can remember.

Charlsie was one of the many people to come and visit Mama after the doctors said it would only be a matter of days. She arrived in San Diego sometime on Saturday, looking shocked that such a terrible thing was happening to her surrogate mother. Mama was not strong enough to communicate extensively, but she acknowledged Charlsie's presence and she made it clear that she appreciated Charlsie's efforts to say a final goodbye.

~ ~ ~

I don't remember the explanation Mama gave us when our cousins Lynn, Debbie and Kay came to live with us at 201 Dewey Street in Newark, but it really didn't matter. One day Mama said that they were coming to live with us. And that was that. Her word was gospel. My cousins arrived shortly after Mama's announcement with suitcases filled with their clothes and their most valuable possessions. We were ecstatic. How lucky could you be? Now we could play with our cousins anytime we wanted.

Lynn, Debbie and Kay were my cousins from my stepfather Gene's side of the family. They were the daughters of Gene's sister Pat. Pat's husband abused her both mentally and physically. One day Aunt Pat decided that she would no longer tolerate his abuse. After she left him, Lynn, Debbie and Kay came to live with us while Aunt Pat financially got back on her feet. When Gene and Mama discussed the matter, there was no hesitation or second thoughts. Family is family. You do what you must to support your family. So it came to pass that the girls came to live with us in the three story walk-up on 201 Dewey Street in Newark, New Jersey.

I had questions that would forever remain unanswered. I wondered how Aunt Pat managed by herself. Where was she living? How did she support herself? Didn't she miss her children? Why couldn't she stay with us too? Why did husbands abuse their wives? Was Gene going to do the same thing to Mama?

Mama and Gene did their best to answer the more straightforward questions like, when our cousins were coming, where they would sleep and would they go to school with us? I was told that they were coming right away. They would sleep in the girls' room. Yes, of course they will go to school with us. No one knew exactly how long the girls would stay. Mama told me to stop worrying about all the details. Enough questions. As it turned out, Lynn, Debbie and Kay lived with us for two years, from 1966 to 1968. We slept five to a bed, three up, two down. Most nights we stayed up giggling until my stepfather Gene came into the room to tell us to quiet down. It was like having a slumber party every night for two years.

In 1968, my three cousins went back to live with their mother, who was better situated by then to take care of her children. Six years later, in 1974, Aunt Pat was diagnosed with breast cancer. Kay, the youngest of the three girls, was in the seventh grade at the time. A year later, they removed one of Aunt Pat's breasts as a life-saving precaution. But the cancer came back with a vengeance in 1979. Aunt Pat died on July 7, 1979. Kay was 17 when her mother died, the same age as Aunt Pat when her mother died. At the funeral, I remember thinking that Aunt Pat was young and beautiful, just like my mother. I remember thinking that life was unfair. I remember thinking that cancer was a deadly, evil, stalking menace to society. I remember wishing there was no such thing as cancer.

~ ~ ~

Mama met Carmen Santana in 1968, when I was ten and a half years old. Carmen had just turned eighteen. We were living on 201 Dewey Street in the three story walk-up in Newark, New Jersey. Lynn, Debbie and Kay had just moved back to live with their mother.

My mother was working as a registered nurse at Beth Israel Hospital in New York City, a short commute from Newark, New Jersey. Working at Beth Israel was a daily drama for my mother. I recall overhearing a conversation that she once had delivered a baby with two heads when she was assigned to the maternity ward of the hospital. In reality, she had delivered Siamese twins who looked like a baby with two heads. She asked the obstetrician if the infant would live. The doctor said that the baby would not survive beyond the end of the week because of internal complications. The nurses let the baby die. They could have lost their licenses, or worse yet, gone to jail. But those consequences did not faze my mother. She wanted no part in saving a severely deformed child who had no chance of survival. The other nurses worried about the ramifications of the death. Not my mother. She told her staff to send any inquiry to her attention if someone questioned the incident. Fortunately, no one ever questioned the circumstances surrounding the baby's death.

Beth Israel Hospital was also where my mother met Carmen. Carmen was one of Mama's pediatric patients. She came from a large family. Some of her siblings lived in New York, some of them lived in Puerto Rico, where Carmen was born. The siblings in Puerto Rico were her half brothers and sisters, many of whom she had never met. They were born after her father left her mother, returned to Puerto Rico and began having children with other women. At the time, I could not imagine having brothers or sisters that I had never met. At the time, I did not know that I had brothers or sisters I had never met.

Carmen was in the hospital undergoing long term treatments for lupus. My mother was the senior nurse assigned to her case. Day after day Carmen's mother returned to the hospital to watch over Carmen. Day after day, my mother returned to the hospital to watch over Carmen. Side by side they stood, the mother and the nurse, tending to the ailing child. One spoke no Spanish, the other no English. One was educated, the other never finished high school. One had learned to manage her world. The other was lost in a morass of bureaucracy and red tape. Somehow, through language barriers, cultural differences, and socioeconomic disparities, Carmen's mother managed to ask for help and my mother responded.

When Mrs. Santana had gathered enough courage, she went to the hospital to confront my mother. She asked her niece, who spoke both Spanish and English fluently, to come with her to the hospital to translate for her when she spoke to my mother. They took the crowded elevator to the general medicine floor and met my mother in Carmen's room. Mrs. Santana politely greeted my mother and then leaned over the bed to kiss Carmen who was resting quietly at the time.

She began, "Yo no se como se dice este, pero...I don't know how to say this, but...I need your help. I can not let another one of my daughters die. I am a good mother and I love my children, but I cannot afford the medicine it will take to keep Carmen alive. Please, I know you care about her, you are here everyday. Carmen tells me that you come to see her all of the time, even during the middle of the night."

"Of course I care about Carmen," my mother began. "I come to see her because I care very much about her, but it is also part of my job to make sure she is comfortable. She is a sweet girl. This must be very painful for you...I can't begin to imagine your pain. Carmen speaks of her sister Maria often. She is afraid that she is going to die just like Maria."

"I can't let her die," Mrs. Santana continued, "I wanted to ask you...I know it is asking a lot, but I thought that perhaps, if you care about Carmen as much as it seems..."

"What is it?" My mother abruptly interjected. "Please, just ask me, if there is anything I can do, I will do it."

Mrs. Santana began to speak rapidly, "I would like for Carmen to come live with you. If you could take care of her, get the medicines she needs, the treatments she needs, I know that she has a better chance, a better chance than I could provide to her sister. I know it is asking a lot, maybe too much. But I have no where else to turn. I do not know what else to do. I cannot stand by and watch her die."

My mother stared at Mrs. Santana and then at her niece who was rapidly translating and trying to keep pace. My mother realized that Mrs. Santana was going to ask for a favor, but even my mother did not expect such an extraordinary request. She was expecting her to ask for money or medicine or help filling out forms. Living with us was a full time, all consuming commitment. It was a commitment that would affect the entire family.

On the other hand, it must be terrible to watch a second child succumb to a deadly illness, my mother thought. Mrs. Santana must be desperate to make such an incredible request. My mother knew that we could afford the medical treatments. She knew that her husband and children would not object to helping someone in dire straits. She knew that there was only one response to Mrs. Santana's request.

Right then and there, Mama and Mrs. Santana decided that when Carmen checked out of the hospital, she would come home to live with us. It was as simple as that, no paperwork, no long debates, no judgments passed. It was the answer to one woman's prayer. It was the solution to one child's dilemma. It was all perfectly normal to me.

When Carmen arrived to our second story walk-up on 201 Dewey Street, Mama explained to us that lupus was a deadly disease that makes you feel sick and tired all of the time. It was a type of blood disease, she told us. "It is a little bit like cancer because the bad cells attack your system and eventually spread the illness throughout the body," she explained. "With the proper medication and care, you can sometimes control the disease, but not always," she added in a grave foreboding voice, a voice to which I was not accustomed.

I remembered how Aunt Pat and little Sherrie were suddenly taken from their loved ones. Cancer was a bad word, an evil word, a word I did not like saying, even to myself. God forbid you should say the word too many times and perhaps become afflicted with some dreaded cancer-like illness. I wished that Carmen's illness was more like a bad cold. People who got cancer or cancer-like illnesses seemed to die.

Although I did not understand much about Carmen's lupus, I understood enough to know that not everyone survived this type of illness, even with the expensive medications and hospital treatments. I understood also that Carmen had a very bad type of illness, because she was always sick and she was always throwing up.

Every morning when Carmen rose from bed, she headed straight for the bathroom. Her morning bathroom ritual was a major part of her day. She dressed in flannel pajamas with a long sleeved shirt, long pants and a matching robe. She always wore big fuzzy slippers on her feet. I wanted a pair of big fuzzy slippers just like them. Sometimes, I would sneak in the bedroom, slip my feet into her slippers and walk around admiring the way they made my feet look all big and furry, like a wild animal.

On good days, Carmen was in and out of the bed all day, her night time clothing often doubling for her day time clothing. She would occasionally get dressed and go out for a walk or a short trek to the drug store. On bad days, she would just stay in the bed. Mama bought Carmen endless matching sets of pajamas and robes, all in the colors she liked. She felt that it was the least she could do. Carmen asked for very little. She rarely even spoke.

Carmen took constant medication which made her nauseous. Mornings were particularly bad. With no food in her system, she would get dry heaves which made her cough and spit over the toilet until she was too weak to stand. When that happened, she would kneel on the little rug in front of the toilet, holding her hair back until the heaving stopped. I would lay in my bed listening to Carmen's morning ritual, flinching with every cough, wishing I could do something to make it go away.

After Carmen finished vomiting, she brushed her teeth and washed her face. She was meticulous about this. First she pulled her hair back with a head band, making sure that not a single strand of hair was left dangling. Then she brushed her teeth for what seemed like an eternity, all the while letting the water run. Mama always told us not to let the water run when we brushed our teeth. Somehow, letting the water run when Carmen brushed her teeth was not that important.

When Carmen finished brushing her teeth, she brushed her tongue. The first time I saw her do this, I asked her why. "The tongue has all the germs," Carmen said with a little smile. "You have to brush your tongue to get rid of the germs." I wondered if Carmen thought it was possible to wash away the germs that gave her the lupus. The thought crossed my ten year old mind.

The pills Carmen took to control the symptoms of the lupus were a type of steroid which made her bloated all over, even in her face. She hated the way the pills made her teenage body look round and portly. She often said, "I look fat."

"Not to me," I said, "I think you look beautiful." I always told Carmen that she looked beautiful, no matter how she looked. Normally, at five foot five, Carmen weighed only 120 pounds. She was thin in comparison to most girls her age. But the pills added an extra 10 to 15 pounds to her frame. None of her clothes fit properly, so she wore either sweat pants or pajamas. She refused to buy clothes in sizes above her normal size four. It was as though buying larger sized clothes was an admission that she had gained weight. In order to minimize the weight gain from the steroids, Carmen compensated by eating next to nothing, which made her even more nauseous.

Carmen was the big sister I never had. I followed her around like a puppy waiting for recognition. Sometimes I would sit down on the bed next to her and ask her if she was all right. No matter how bad she felt, she looked at me with her dark eyes and long lashes and said with a little smile, "I'm fine. Don't worry." But I did worry.

If Carmen was feeling well enough, she would tell me stories about her two sisters Maria and Elena. Maria was a year older than Carmen and was diagnosed with lupus when she was 18. She died six months after the diagnosis and one year before Carmen came to live with us. Elena, who was my age, had not developed any symptoms of lupus, yet. Everyone fearfully waited for the signs to surface because the illness is genetically linked. Carmen had pictures of Maria and Elena everywhere, on her nightstand, in her wallet, tucked away in her lingerie drawer amidst sashays of potpourri, between the pages of her bible. The scattered worn photographs were the cherished remnants of happier times, when life was good and worries consisted of childhood frivolities like the uncertainty of the ice cream truck arrival.

The image of Maria indelibly etched in my mind is the picture used for her prayer card. It was Maria's high school graduation picture. Carmen placed the wallet sized card on the wall above the headboard of her bed. Maria was wearing an emerald blue strapless top made of a shiny silk material. She wore a single strand of cultured pearls around her neck with dainty matching earrings. They looked real. Her long dark hair, which she normally wore down to her waist, was pinned up in an elegant French twist.

Maria looked like an angel, gazing down upon Carmen with a mesmerizing Mona Lisa smile. She had a tiny svelte figure which was evident even from the wallet sized bust shot. Her creamy brown complexion was clear and smooth. But her best features were her eyes. They were the most mesmerizing eyes I had ever seen. They were almond shaped with pupils as black as midnight surrounded by long thick eye lashes. I imagined her up in heaven, smiling down on us from above the clouds. No pain, no sadness, no lupus.

The inscription beneath the picture on the prayer card read, "Our beloved Maria Elena Santana." The inscription below the name read, "Yea, though I walk through the valley of the shadow of death, I shall fear no evil, for thy rod and thy staff they comfort me."

I wondered if at the tender age of 19, Maria feared no evil when she walked through the valley of the shadow of death.

Maria was a popular, outgoing girl, not at all shy and quiet like Carmen. All the boys in the neighborhood liked Maria. She had a boyfriend who took her to all the dances and all the parties. Maria could salsa and merenge better than all the other girls. She and her boyfriend looked like Fred Astaire and Ginger Rogers when they danced.

I sat on the edge of the bed listening to Carmen and asking a million questions along the way. What did Maria wear to the party? How old was she when she first kissed a boy? Did she get in trouble for staying out that late? Can you dance like Maria danced? Can you teach me to dance like that? Oh please, oh please, oh please?

Carmen was never annoyed by my incessant questions. She mostly smiled when she talked about Maria, until she finished her story and her thoughts inevitably drifted to Maria's untimely death and her smile gradually faded with her lingering words.

Maria's original diagnosis of lupus came as a shock to everyone. At first, Maria felt tired and achy. Initially, their mother dismissed these ailments away and attributed them to less than perfect eating habits. The remedy was more vitamins, more fruits and vegetables, more chicken and beef, more rice and beans. But then Maria began to feel weak and tired all of the time. Some unknown malady was slowly extinguishing the life from her body. One morning when Maria refused to get out of the bed, her mother knew that something was seriously wrong. Mrs. Santana decided to take Maria to the emergency room at Beth Israel Hospital, the same hospital where Mama would meet Carmen a year and a half later. During her brief stay at the hospital, Maria received a battery of tests. The test results revealed a diagnosis of advanced lupus. The family was devastated. No one had ever been seriously ill.

The doctors told Mrs. Santana that Maria would need expensive treatments and medications to keep her alive. Without money or insurance, Mrs. Santana was not able to provide Maria with the medicine she needed. Like all faithful Catholic families, the Santana family turned to prayer for consolation. They prayed that Maria's health would miraculously improve. But the Patron Saint of Miracles granted no miracles at the Santana household that year.

Not long after Maria was diagnosed with lupus, the fatigue and joint pain became so excruciating that she required hospitalization. Again, her mother rushed her to the emergency room at Beth Israel Hospital. They hooked Maria's slender arms up with intravenous tubes of food, water and pain killers. After the tubes were in place, the doctors told the family that Maria would probably slip into a coma and die. As soon as the pain medication penetrated her system, Maria relaxed, closed her eyes and slipped into a coma. She never spoke another word.

The last thing Mrs. Santana said to her dying daughter was, "It will be all right."

But it was not all right.

The family came to the hospital everyday for a week and stayed all day until visiting hours were over, hoping with each passing hour that Maria would show some sign of improvement. After the seventh day, the doctors said that Maria's vital signs were negligible. They took her off the respirator and she died hours later. The entire Santana family was at the hospital. Mrs. Santana was screaming at the top of her lungs in Spanish, "Ay Dios mio. They took my baby! Ay Dios mio. They took my baby." Aunts and uncles, cousins and siblings were all crying and screaming in the waiting room, barely cognizant of the people around them. One of Maria's aunts was holding her mother back, trying desperately to console her.

"You must calm down. Your family needs you now," they told Mrs. Santana while grabbing her arms and pulling them back to keep her from hitting some unseen object of her aggression. "It is God's will. Maria is resting peacefully now. It will be all right."

But it was not all right.

Carmen said that her mother was never quite the same after Maria died. The family thought that Mrs. Santana lost her faith in God. She prayed less often. She went to church less often. She smiled less often. Then, when Carmen was diagnosed with lupus one year later at the same age as Maria, her mother became bitter and angry. She blamed God. She blamed the government for supplying contaminated water to the projects. She blamed her ex-husband for bad sperm. She swore she would not allow another daughter to die, even if it meant sending her away to live with another family, our family.

In 1975, eight years after Carmen came to live with us, I flew off to college, leaving Carmen and the rest of my family behind. At the beginning of my sophomore year in September of 1976, Carmen's real mother decided to return to Puerto Rico where life was simpler and where everyone spoke Spanish. She never learned to speak English. In May, 1977, Mrs. Santana called our house and asked Carmen to join her in Puerto Rico. Mrs. Santana wanted her daughter back. Without much discussion or fanfare, Carmen left for Puerto Rico intending to return to us at the end of the summer. She never came home.

Shortly after Carmen's arrival in Puerto Rico, she began to experience severe pain and headaches. Her mother took her to the hospital where she died days later. I learned about Carmen's death two weeks after the fact when I flew home for summer vacation. I never had a chance to tell her goodbye.

I asked my mother why no one had called me at school to tell me about Carmen's death. I was confused and upset. Carmen had lived with us for nearly a decade. She was essentially my older sister. Had I known she was dying, I would have flown to Puerto Rico to stand by her bedside. I would have told her that I loved her one last time.

"But Terri," my mother tried to explain, "No one called me until a week after Carmen's death. You were already scheduled to come home from school. By that point, there was nothing any of us could do."

It was as though Mrs. Santana didn't care about our feelings for Carmen. She didn't bother calling when Carmen was first hospitalized. Calling us was an afterthought. We were just more people on a long list of too many people to contact.

Like all those who give without expecting anything in return, my mother understood Mrs. Santana's apathetic attitude. Mrs. Santana appreciated my mother's help, but she did not feel like she owed us anything. In fact, it seemed that she even resented our help. Our assistance only reminded her that she was unable to provide for Carmen herself. She had been forced to send her daughter to live with another woman because she could not afford to take care of Carmen herself. And to make matters worse, when Mrs. Santana was finally able to send for Carmen, Carmen died weeks later.

It was ironic, to say the least.

My sister Carmen, who lived with us for nine years, died with no fanfare and no goodbye. Sometimes, when I wash my face and brush my teeth in the morning, I think about Carmen. Cuidate mi mayor hermana. Take care big sister, till we meet again.

~ ~ ~

My cousin Darryl came to live with us when I was 17. Darryl was my stepfather Bob's nephew. He was tall and thin with a thick well trimmed afro. Sometimes he wore a little mustache and beard, but it never grew in very thick. He and I actually attended the same college and then spent summers together at our house in Houston, Texas. He was one of the funniest people I ever knew. He lived life to the fullest. He smoked and drank and partied with his friends until the wee hours of the night. His friends were just as wild and crazy as he was. On several occasions, I went out with him to the gay bars he frequented in Houston, Texas, admiring his carefree attitude and wishing I had the same laissez-faire approach to life. We danced rowdily with his friends, no one in particularly dancing with anyone else in particular.

When we went back to college, Darryl settled into school life and fell in love with a gorgeous Italian guy named Dan who had straight brown hair, a chiseled profile and a perfect physique. They spent all of their free time together. It got to a point that if you saw one, you saw the other. Their relationship soon became monogamous. But it was already too late by then.

Darryl started missing classes. When I asked him about it, he said he wasn't feeling well. Frequent visits to the health center were of little consequence. He grew pale and thin. His doctor in Houston said that a large percentage of the gay population in Houston had become afflicted with a similar illness. She said that no one knew what type of virus was causing the epidemic. In the early 1980s the medical community was just learning about HIV and AIDS.

Darryl and Dan made it to graduation and then moved together to Colorado. I never say Darryl after that. He died less than a year later. I don't know what became of Dan. Shortly after Darryl's death, I had a dream about him. He was sitting on a chair, telling me that he was sorry. I wasn't quite sure why, but I kept telling him that he had no need to be sorry. I loved him no matter what. It saddened me to think that his life had ended in such a miserable fashion.

9
The Disappointment

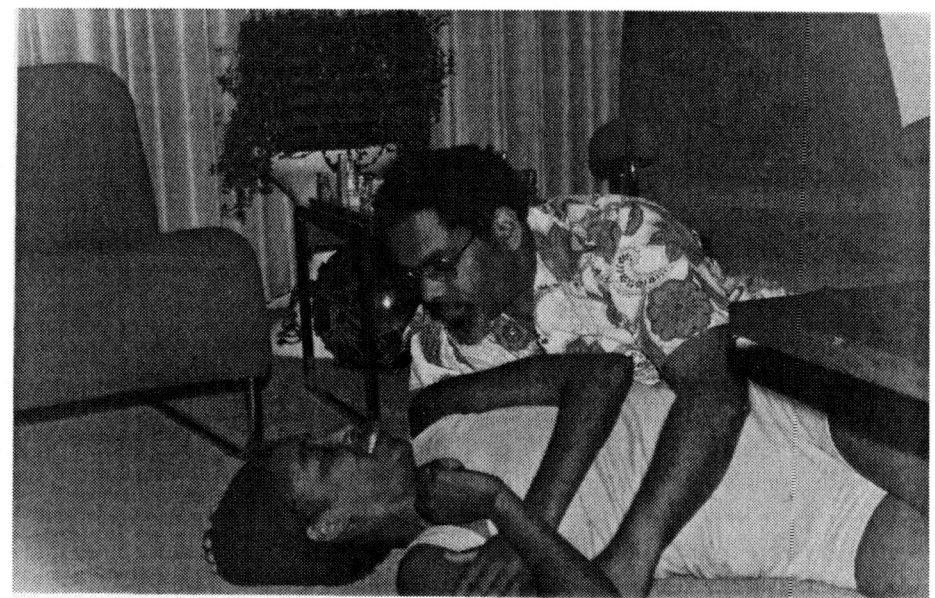

My mother and Bob were true soul mates. I have never seen two people who were so much in love. They were married in 1973, in the back yard of our house outside of Syracuse, New York. There is a picture of my mother with her hair shaped in an Angela Davis afro, wearing a pair of white shorts. Bob has his arm around her waist. They both looked so happy.

But the happiness did not last long.

She met Bob during the pursuit of her doctorate degree in clinical psychology from Syracuse University. At the time, we were living in Potsdam, New York and she was married to my stepfather Gene. She traveled back and forth to Syracuse spending most of the week studying and working part time in Syracuse. She came home to Potsdam every weekend to spend time with us. None of us liked the long absences, but we understood that it was a short term situation.

My stepfather Gene had a harder time dealing with my mother's absences. Her relentless drive for education and the demanding schedule it required put a tremendous strain on their marriage. His insecurity about his own educational accomplishments and financial success caused arguments over the most trivial issues. As soon as Mama walked in the door on Friday evening, the arguments began. Gene wanted to know where she had been, who she was with and why she hadn't called. The questions didn't stop there. He questioned the clothes she wore, the way she wore her hair and almost everything else. Mama tried to calm his fears, to assure him that she was not leaving him for another man. But eventually, the constant bickering caused her to do just that. It drove her to the arms of another man. That other man was Bob.

My mother eventually obtained her doctorate degree. She did not allow the long commute or the divorce from Gene to impede her progress. My brother, sister and I all attended the graduation. It was a bright sunny day, unusual for Syracuse. What I recall most about that day was her beautiful smile. She was so happy. She finally proved to herself and the world that a poor little black girl from Birmingham, Alabama could become an accomplished scholar.

During the graduation ceremony, I thought about a story my mother once told me. When she was in grade school, first learning how to read, her teacher told her that she was retarded and that she would never amount to much. The remark devastated my mother. At first she was hurt, and then her impressionable mind began to doubt her own abilities. The comment became part of her permanent school record, making it even more difficult to disregard. Racism during the 1930's and 1940's in Birmingham, Alabama was not well disguised. Discouraging black children from academic success was a way to keep them down. It took years for my mother to truly believe in herself. I secretly wished that her teacher could see my mother now, accepting her Doctorate degree and proving them all wrong.

Bob ultimately left my mother in 1982, to marry his office manager. The divorce was brutal, driving her into bankruptcy. Bob treated her this way despite the fact that she helped care for two of his adopted daughters and his nephew Darryl.

My mother and I spoke often during this time period. It was one of the most difficult times of her life. I wrote a poem reflecting her sentiments at the time.

Take me away from this madness
to where placid waters flow.

*The time has arrived long overdue
for peace and love to grow.*

*Tell me only sweet words
for that is the fruit of my search.
I want to hear the thorn bird sing
But it has yet to find its perch.*

*Wildflower growing wild
leaning in the wind,
Do you hear the voice calling
Will this journey never end?*

*You promised to bring me gladness
never ending love,
But alas the words were empty
as vast as the skies above.*

*Now as I come to rest
I find all my dreams the same.
Has life's promises passed me by,
Was it all for naught, in vain?*

Life's Promises, March 28, 1983

 My mother and I both moved on, she from her divorce with Bob, I from my long term relationship. Mama started a new management consulting business in California which took off like wildfire. I helped her negotiate a number of successive lucrative management consulting contracts. She began to make substantial amounts of money. She met and married Larry. She was finally content with both her professional and personal endeavors.
 It did not last long.

10
The Last

Larry never liked me, he never seemed to like anybody, but he really didn't like me. He was extremely jealous of my relationship with my mother. He treated me with callous disdain, often criticizing my actions and rebuking my approaches. He had no patience or tolerance, even for his own children and grandchildren, especially for his own children and grandchildren.

Once, when my sister's three boys were quietly watching cartoons in his living room, he walked defiantly towards the television and turned it to another channel. When the boys asked why he had turned the channel, without hesitation he said, "This is my house, we watch what I want to watch." Never mind that there were multiple television sets in the house. Never mind that Larry did not sit down to watch the television once he changed the channel. And never mind that the boys only had the opportunity to visit Papa Larry and Dah once or twice a year.

Larry has two daughters from a prior marriage, Kathy and Barbie. He also has an estranged son named Doug who lives somewhere in the State of Washington. I often wondered how someone could have an "estranged" son. The word was generally reserved for spouses, not blood relatives. Larry must have done something pretty awful for his son to run away like that and sever all contacts with everyone in his entire family. Apparently, the brother left one day and refused to return or provide contact information. Then he stopped calling all together. That was over 10 years ago.

Larry's daughters did their best to maintain a decent relationship with Larry, but the relationship was strained at best. Mama seemed to be the only one who could handle him, and even she had her moments.

~ ~ ~

The first time I met Larry was in Bethel, Maine, the spring of 1989, a few months before my daughter Nicole was born. Mama and Larry were spending the summer in Bethel to attend diversity training sessions at NTL, the National Training Laboratory for clinical psychologists. Mama had described him to me, but only briefly. She told me that he was funny and smart. They met several times during their travels, were intrigued with each other, but never connected. When they finally got together, the chemistry between them was undeniable. They were totally infatuated with each other. In a matter of a few short months, they decided to get married. It would be the fourth marriage for both of them.

I was delighted to hear the news of their relationship and their imminent marriage, even though she had never even mentioned his name before. I wanted to know everything about him, what he looked like, where he was from, what his personality was like. She was leaving something out, or so it seemed to me. I sensed that she wanted me to form my own conclusions, uninfluenced by her opinions. Not wanting to sound discouraging or pessimistic, I told her that I was thrilled by the news and that I could not wait to meet him. Secretly, I thought that she was moving too fast. I worried that she would be hurt, again.

Mama and Larry picked me up from the airport in Portland, Maine, two hours north from our ultimate destination in Bethel. I hugged and kissed Mama with my big belly protruding out between us. We were both so excited about seeing each other, about my pregnancy, about their impending marriage, about everything.

I turned to say hello to the man standing next to my mother, the man who would soon become my stepfather. He was not especially good looking. His face was old and wrinkled, bearing the imprints from 70 years of a long life, yet lacking the gentle aura that often comes with age. The hair on his head was long and gray and it continued down his face into a scraggly beard and mustache as unruly as the hair on his head. He was average height and weight with a small round belly that protruded slightly over his belt. And he was white. Not that this mattered, but it was a totally unexpected detail which Mama completely neglected to mention.

The drive to Bethel was long and uncomfortable. I sat in the back seat behind my mother on the passenger side, squirming to find a comfortable position. I stared at the back of Larry's neck and the right side of his head for most of the trip searching for clues about his personality. He didn't say very much in the car, which was an old outdated Toyota Celica. He sat straight up, leaning slightly over the steering wheel with his hands at the one o'clock and eleven o'clock positions. Any closer and his thumbs would have brushed each other. He stared straight ahead at the road, never glancing to the left or right to see what might be coming from another direction, as though his direction was the only one that mattered. He seemed obsessed with his driving, which was far too fast for my comfort. I wondered why he was driving so fast and so recklessly. We were not scheduled to be anywhere by a certain time. I buckled the seat belt around my fat pregnant belly, just in case.

He drove like a bat of hell, as my mother would say, but didn't. Bats driving out of hell could not have been more reckless than Larry driving on the one lane highway to Bethel, swerving in and out of oncoming traffic to gain the slightest edge over the car in front of him. On more than one occasion, I felt like shouting from the back seat, "Slow down, look out for that car," or "Be careful, the light is turning red." But, I held my tongue, taking my cues from Mama who remained conspicuously silent.

She must have known what I knew, that all men detested back seat drivers. Such knowledge was not usually enough to keep me quiet. But, Mama's body language told me that in no uncertain terms I should remain quiet. She looked as though she had placed her fate in God, to protect us from being killed in some horrendous car accident. I decided to say the Serenity prayer and do the same. For as long as I can remember, Mama kept the Serenity prayer prominently displayed in the house. It was a perfect description of how she approached life, and now, the way I approached it as well. "God, grant me the serenity to accept the things I cannot change, the courage to change the things I can and the wisdom to know the difference." I was having difficulty with the part that says, "and the wisdom to know the difference." Perhaps this was one of those situations I should be changing instead of accepting and the wisdom to know the difference had escaped me. As we approached the little town of Bethel, I said another prayer, "Dear Lord, thank you for allowing me to live yet another day. And also, I'm sorry for missing so much church. I will do better. Amen."

When we reached the small cottage where we were staying for the week, Larry parked the car and hastily took the bags inside. He looked at his watch and declared that we should be ready to go to dinner by 6:00 p.m., in less than an hour. I looked at Mama for a reaction, thinking that I would rather relax for a little while and go to dinner a bit later, say 8:00 p.m. when most civilized people go out to dinner on a Saturday night. She smiled and just said, "Honey, why don't you go upstairs and wash up."

Again, I knew from Mama's body language that something was not quite copacetic. She was always very outspoken, never one to hide her feelings or withhold her opinions, a character trait which, for better or for worse, had clearly passed on to me. But I did as I was told, quickly and quietly. When I was finished getting ready, I walked throughout the cottage looking for Mama and Larry to see if they were ready to go. As I passed by the front screen door leading to the porch, I saw Larry, out of the corner of my eye, sitting alone in the car which was parked in the driveway. He was sitting in the driver's seat, looking straight ahead with his hands at the 11:00 and 1:00 o'clock positions. Waiting. Just sitting there in the car, all alone, waiting.

A chill ran up and down my spine. This was just creepy, plain and simple. All kinds of crazy thoughts ran through my foolish head. Larry looked possessed to me. What had he done with my mother? Just how long did she say she knew him? Where was he planning to take me in my vulnerable pregnant state? I searched the rest of the house for Mama and saw the light on in the upstairs bathroom where Mama was getting ready. I knocked tentatively on the bathroom door, half thinking with my wild imagination that I would find her sprawled out in the middle of the floor in a pool of blood. "Mama, you in there?"

She cracked the door and peeked out from behind the mirror on the medicine cabinet where she was applying her lipstick. "Are you ready honey?" she calmly asked me, pursing her full lips together to evenly spread the lipstick.

"Yes," I said in a quiet, relieved voice. "But Mama," I continued hesitantly, "did you know that Larry was sitting outside in the car, all by himself? He's just sitting there staring straight ahead. Is everything all right? Why is he sitting there like that?"

"It's all right honey, he does that. He's just ready to go, so he's waiting for us in the car."

"But it's not even six o'clock yet. Why doesn't he just wait inside for us?" Like a normal person, I wanted to say.

"That's just his way honey. When he starts to get impatient, it's better that he just go somewhere else to be alone and deal with it."

"Ohhhhh kaaaaay," I said. "Anything else I should know before we get going?"

"Don't be silly," Mama said with a little smile. "Go outside and wait in the car with Larry. I'll be right along."

"I'd just as soon wait in here with you, if that's o.k.?"

"Of course honey, but it's not like he's going to bite your head off."

She was wrong. Contrary to Mama's assertion, I soon discovered that Larry would bite your head off, with little or no provocation. He and I were constantly involved in a plethora of arguments too numerous to count, ranging from major political topics to how one should properly wash a water glass. I took little comfort in knowing that he argued with most everyone like that. My mother remained by his side, however, to the bitter end, which was nearer than any of us could have imagined.

11
The Diagnosis

Crone: n. A wise old woman who is not afraid of growing old. (Webster's Dictionary)

December 17, 1994. Today was my mother's sixtieth birthday. No one thought it might be her last. Twelve of her closest friends and relatives gathered around her to celebrate this momentous occasion. She wore a royal blue shawl dress with delicate red lace trim. She carried a few extra pounds in these later years, but she carried them well. Her gray speckled hair, which she usually wore short, was soft and wavy. Her make-up, which she rarely wore, was applied sparingly, except for the luscious red lipstick gently spread across her full lips.

As I unpacked my bag to prepare for my weekend stay in Los Angeles, my mother sat back quietly in a white wicker rocking chair savoring me and listening as I rambled on about my flight from New York. Then, in a voice just above a whisper, she said, "Terri, I haven't said anything to anyone, but I don't feel so well."

I stopped unpacking momentarily to look at my mother. Admittedly, she looked tired. In fact, she looked exhausted. Every move was a tremendous effort. I could tell that something was terribly wrong.

"What's the matter Mama," I said, "What hurts?" I was waiting to hear her say that her stomach was aching or that her throat was sore. Instead, she said she couldn't really describe how she felt, just tired and achy, a feeling she had not been able to shake for weeks, maybe even longer. She couldn't remember exactly how long. Accompanying her general malaise was a persistent cough. We decided that she should go to the doctor as soon as the weekend celebration was over.

We celebrated Amanda's 60th birthday that weekend in the quaint cottage by the ocean underneath exceptionally blue skies, having no idea of the extent of her illness. But somehow I knew this was not just an ordinary cold or flu. Mama's energy was not the same. Something immense, something hideous was draining her from the very core.

Both of her sisters (Yvonne and Adrienne), both of her daughters (Terri and Cathy), and both of her stepdaughters (Barbie and Kathy) flew into Los Angeles from all parts of the country to participate in the celebration of my mother's 60th birthday. Five of her closest friends also joined her for the two day celebration. These women worked together and had developed an incredible bond, the center of which was Amanda. The women included Nancy Brown Jamison who was Amanda's best friend, Anne Litwin, Marylou, Marilyn and Brenda. At one of their many gatherings, the five women decided to give their group a name. They liked the name "Maude," it was the name of Anne's cat. So they called themselves the Maude women.

Months before her 60th birthday, Mama located this beautiful cottage beside the ocean right outside of Los Angeles. The cool ocean breeze swept through the upstairs bedrooms filling the cottage with a fresh tropical scent. Attached to each of the precisely decorated rooms was a full bathroom with a tub, sink and toilet. There were fresh cut flowers in all the rooms and potpourri in all the bathrooms.

Each of us shared a room with one other person. The room I shared with Brenda was all white with wicker furniture. The room Mama shared with Barbie was painted pink with mirrored furniture. The room my sister Cathy shared with Anne Litwin was brown with wooden furniture. The rest of the bedrooms were equally attractive. The beauty of the house made me yearn for a home of my own to decorate lavishly. After living in cramped quarters in New York City, I appreciated the beauty of a spacious home.

The invitation said it was a Croning Celebration. I had never heard of such a thing. I assumed it was one of those terms that psychologists use, something related to management consulting or diversity training, two areas my mother mastered long before they became corporate buzz words. I pulled out my dictionary to determine the precise meaning of the word "Crone." It said a wise old woman who was not afraid of growing old. That pretty much described my mother.

Most of mom's friends were trained psychologists working as management consultants, just like her. They generally organized and led workshops to assist large and small companies in managing personnel. Their work was nothing like the sterile legal profession to which I was accustomed. Even when their work did not bring them together, they managed to find excuses to see each other.

The Croning Celebration turned out to be one of those excuses. It was an excuse to relax and enjoy the company of good friends. We celebrated Amanda's sixty years in a style to which I was not accustomed.

Each of the activities planned that weekend was perfectly orchestrated. Nancy Brown Jamison brought her camera to capture the event for all eternity. She caught all the important moments and some of the not so important moments. She took so many pictures that after a while we hardly noticed she was taking pictures at all.

At my mother's request, I eventually compiled a photo album of the weekend. By the time the pictures were developed, Mama was too sick to put the album together, so I did it for her. The project was not a huge effort on my part, but Mama was eternally grateful. The album contained pictures of us laughing, crying, hugging, eating, drinking and playing games. My mother told me that it was one of the best weekends of her life. It would be the last weekend before knowledge of the cancer changed everything.

One of the weekend activities included sewing a quilt together. The idea was for each of us to design a piece to go into the quilt. We were supposed to create a patch which reminded us of Mama. I didn't think I would be creative enough to design a piece. But I did. I cut out a red heart and sewed it onto a blue patch. On top of the heart I placed beads which looked like little tear drops. For some reason, love and sadness came to my mind; hence the heart and the tears. Perhaps my subconscious intuition foretold the deep sadness which would soon loom over us.

Barbie, Larry's oldest daughter, shared my anxiety about creating a presentable patch. As it turns out, her patch was my favorite. It looked like a playful little girl with a big floppy hat, stylish and free spirited, like Mama.

We teased Aunt Adrienne about her patch because it took so long for her to finish it. Unlike the rest of us who glued most of our materials, she sewed each bead individually onto her patch. She designed two connecting hearts made of little white beads which looked like tiny pearls. Late into the night, while we talked and laughed and drank too much wine, Adrienne sewed her magnificent patch.

After we finished the quilt, we reminisced about time spent together with my mother. There was a lot of crying as we circled the room describing our first and best memories of Mama.

I told the group that one of my first memories of Mama was an incident that took place when I was four or five years old. We were walking down the street and I did not feel like holding her hand. Instead of making a fuss or demanding that I hold her hand, Mama told me that I was free to walk beside her, so long as I did not run out into the street. She knew that when I was ready, I would reach for her hand. Seconds later, I reached up for her hand, on my own free will. There was never a question of control, only guidance.

On the second evening of the Croning, we went to a nearby seafood restaurant for dinner. We all maneuvered for a seat next to Mama, or at least at her table. The restaurant was small and the tables were tight. I felt lucky to sit next to her. I would have felt the same way even if it had not been her birthday. She had that effect on everyone.

There was something about Mama, she had a special aura. Everyone wanted to be close to her. When she spoke, she chose her words carefully. She didn't need to hear herself talk. Instead, she listened carefully to her audience and only commented when it was time. Her observations were often profound.

And there was no mistaking that smile. It was definitely a Fouther smile, large and wide with pearly white teeth shinning through her full red lips. Her entire face lit up when she smiled. Behind her large brown eyes she held the secrets of the world. When she smiled she shared a glimpse of those secrets with her audience.

That night she drank her wine, laughed and talked, so happy to be with all of us. I wanted the night to last forever, but alas, we all grew tired and returned to the cottage. I slept well that night. Fortunately, so did my mother.

Although I missed my children during the weekend celebration, I realized that if they had accompanied me on this trip, I would not have been able to relax or share special moments with my mother. Besides, I thought, we would all be together soon enough. Christmas was right around the corner and for the past five years since Mama and Larry were married, the family had gathered in San Diego for our annual Christmas reunion. It tuned out to be the last Christmas together as an entire family.

~ ~ ~

December 23, 1994. As promised, Mama went to her regular physician a few days after our weekend celebration. When the results of the laboratory tests were abnormal, Dr. Ruderman sent her to Dr. Sabina Wallach, an oncologist. I liked Sabina from the moment I first met her. She insisted that we call her Sabina. She was honest and down to earth, just like Mama. I could tell that Sabina was equally struck with Mama. She sat close to my mother. She lingered with her touch. She took her time during her lengthy exams to thoroughly review every detail.

During the initial exam which Mama attended with her husband Larry, Sabina took all kinds of tests including blood, urine and x-rays. Her initial report was alarming to say the least. It was to become the first of many such reports.

<u>New Patient Consultation</u>   **<u>Sabina R. Wallach, M.D.</u>**

Dr. Amanda Fouther is a charming 60 year old lady referred by Dr. Steven Ruderman for management of newly diagnosed malignant left pleural effusion. She had a chest infection eight weeks ago but was well until she developed progressive exertional dyspnea and irritative cough over the past week while traveling in the course of business. Upon her return to San Diego, she was promptly evaluated by Dr. Ruderman. Chest x-ray three days ago showed a large left pleural effusion. Thoracentesis by Dr. Fredrick Hanson the next day showed malignancy, presently not further characterized. Her symptoms have improved and staging today by CT has not shown any significant abnormality outside the left hemithorax.

Apart from symptoms relating to pleural effusion, she has no complaints. Recent weight, appetite and energy have been normal, and she has no fevers. There is no history of bleeding or pain.

There is a family history of malignancy: Her mother died of a primary brain tumor at age 87, possibly meningioma; a brother who was a heavy smoker died of lung cancer. She had 12 siblings with a strong family history of vascular disease including hypertension, coronary artery disease and stroke. There is no family history of TB or diabetes. Her three adult children are in good health.

She is a former nurse with a Ph.D. in Psychology who now has her own management consulting business. She remarried five years ago and her husband accompanied her today. She has not smoked in 20 years but smoked lightly before this (one pack per week). Alcohol use is occasional and she has never received blood products. There is an ALLERGY TO PENICILLIN WHICH CAUSES ANAPHYLAXIS).

Current medications include Synthroid, Provera and Premarin, multivitamins and occasional Feldene.

She is G5 P3 and had premature ovarian failure in 1972. A follicular adenoma was managed with thyroidectomy in 1960. A right breast biopsy in 1982 was benign. An abnormal Pap smear was managed with colposcopy one year ago. Rectoplasty was required in 1972 to correct episiotomy complications.

There is no known cardiac disease. Her only pulmonary symptoms relate to the effusion. There is no history of hemoptysis, gastrointestinal or genitourinary blood loss. She has chronic low back pain managed with nonsteroidals as needed, and this has been stable. There is no history of thromboembolism. Annual screening mammography in August was unremarkable. System review is otherwise noncontributory.

Examination revealed an adequately nourished black lady in no acute distress, appearing younger than her stated age. There was no conjunctival pallor or icterus, nor stigmata of chronic liver disease. She was clinically euthyroid. Subtle mobile left supraclavicular and axillary thickening was appreciated without obvious breast masses. There was some left basal percussion dullness with decreased air entry. Abdomen was soft and benign without masses, tenderness or visceromegaly. There was no bony tenderness. Extremities including calves were normal. There was no focal neurological deficit.

Recent laboratory studies include normal CBC and chemistry panel, including hepatic and renal function. LDH was modestly elevated. Today's imaging studies confirm residual left pleural effusion with pleural thickening and left lower lobe density without mediastinal change; liver, pancreas and retroperitoneum are normal. The only pelvic abnormality identified is rectosigmoid thickening consistent with past surgery.

This malignant pleural effusion is asymptomatic in terms of tissue of origin. Clinically, minor left axillary adenopathy could be suggestive of occult breast cancer. Similarly, subtle left supraclavicular changes could represent an intra-abdominal primary. Breast and ovarian cancer, in particular, should be considered since there are effective treatment options. With the history of recent Pap smear abnormality, repeat pelvic examination has been requested of Dr. Steven Russo who will see her next week. Stool guaiacs will be checked. Tumor markers, ESR and U/A will be performed today.

There are plans to proceed with thoracoscopy and pleurodesis, and I have encouraged her to proceed with these. Perhaps lymph node biopsy could be performed at the same time. Bronchoscopy would also be of interest because of left lower lobe consolidation.

The situation was reviewed in detail with the patient and her husband, and their questions answered to the best of my ability. They understand that definitive treatment recommendations will depend on additional studies and will be as specific as possible if tumor origin cannot be identified. She has been advised to avoid ASA and NSAIDs in preparation for surgery. Bone scan will be ordered to complete staging. She will return after the studies have been performed.

Sabina R. Wallach, M.D. 12/23/94

cc: Steven R. Ruderman, M.D.
　　Frederick Hanson, M.D.
　　Scott Brewster, M.D.

12

Christmas

December 24, 1994. It was Christmas eve and I called to tell Mama that I might not be able to make the annual trip to San Diego for Christmas because Nicole, my five year old, had contracted the chicken pox. I heard silence on the other end of the phone and I asked Mama if she was still there. "Terri," she said, "I think that you should do your best to come out here. The doctors did some tests and they said the tests reveal cancer."

I nearly forgot that Mama had not been feeling well during her birthday celebration the week before. "Cancer, what kind of cancer," I demanded to know. She said that they were not exactly sure, either breast or lung, the only thing they knew for sure was that cancerous cells were found in the pleural cavity next to her left lung. It was the type of cancer that metastasized very quickly.

'Metastasized very quickly,' what exactly does that mean I thought? Whatever it was, it did not sound good. "How serious is this Mama?" I asked in a very measured tone.

"I'm afraid it's very serious Terri."

"We'll be there Mama, one way or another, we will be there."

~ ~ ~

December 27, 1994. As we flew from one coast to the other, I thought about my mother's illness. Cancer was something that happened to other people, to other families. The journey seemed a bit surreal, interwoven with thoughts of life and death. At times, I wondered if everyone could read my thoughts. It seemed as though I thought of nothing else but Mama and her illness. This feeling would come over me often in the days and months ahead. I didn't know much about the disease, except that two of the worst types of cancer were liver and lung.

When my thoughts wandered too far off, Nicole and Christopher would bring me back to reality with cries for juice or cookies or both. The kids and I managed to travel after Nicole's contagious period and before Christopher contracted his first bump. To be on the safe side, I made sure they kept there distance from everyone. Although the children were only five and three at the time, they were remarkably good on the flight. As a single mom, I was grateful for this. They played with their coloring books, ate their animal crackers and essentially entertained themselves for a major portion of the flight. The rest of the time they slept. It was almost as if they knew my mind was preoccupied.

Mama was already in the hospital by the time we arrived in San Diego. Sabina, the oncologist, advised us that the fluid which had accumulated in Mama's lungs had to be drained immediately. As usual, the rest of the family was already there when I arrived: Mom's husband Larry and his two daughters, Barbie and Kathy; Barbie's husband Rick and their two children, Liam and Joshua; Kathy's husband Mark and their two children, Heather and Alexander; my sister Cathy and her three boys, Isaiah, David and Daniel; and finally my brother Benji.

As in the past five years, we rented a beach house within walking distance from Mom and Larry's condominium. San Diego was beautiful this time of year. In point of fact, San Diego was beautiful every time of year. The days were warm and sunny and the nights were clear and cool.

I had grown accustomed to leaving New York this time of year, though I never thought I would. Christmas in New York is like no where else in the world. The bright lights and lavishly decorated store windows brought joy and excitement to the season. And of course, the tree in Rockefeller Center was beyond compare. I so enjoyed taking the children to behold this awesome spectacle each year. For these reasons, I tried very hard to return to New York by the 31st to at least bring in the New Year.

For obvious reasons, the mood was very different this Christmas. We tried not to talk much about "the cancer." There was no sense in making the children worry needlessly. But they knew; they could see it in our eyes, in the words not spoken, in the lingering embraces.

We spent most of the time feeding and cleaning our nine children who ranged in age from two to twelve. As usual the women did all the work. Once the breakfast dishes were put away, it was time to start planning lunch and then dinner and so forth and so on.

We were forced to take turns visiting Mama because at least two of the sisters needed to stay at the beach house at any given time to take care of the kids. The men were useless in this regard, so their roles were relegated to entertaining the brood or running to the store.

Larry insisted upon driving us all back and forth to the hospital. He spent most of his time by Mama's bedside or back at his apartment alone. He had a difficult time relaxing around all the children and chose instead to avoid the beach house where we all stayed. It almost seemed to me that he considered his grandchildren a necessary nuisance at best, though deep down inside I had to believe that he loved them.

Each time we went to the hospital, someone from the staff had to personally escort us to the intensive care unit. The unspoken words of the hospital staff said, "Your mother is very ill. We do not let all visitors through these doors. But you are special because your mother is very sick. So we will let you through these doors to visit with her. You may not get another chance like this, so make your visit a good one, make it count."

Most of the patients in the intensive care unit were old, older than my mother's sixty years. They all looked feeble and sickly. Their faces were pale and paltry. Their hair was gray and unkept. The covers on their beds were undone and their clothing was disheveled. All except for Mama.

Even though she was tired and weak, Mama's skin was clear and smooth, her lips were moist and her hair was combed. The starchy white bed linens were draped over her legs and neatly tucked into the sides of the bed. She had a huge tube projecting from her chest and two smaller tubes coming from her nostrils. The large tubes were connected to a machine, one of which made loud pumping noises. Another machine, the heart monitor, made that high pitched single beep that you hear in all hospital rooms. Within seconds of entering the room, I completely forgot about both noises. The smells, however, were harder to ignore. Rubbing alcohol, fresh cut flowers, an un-emptied bedpan, an uneaten lunch tray. Familiar smells in an unfamiliar setting, together forming the smell of a typical hospital room.

It seemed to me that the nurses were pampering Mama, making sure that no need was left unattended. Just like Mama, I thought, wherever she goes, she manages to charm everyone she meets.

Mama tried to smile when I came into the room, but she was obviously in great pain. The expression on my face couldn't hide the fact that I was upset and worried, though I tried hard to look positive. My eyes immediately began to swell with tears.

I had never seen my mother look so vulnerable. Once, when I was much younger, I remember she was hospitalized because of a thyroid problem and years later for a tissue biopsy. But never anything like this. The magnitude of this situation suddenly hit me when I saw her lying there. Mama was very sick, she had a very serious cancer. Our lives were about to change forever.

I leaned over the bed and grasped her hand, afraid to sit. She squeezed back ever so slightly. The water filling my eyes made it difficult to see clearly. I tried hard to be strong, I didn't want her to worry about me. But her eyes told me that she would say or do anything to take my pain away. I asked her how she felt and when she could go home. She said it felt like this gigantic tube was stuck in her chest and sucking her blood out. Then she smiled. A second later I smiled too. It would take a couple of days to recover, but she hoped to be out of there before our vacations ended.

The December 27th Surgical Pathology Report which analyzed a specimen identified as the left parietal pleura read in part:

> "One can virtually exclude an endometrial, hepatocellular, renal, or squamous origin, as well as melanoma, mesothelioma and malignant large cell lymphoma. The lesion is very likely of endodermal origin in the general sense, but carcinomas of the stomach, pancreas. and colon almost always produce stainable mucin. As a result, it is quite likely that this lesion represents metastatic

large cell carcinoma from the lung, despite the patient's previous negative bronchoscopy and the absence of a clear-cut intrapulmonary mass on chest radiograph. Salivary gland carcinoma must be considered as a theoretical possibility, but usually is so obvious clinically that it poses no diagnostic problem."

Although the origin site of the cancer was unclear, the diagnosis, according to the end of the report was, "Metastatic poorly-differentiated carcinoma, left parietal pleura, biopsy." The final notation of the report indicated that the laboratory physician telephoned his findings to Sabina on December 28th.

It dawned on me that Mama might spend the entire holiday in the hospital. I prayed that she could be discharged before we all had to return home because otherwise she would not have a chance to see the children. The kids made her so happy. I thought about the possibility of sneaking the children into the hospital to see Mama, but I knew Larry would seriously object. It wasn't worth the aggravation and turmoil.

Ironically, I spent the following afternoon in the same hospital as an outpatient. Scripps Memorial Hospital is a huge facility with all kinds of services. Long before Mama was even diagnosed, she made arrangements for me to have a mole removed from my nose. We decided to schedule the relatively minor outpatient surgery during the Christmas holidays because it would give me an opportunity to heal away from New York and away from the office.

As I walked through the vast corridors looking for my assigned room, the irony of the situation struck me. Within these same walls my mother was struggling for her life, while I was seeking cosmetic surgery.

I thought about my mother throughout the entire procedure. I thought about the tremendous amount of pain she must be experiencing in comparison to the slight prick I would feel as the doctor removed my mole. I thought about the trivial scar my surgery would leave in comparison to the gaping hole in Mama's chest. I mentioned to the surgeon that my mother was in the hospital undergoing surgery to remove the cancerous fluid from her lungs. When I told him that the cancer was diagnosed as "metastatic large cell carcinoma from the lung," he paused slightly and said nothing. "Is that a really bad type of cancer?" I asked.

"Yes," he admitted, "but I am sure they will do all that they can do for her." His measured tone frightened me more than his words.

I prayed that they would perform miracles and make the cancer disappear completely. I hoped that the gigantic tube in her chest would suck out all of the cancer from her body, never to be seen again. I was scheduled to return to New York and back to work by the first of the year. Mama was finally discharged the day I was scheduled to return. She asked me if I could possibly prolong the trip back to New York. Most of the other siblings had done the same. I picked up the phone, changed my reservations, paid the $50 change fee for all three tickets and hung up the phone. "All set," I told Mama.

We all spent one glorious day together as a family. It was finally Christmas, now that Mama was out of the hospital at the beach house with us. Even though she spent much of the time resting, even though she was not cooking in the kitchen or cleaning, even though she was not running around with the kids, it was finally Christmas because Mama was home.

We took the family picture, as we did every year, Mama in the middle, being held up by sheer love and determination. She squinted to keep the bright sun from blinding her. She looked, as I am certain she felt, weak and tired. The thought occurred to me that this may be the last Christmas picture with Mama. I wondered if anyone else was thinking the same thing. If so, no one dared verbalize it. Stop thinking such morbid thoughts I told myself. We all counted to three with the timed camera lens and said "spaghetti" at the same time. We were going to beat this cancer thing. No doubt. Feet forward, one step at a time.

If you look closely enough at the picture, you can see that I have a band aid on my nose, covering the incision from the removal of the mole. The scar on my nose now has a special meaning for me. It reminds me of Mama. I think of her everyday, especially when I look in the mirror, plain as the nose on my face.

After my surgery, I took a long walk along the beach with my brother Benji allowing the warm embrace of the bright sun to engulf me, and the cool ocean breeze to refresh me. I removed my sandals so that I could feel the grains of sand as they rubbed against my feet and between my toes. We didn't say much. Benji was never one of many words. But we didn't have to talk. I knew he was thinking about Mama, hoping and praying that soon she would be well.

As for me, I thought about how Mama would enjoy this walk. I wondered whether she would be able to continue taking her daily walks that she loved so much. Before the cancer, I had taken such things for granted. It would have been nice to see Mama's footprints in the sand, walking along next to ours. I thought about the words from the poem "Footprints." God told his weary disciple that in difficult times if he could not see God's footprints next to his, it was not because God had abandoned him, it was because God was carrying him. It occurred to me that if Mama could no longer walk with us, her strength would carry us, always.

~ ~ ~

January 3, 1995. Report of Sabina R. Wallach, M.D.

FOUTHER, Amanda

She is recovering well from last week's thoracoscopy and pleurodesis and is pleased that dyspnea has resolved. The operative findings are not yet familiar to me. However, bronchoscopy showed no endobroncial lesion. Bone scan showed no metastases. Histopathology of the left parietal pleura confirmed an anaplastic neoplasm likely endodermal origin. Extensive immunohistochemical studies have excluded many common malignancies; metastatic large cell lung carcinoma is likely. Serum tumor markers included normal CEA, CA-125, CA 189-9 and modest CA 15-3 elevation. Serial stool guaiacs showed no occult hemorrhage.

These findings were reviewed extensively with the patient and her husband, together with implications for treatment. Since the organ of origin remains clinically obtuse and she feels well, she would like to defer empirical chemotherapy until new symptoms arise or further unresectable and probably incurable. She plans to decrease her work schedule and will return in two weeks for reassessment. She will continue taking Vicodin as needed to manage residual left chest pain.

SRW/weh

cc: Steven Ruderman, M.D.
    Fredrick Hanson, M.D.
    Scot Brewster, M.D.

January 20, 1995. Report of Sabina R. Wallach, M.D.

FOUTHER, Amanda

She continues to convalesce after thoracoscopy with improved breathing. She still takes several Vicodin daily to manage pain but generally is progressing well. She has now liberalized her diet after a trial of vegetables exclusively. Her appetite is satisfactory. She has no new complaints nor focal symptoms.

Examination confirms healing thoracoscopy incisions with good air entry to both lungs. Breasts remain normal without adenopathy. Remainder of examination is unchanged and unremarkable.

Counts remain normal. Chemistries are pending including repeat tumor markers. Histopathology has again been reviewed with Dr. Cooley Butler who will send it to Stanford for further opinion. If there is no further diagnostic elucidation, then I have recommended a trial of tamoxifen. She will return in two to three weeks for review. She has chosen to start shark cartilage and Natcell thymus and will visit the Optimum Health Institute for alternative cancer remedies. She will also try Paxil to manage situational depression.

SRW/weh

cc: Steven Ruderman, M.D.
   Fredrick Hanson, M.D.
   Scot Brewster, M.D.

~ ~ ~

January 24, 1995

Dear Nancy and Bill,

"Friendship," said Christopher Robin, "is a very comforting sort of thing to have." A. A. Milne

You will never really know how important the two of you are for me during this cancer journey. Your love and support helps me stay focused on the real treasures in my life. However, nothing helps with this diet of live foods, wheat grass and enemas. It requires my full attention and total coordination. Larry's willingness to move on this journey with me makes it easier. We will be so squeaky clean when you see us again we may even look like someone else. But don't worry we will wear purple.

Love Amanda.

One month had passed since Mama was diagnosed with cancer, still at this point, of unknown origin. She consulted with doctors, friends and family members to determine the proper course of action. She reasoned that because of its destructive nature, chemotherapy and radiation would be a last resort. Rather, she would select an aggressive cleansing program designed to eliminate the cancer cells from her body. She had read about a program at the Optimum Health Institute which offered a wheat grass diet that consisted of consuming large amounts of wheat grass followed by daily enemas. Losing weight would be a by-product of the diet.

In addition to the wheat germ program, Mama decided to investigate an aggressive holistic program which would include large doses of vitamin supplements along with daily colonic cleansing. She had read about a physician in New York, Dr. Gonzalez, who had been successful in treating cancer patients with this approach. The vitamin regimen would follow the wheat germ program. I was pleased to learn that one aspect of her treatment would take place in New York which meant an additional opportunity to see Mama.

Concurrent with the wheat germ and vitamin programs, Mama began to consult a creative visualist located in Los Angeles who would help her to visualize a cancer-free body. If nothing else, the visualization sessions were relaxing and put my mother in a positive frame of mind. Staying focused and positive, we were told, was crucial in the fight against cancer.

The family discussed the pros and cons of these natural remedies. Would it be enough? What if it did not work? We decided that we would support Mom's decision, no matter what. It was important that she took control of her illness and the treatment of her illness. She told us long ago that if she ever became ill, she did not want to linger, hooked up to machines and IVs and dependent upon a life support system. She would fight this cancer as best she could. But ultimately, if the situation became intolerable, she would relinquish her spirit to God and the Universe.

Nancy, Mom's best friend, and I discussed Mom's course of action. We were pleased that she was cleansing her system, but we were concerned that she needed a program directly aimed at eliminating the cancer.

Larry was clearly hesitant about any holistic approach to medicine, and consequently, encouraged her to seek a more traditional course of action. The wheat grass diet was an interim compromise solution. He agreed to partake in the wheat grass diet with her to provide moral support. He also agreed to investigate the Gonzalez vitamin program in New York. He seemed indifferent about the visualization sessions.

February 14, 1995. Report of Sabina R. Wallach, M.D.

FOUTHER, Amanda

She feels well without significant breathing problems but reports occasional left hemithoracic discomfort likely related to pleurodesis. She has lost 20 pounds on the Optimum Health Institute Life Diet, including colonic wheat germ placement. She would like to resume work next week.

Apart from obvious weight loss, examination is unremarkable. The thoracoscopy scars have healed well with excellent air entry to both lungs bilaterally. Breasts and abdomen remain benign. Calves are normal.

CA 15-3 levels are rising. Review of the pleural material at Stanford confirms the diagnosis of poorly-differentiated adenocarcinoma, metastatic. Immunological studies do not support mesothelioma and a breast primary is favored. This was reviewed in detail with the patient, with recommendations to start tamoxifen. She will consider this in the context of repeat CA 15-3 levels which were drawn today. She will return in two weeks for further discussion and recommendations.

SRW/weh

Cc: Steven R. Ruderman, M.D.
 Scot Brewster, M.D.
 Fredrick Hanson, M.D.

March 7, 1995. Report of Sabina R. Wallach, M.D.

FOUTHER, Amanda

Apart from residual left chest pain managed with Vicodin, she is well and active without new complaint. Weight is up eight pounds.

Serial CA-125 levels continue to rise consistent with metastatic breast cancer. This was reviewed in the context of a similar pathological diagnosis. Accordingly, a trial of tamoxifen has been suggested, with detailed review of the potential risks, benefits and side effects in this context. Her husband was here today and we had a long discussion regarding metastatic adenocarcinoma of unknown primary and possible management options, including prolonged observation. She is interested in isotope mammography and I will check availability locally. She has been encouraged to seek a second opinion on the East Coast, planning to return in four weeks for reassessment.

SRW/weh

cc: Steven Ruderman, M.D.

March 14, 1995. I can't remember now who called, but in retrospect, it must have been Larry. They had gone to the doctor and received a detailed report explaining Mama's condition. The Serial CA-125 levels, the cancer markers, were rising. This was a very bad sign. I remember hearing that the cancer may have started in the breast and not the lung. I remember hearing that it was extremely widespread and therefore would not be responsive to chemotherapy. I remember walking to the Wall Street subway station on my way home from work totally numb, like someone else was actually doing the walking and I was out there somewhere watching. Up until this point, I honestly believed that Mama was going to beat this thing. Now, my optimism seemed foolish.

An old friend from law school, David, called earlier that week to make plans with me to hear Desiree' sing at The Supper Club. Although I looked forward to going, I had second thoughts after hearing the news about my mom. David encouraged me to go. He had met my mother on several occasions and he said that he was sure she would want me to go. He was right. When I mentioned on the phone that I had tickets to the performance, she begged me to go.

In the middle of the performance Desiree' paused to dedicate a song to her mother. She then proceeded to sing her hit song entitled, *You Gotta Be*. It spoke of all the things you gotta be: bad/bold/wiser, hard/tough/stronger, cool and calm. It was one of my mother's favorite songs. I began to sob uncontrollably. The club was so loud and so crowded that no one even noticed. My friend tried to comfort me, but I was inconsolable.

I held my head down low and noticed a hand with a Kleenex reach across in front of me. I looked up and saw this woman, this sweet woman with a tissue and a warm face. I cried harder and she offered her hand. I took this stranger's hand and felt like she knew exactly what I felt, exactly what I was thinking. We embraced and I cried even harder. When I was finally able to talk, I told her that I had just learned that my mom was dying of cancer.

"I know," she said. "I came over to tell you that I lost my mother too." This woman, whose name was Jamie, continued to say that I would never really lose my mom. She told me that even though her mother was no longer part of this world, they communicated constantly.

I thought about what this woman said and then about what my mother once told me. My mother said that when she died she would find a way to communicate with me from beyond. I remember telling her that I hoped she would come unobtrusively in a dream or give me some kind of warning before appearing out of nowhere. She promised she would. She seemed so certain about that.

I am convinced that Jamie was placed beside me that night to give me hope, to give me courage and to give me strength. I never saw Jamie again after that night. But I left the concert knowing that I would be stronger, tougher and wiser.

~ ~ ~

March 21, 1995. After much debate regarding how to treat the cancer, Mama and Larry decided to follow the Gonzalez regimen. It was an alternative medicine program which appealed to Mama because it was all natural and because the success rate, at least for those who were diagnosed early, was high. I was pleased with this development because it meant that she would be coming to New York for treatment. Dr. Gonzalez's office was located in the City.

Mom and Larry arrived at our pink brownstone and climbed the long flight of stairs. Nicole and Christopher were thrilled to see Dah. She spent most of her time in the apartment stretched out on the bed with the kids jumping all around her. I kept saying, "Stop jumping," and "Get down," and "Be careful." None of which made any difference. They could not control their excitement. Neither could I.

Larry did not spend much time in the apartment. He paced up and down, like a caged animal. Maybe it was too cramped for him, maybe he was in unfamiliar territory, or maybe he just hated to be around me. Whatever the reason, he quickly excused himself and went for a walk in the neighborhood. As soon as he left, a huge weight was lifted. I felt like Mama and I could finally relax and talk.

I wanted this trip to be as comfortable as possible. Maybe if Mama felt comfortable, she would consider staying in New York where she could have easy access to Dr. Gonzalez and where we could see each other often. I offered her something to drink and poured myself a Diet Coke. She asked for bottled water which I had purchased from the grocery store in preparation for her arrival.

She told me that she wanted me to cut back on the Diet Coke, altogether if possible. She was worried that, like most artificial foods and beverages, it may be carcinogenic. She looked very somber when she said this. If what she said was true, I thought to myself, I am in serious trouble. The idea of eliminating Diet Coke from my diet was unthinkable. When I didn't have time to make a fresh pot of coffee in the morning, I often started the day with a Diet Coke instead. I told her that I would try to heed her advice. She sighed a small breath of relief. A mother's breath.

Larry returned from his walk much too quickly. I called the babysitter to watch the children while we went to visit Dr. Gonzalez. After the sitter arrived, the three of us took a cab to his midtown office. I looked around the waiting room as Mama and Larry completed the preliminary paperwork. The patients did not look sick. No one was losing their hair. No one looked emaciated or weak. There were casual conversations with occasional smiles. Maybe, just maybe I thought, this vitamin regimen would work.

The nurse entered the waiting room and called my mother's name. The three of us rose to head toward the back office. Larry glanced back at me as if to say where are you going? My mother motioned for me to join them. She looked at Larry and said, "She can come back too." I knew this perturbed him. In his little mind it meant that he was not the only special person in her life.

Dr. Gonzalez was cordial, but he did not mince words. My mother was very sick, he said. Statistically speaking, his program was more successful when the cancer markers were not quite so high. He recommended his program, but cautioned her to continue consultations with her oncologist. After signing the check and the appropriate release forms, we walked out of the office with a slew of pills.

April 2, 1995. Journal Entry

It's been a long time since I've taken the time to write down my thoughts. Too long. The kids are great and thriving here in the City. I love them so much. They are my life.

It's hard to believe that Mama is as sick as they say. She is everything to all of us. It will be hard to imagine life without her. Plan for the worst. Hope for the best...I wish we had videotaped Mama's 60th birthday. I hope she likes the [photo] book.

April 8, 1995.

Dearest Terri,

My illness has slowed down my world, only to discover what a very rich world I have. You are a critical part of this richness.

Without seeming to try at all you give. Thank you for selecting me as your Mother. My world would not be complete without you. With you I am surrounded by life's gentle gifts and can comfort myself in blankets of memories you've woven.

Love,

Mama

In one short note Mama managed to say everything she needed to say. It was as though she wanted to take this opportunity to tell me how she felt, in case she didn't have another chance. I read the words she wrote over and over again. They made me feel good. She wrote that I was giving, but I thought I should have given more. She thanked me for selecting her as my mother, but I was eternally grateful she had selected me as her daughter. She said her world would not be complete without me, but I could not imagine a world without her. She said that she was comforted by her memories. Memories, I thought, which I will never forget.

These words were written inside a blank card. The front of the card pictured a Navajo woman surrounded by swirls of turquoise and a full white moon. She was listening to the calls of a flock of owls. The back of the card said that the midnight counsel of the owls guides the woman and her family to safety. Oh wise owl, I thought, show my mother and her family the way to safety.

April 11, 1995. The phone rang. When I picked it up, my mother was crying on the other end of the line. She said she was calling so that I could cheer her up. I asked her what was wrong, but she was hesitant to answer at first. So I sang a frame from the musical, *The Sound of Music* and it went something like this:

> *Raindrops on roses and whiskers on kittens/Brown copper kettles and warm woolen mittens/Brown paper packages tied up with strings, these are a few of my favorite things/When the dog bites, when the bee stings, when I'm feeling sad, I simply remember my favorite things and then I don't feel so bad.*

When we were young, Mama sang this song to us whenever something made us sad. All of a sudden she would break out in verse, swirling her arms around and sashaying her feet, like she was on stage. This would always get our attention. Then, she would come up close to us at the part where the dog bites and the bee stings and she would gently grab our nose and tickle our tummy, making believe she was a dog biting or a bee stinging. That's when we would start laughing and join her in the song, just like the Von Trapp children from *The Sound of Music*. It worked every time. I used to imagine that my mother was just like Julie Andrews who played the part of the beautiful caretaker who ultimately married Mr. Von Trapp.

Alas, if only it were so simple now. When I began to sing the song over the phone to cheer up my mother, it only made her cry harder. I knew something was terribly wrong, even beyond the cancer. "What is it Mama?" I pleaded. "Please tell me what is wrong."

"He has to leave," she said, "I can't live with him here anymore. He is so needy, he is draining all my energy. I have nothing left to fight the cancer. One minute we are fighting about the way he is preparing my meals, the next minute he is trying to have sex. He doesn't understand that having sex is the last thing on my mind right now. How can I have sex? I barely have enough energy to get up and go to the bathroom."

I could not believe my ears. I sat speechless on the other end of the line for a second to make sure I was getting this straight. Was Larry crazy? Had he completely lost touch with reality? Was it possible that he was too self absorbed to understand that she was in no condition to have sex? I wanted to make him disappear. Truthfully, for a split second, I wanted him dead. I held my tongue knowing that I dare not utter such thoughts.

"Isn't there someone he can stay with?" I asked. I hesitated to make the suggestion, but she seemed amenable to the idea.

"No, not really," Mama said. "Where could he go? I can't ask Barbie or Kathy to take on such a burden, they are managing enough already with their families. Unfortunately, he doesn't have any close friends we could ask. And frankly, I don't know how long I will need to recover?"

She was right. There was no place he could really go. His daughter Kathy lived in Los Angeles with her six year old daughter Heather and her three year old son Alexander. His daughter Barbie and her husband Rick lived in Malibu with their two sons Liam and Josh, who were eight and six. Both families lived close enough to San Diego and both families would be willing to help, but it would not be fair to ask either household to make room for an ornery old man for an undetermined length of time. Mama and I briefly debated the issue and agreed that we should not ask for such a huge imposition. In any event, Mama doubted that Larry would agree to stay with his children and grandchildren. He could never tolerate the hectic pace.

The alternative, I told Mama, was to tell Larry that she was leaving to go somewhere to exclusively focus on her recovery. "We could find a place for you to rest and relax," I said. "You could come to New York and stay with me. That way, you would be closer to Dr. Gonzalez enabling you to better manage your recovery program. You keep saying how difficult it has been to contact Dr. Gonzalez. If you were here in New York, it would be much easier," I said.

Mama sat silently for a few seconds on the other end of the phone line, leading me to believe that she was not thoroughly convinced. So I continued, "If staying with me is too much because of the kids, you could stay in Anne's apartment. It's just a few blocks away. That would be perfect because Anne rarely uses it and it's just the right size."

I held my breath, hoping that Mama would agree that coming to New York would be the best solution to her dilemma. Anne was one of Mama's closest friends. One of the Maude women. I was certain that she would gladly agree to let Mama stay in her apartment. If Mama stayed in Anne's apartment, I could check on her daily. It seemed to be the perfect solution.

Mama and I discussed the possibilities at great length. She was convinced that she would not be able to recover while living in the same house with Larry. But she was ambivalent about asking him to leave. He was, after all, her husband.

She ultimately decided to speak frankly with him about the situation. They both ended up staying. I knew they would.

The only other time I remember my mother calling me in tears was ten years earlier when Bob, her third husband, left her. The men in her life made her vulnerable. She was inexplicably attracted to the flame, only to get burned when she drew too close. She managed to survive the relationship with her third husband. I wondered if it was too late for her to escape her fourth.

13
WalkingHome

April 26, 1995. San Diego. I decided to take the kids to go see Mama, before it was too late. The flight was unbearably long, but as usual, the kids were great. To my dismay, Larry arrived at the airport to pick us up. I had hoped that Mama would be feeling well enough to accompany him on the ride. It was wishful thinking on my part. She was not well enough to travel, even short distances in the car. But the thought of dealing alone with Larry concerned me. I decided to focus on the kids. No matter what, I would not allow him to upset me.

My resolution did not last long. Soon Larry was complaining about the noise Chris was making in the car, about my lack of correspondence from New York, about how I was not setting a good example for the children. Then he started explaining the rules of the house, no running, no loud noises, etc., etc., etc. It took every ounce of energy to restrain myself from telling him to shut the hell up. I concluded that it was not a very good way to start the trip.

When we arrived at the apartment, Mama was in the bed, but she was wide awake, obviously awaiting our arrival. I brought Nicole and Christopher into the room explaining to them that they had to be quiet and that they couldn't jump all over the bed because Dah was sick. They gingerly sat on the edge of the bed causing her body to roll slightly towards them. She grimaced ever so slightly. They didn't notice, but Larry did. He told them to get up from the bed. Mama said no, that it was all right. She was elated to see them. She said that the children were a sight for sore eyes. The same thing Mother Dear used to tell me. "Girl, you sho 'nough are a sight for so' eyes." I didn't fully understand what Mother Dear meant at the time, but I knew just what Mama meant now.

The next day I arose early and asked my mother if she wanted to go for a walk on the beach. Next to taking baths, walking along the beach was my mother's favorite past time. She would wake up every morning and walk along the beach for miles, returning only when her body could not go any further. She loved the water, the sand beneath her feet, the sun and wind at her back. When she turned around to go back home, she would put on her shades and her baseball cap, passing other young runners and older walkers. When I was in town, I would run by her side, sometimes running ahead, sometimes running behind, to stay at her pace. She spent these early morning hours contemplating life, thinking about how far she had journeyed, how peaceful this phase of her life had become, until the cancer.

Mama made it down the steps of the apartment building and onto the sidewalk. By the time we got to the beach, she was tired and out of breath. She told me to walk ahead with the children while she rested a bit on the bench. She wanted to walk with us, but her body would not let her. So I sat next to her on the bench while the children played in the sand. It was enough that we were there. As I sat next to her, we talked about the future. I told her that I wanted to run a marathon in her honor. "You know baby," she said, "I would like that."

~ ~ ~

May 6, 1995. After many pictures and long goodbyes, we flew back to New York. It would be the last time Nicole and Chris saw their grandmother. It would be the last time we all walked along the beach with my mother.

> May 7, 1995. Journal Entry
> *Dear Lord, I pray you make my mother safe and well this Sunday night. My time in San Diego was so beautiful. I long for more. God willing.*

I had not been home long when a card with an article folded inside arrived from Mama. At the top of the article she wrote, "I see us—you and me—reflected everywhere. Love, Mama." The article was entitled, "Walking One Another Home." It read as follows:

> *About three years ago, my mother had deteriorated to a point where she needed to leave the little house that we had all grown up in, and that she had lived in for sixty years. She said she'd already started packing. We were going in shifts. I was "the advance team." Then my two sisters were coming and finally my two brothers. When I arrived, the packing she had done was in two cardboard boxes. One had two rolls of toilet paper in it, the other had a little doily that she had made before her wedding.*
>
> *My task was to just be there with her. To sit and rock and look out at the lake and reminisce. Not to take any pictures down, not to change anything, but just be with her. So I was there for about ten days. I was to take her to get her last hair perm by the woman who had done it for thirty-four years. Take her to get the taxes done. Take her cronies to lunch. Say goodbye to the church. All those things.*
>
> *We lived across from the little lake. A tradition was that we always walked around the lake together. For all these years, when we were growing up, every time I'd go back home to visit that was part of the tradition. Mother wasn't walking very well these days. She hadn't been able to go around the lake for quite some time. But, I always asked. So the first morning that I was there, I said, "Mom, I'm going to go walking around the lake. Do you want to go?" She sad, "Yeah!"*
>
> *The lake is about one-third of a mile. So we walked all the way around the lake. She said, "Are you going to go around again?" I said, "Well, I don't know. What about you?" She said, "Yeah." I couldn't believe it. She walked on around, and she did it a third time, which made it a mile. It was incredible!*
>
> *So then we went home, which was just right across from the lake. Each morning then, I would say, "Mom, I'm going to go walking. Do you want to go around the lake?" She couldn't go any of the other mornings…*
>
> *On my final morning I said, "Well, Mom, I'm going to go walking around the lake. Do you want to go?" She said, "No, no I can't go around the lake." It was a northwest morning back there in Illinois, it was cloudy and overcast and misty. I went on to walk around the lake, briskly as I always loved. I went around, I don't*

know how many times. There were figures passing me but at some point I saw a figure coming, probably a little farther than the back door back there, with some kind of a long something on, just coming very slowly. It didn't strike me at first. Then suddenly, as I got closer, I saw that it was my mother! I hurried to meet her. She had come with her raincoat and her nightie on to meet me.

She said, "Rita?" It was always a question. "Are you going to walk around again?" I said, "Mom, did you want to go walking? Did you want to go around?" I could feel that every muscle and every bone...her whole spirit was saying, "Yeah, I want to go around," but no muscle and no bone could muster any strength to do that. So she looked at me and she said, "Oh Rita. Let's just walk one another home." So we tucked our arms into one another and walked very slowly back, what must have been about maybe a block or a block and a half. We both started crying. We knew that was our last walk together at the lake.

I thought that really, this is what we are all about—is walking one another home. That's what we Crones are about. One person is not doing the walking home to the other person. We are walking one another home. My mother was walking me home every bit as much as I was walking her home.

I carefully folded the article and placed it back inside the card. The tears did not wait for the card to reach the inside of the envelope.

~ ~ ~

May 19, 1995. Everyone you meet in life serves a purpose, though initially it may not be self evident. HW was one of those people.

A mutual girlfriend arranged the blind date. I never really got the whole story from either one of them. Clearly one of them liked the other at some point, but it never quite worked out. He said that she was too skinny. She said that he was too arrogant. They were both right.

HW and I spoke at length over the phone on several occasions before we actually met. He could talk for hours at a time. I had never been a phone enthusiast and I wondered how anyone could talk for so long. Conversations with HW began to replace conversations with my mother, whose weakened condition made it difficult to talk on the phone.

I decided to take my chances with HW, who seemed too good to be true. He spoke highly of himself. He boasted about his looks, his lifestyle and the incredible way he treated the women in his life. I was leery but intrigued.

It had been ages since I dated someone seriously. In fact, I hadn't dated anyone seriously since my ex-husband left me three years earlier. As a single mom with two young children, I had neither the time nor the opportunity to meet people. When I finally met men worth considering, they were intimidated by the single mom issue. On those rare opportunities when I did go out, the guilt was enough to quickly send me home. I needed an occasional break to talk to an adult, an adult outside of the work setting. I also needed to talk to someone about my mother's illness. I knew that I shouldn't burden a new date with talk of cancer and death, but I also knew that the subject would inevitably come up in the conversation. It always did.

We decided to go to Swoozi's restaurant near Lincoln Center because it was close to both of us. I remember when he picked me up I thought, my God, he *is* gorgeous. He was at least 6'4", well built, a full head of dark wavy hair, medium brown smooth complexion, an all around great looking guy. His nose was slightly large, but even that was attractive because it had sort of an exotic European shape with the little bump in the middle. He wore jeans and a white shirt with a navy blue jacket.

I wore a long black skirt with buttons down the front. I left half of the buttons undone to show my legs, which were lean and shapely. He noticed. I shopped that day for the perfect top which I found in the little store I loved so much on Broadway and 75th Street called *Lord of the Fleas*. The shirt was a crimson red cotton and knit blend which tightly hugged my small frame. I even went to the lingerie shop across the street and bought one of those wonder bras, just to make the shirt look better.

I spent half the evening getting dressed and anxiously awaiting his arrival. My makeup was just right, not too much, not too little. I took the time to get my hair done and to get a manicure and a pedicure the day before. I looked in the mirror and thought, perfect.

When the doorbell rang my heart leapt into my chest and the kids ran to the door to see who was there. After I left, they stood in the window of the little pink apartment, looking down, calling my name, begging me not to go. I wanted this first encounter with HW to be just between him and me. Oh well. He knew I had kids. And great kids they were. So what if they stood at the window shouting after their mother whenever she left the house. That's normal. Isn't it?

I had been on a number of blind dates, but somehow I felt this one would be different. I was right. Unlike the rest, he turned out to be patient and giving. In due course, I realized that he was placed in my path at that moment in time to help me through a very difficult journey. And yet, somehow in the back of my mind I knew that he would not be with me forever. It was almost as if he were too good to be true. In fact, whenever I described him to anyone, they always said, he's sounds too good to be true.

That night we talked and joked through dinner. He made me laugh out loud. For the first time in a long time, I relaxed. After my second glass of wine, I completely let my guard down. It felt good. He took me home and walked me into the foyer of my building. We were standing at the bottom of the staircase and he had to lean over to kiss me. I'll never forget that first kiss, it put me into an instant trance. It wasn't even a big kiss, but when we touched, a chill rushed through me. I knew that we would see more of each other. He had already begun to occupy my thoughts, thoughts that previously were consumed by illness and death. Now, there was a place to go, if only for a minute, to escape the harsh reality.

~ ~ ~

May 20, 1995. Aunt Yvonne, my mother's oldest sister, arrived in San Diego to take care of my mother until she recuperated. Her plan was to finish her class work, stay in San Diego for the summer, nurse Mama back to health, then return to Birmingham in time to resume teaching in the fall. Yvonne taught college English at Birmingham Southern University. She taught her final class, graded her final papers and took off for San Diego. We were going to beat this cancer thing, she thought.

Like all of Aunt Yvonne's plans, it was well laid. Unfortunately, events did not unfold according to plan.

The rest of the family was grateful that Aunt Yvonne could take the time off. No one could take care of Mama better than Aunt Yvonne. After all, she practically raised Mama herself.

Since Amanda's diagnosis in December, Yvonne thought of little else but the cancer her sister was now battling. She dreaded the possibility of Amanda dying. She dwelled on the thought so much that her twin brother Bubba appeared in her dreams on two separate occasions to tell Yvonne to relax. He reassured her that it was not time for Amanda to leave this world.

But after Yvonne arrived in San Diego, Uncle Bubba did not reappear in her dreams. Yvonne interpreted his absence as a bad omen. Sure enough, when Yvonne arrived in San Diego, the doctors told her that the cancer had already metastasized from mom's lungs, to her liver and to now to her lymph nodes. Sure enough, the doctors said that the rapid movement of the cancer was a bad sign.

May 29, 1995. Aunt Yvonne and I spoke longer than usual today. I sensed a higher level of anxiety in her voice. She said that Mama was having chest pains and trouble breathing. She also said that Mama had lost a great deal of weight.

She now weighed 132 pounds, down from about 157 before the cancer. I noticed that Aunt Yvonne, like me, was measuring time before and after the cancer.

The most disturbing news was that Mama began having terrible headaches, headaches that were severe and long lasting. We didn't know what was causing these headaches, but we tried everything to relieve the pain. She had not been eating her normal intake, so I told Aunt Yvonne that maybe if she ate a bit more, she would feel better. Yvonne tried giving her more food and regular pain medication, but it did little to ease the pain.

To complicate matters, Mama did not recognize Aunt Yvonne when she brought her morning breakfast. "Who's there?" Mama asked, according to Aunt Yvonne.

"It's me baby, it's Yvonne, your sister."

"Thank you for being so good to me," Mama said to Aunt Yvonne, almost like she was thanking an attending nurse.

"That's o.k., just try to eat something." Aunt Yvonne told her.

Yvonne was devastated. Amanda was becoming delirious and failed to recognize her own sister. I agreed that the headaches and delirium were bad signs. It was time to take Mama back to the oncologist for more testing. Our fear was that the cancer was spreading even further.

May 31, 1995. Report of Sabina R. Wallach, M.D.

FOUTHER, Amanda

She has been following a strict alternative program involving dietary modulation, supplements and daily enemas. She has lost weight and energy on this regimen. She has a three week history of progressive left sided chest pain, worse at the left shoulder, associated with exertional dyspnea. She also has considerable nausea and epigastric discomfort. She takes Vicodin to manage pain and occasional Compazine suppositories for nausea.

She appears chronically ill and pale with signs of recent weight loss. Non-bulky adenopathy is present in the left axilla and supraclavicular area. There is persistent left lower chest percussion dullness and decreased air entry but no subcutaneous tumor. The thoracostomy site has healed well. Breasts are symmetrical although the right is smaller without masses or tenderness. Abdomen is soft with epigastric fullness and tenderness but no distinct mass or ascites. There is no focal bony tenderness or neurological change.

She clearly has progressive nodal disease, with likely intrathoracic involvement. For now, she will try Duragesic to manage pain together with Compazine for nausea. She will return in the next few days for reassessment and further management.

SRW/weh

cc: Steven R. Ruderman, M.D.

June 2, 1995. Something told me to call. The last two weeks have been very bad because she's been throwing up and unable to keep any food or medication down. When I called I got the answering machine so I left a message. "Called to see how you're doing Mama. Love you much. Feel better. I'll talk to you later."

I was going out tonight with HW, only our second date, but he had been very supportive during our many conversations over the phone. I almost felt guilty going out on a date when my mom was across the country, dying of cancer. I should be there, or at least here at home. The last thing I should be doing is having fun.

I could not keep my thoughts off of Mama, so I called home from the restaurant with HW's cell phone, still considered a luxury item for me at the time. The babysitter said that one of my mother's friends had called, but unfortunately she couldn't remember which one. Her lack of information annoyed me. My mother was deathly ill. The call could have been news about her condition. She should have at least written down the name of the person who called.

I told HW that I wanted to go home to figure out who had called. I was on the verge of tears. He was incredibly supportive. I assumed the call was from Nancy Brown Jamison, but when I called her house, Nancy was not home. Anxious to calm my fears, I called Mama directly. For the first time in weeks she was able to speak. Larry had left briefly to run an errand. Her words were slurred from the medication, but I was relieved when she laughed at one of my jokes. It meant that she was lucid.

As I sat in my living room with HW and the babysitter, Mama and I talked about this new guy in my life. She sounded pleased about my new found companionship. I whispered that HW seemed too good to be true. "I think God sent him," Mama told me.

The conversation with Mama lasted only about ten minutes, but it made me feel much better. We talked about the food she ate and the way she felt. Then she abruptly changed the subject, as if she wanted to make sure she said this before Larry returned. "I want to get my affairs in order before I die," she said. After I told her to stop talking about dying, she told me in a very serious voice, "Terri, I want you to help me rewrite my will so that Larry doesn't have total control of all the finances after I'm gone. You know he has difficulty giving, even to his own children."

I was well aware of his miserly nature, but I simply listened. She said that she would call back tomorrow when Larry was out of the house again to discuss exactly how she wanted her estate handled. She didn't get a chance to call back. Somehow I knew she wouldn't. It was virtually impossible to get Larry away from her. I was certain that he knew she wanted to discuss something serious with me. I knew that he would do everything in his power to keep her from speaking to me, including giving her medication so that she was too drowsy to talk on the phone when he was out of the house.

HW sensed that I was feeling better after I spoke to my mother. He suggested that we could go back to his place because "the night was still young."

We took a cab to his apartment a few blocks away on 57th Street. It was breathtaking, not a bit like my little pink apartment. It overlooked Central Park and had a breathtaking view of the City. You could see the entire northern half of the City, clear to the George Washington Bridge. I had never been inside an apartment with this type of view. It literally took my breath away.

The apartment was decorated with metal and glass bookcases and black leather furniture. There was original artwork on the walls and tasteful sport figurines on the bookcases. It was surprisingly neat and clean. "Wow," I said to myself. "Nice apartment," I said to HW.

"Thanks," he said. "It's comfortable. Can I get you some wine?" We drank half a bottle of red wine and watched part of a movie on one of his many movie channels. When the time was right, he took me by the hand and led me into the bedroom. He switched on the stereo and the smooth sounds of Marvin Gaye filled the room. For the first time in a long time, I thought of nothing else but that moment in time.

June 3, 1995. Anne Litwin, another close friend of my mother, finally caught up with me. It was she who had called the night before. Mama was doing poorly today. She was unable to talk and again unable to hold down any food. I realized that this journey would truly be a roller coaster ride.

June 6, 1995. It was another very bad day. The headaches my mother was experiencing had become intolerable. Larry and Yvonne took her to the clinic for a CAT scan and the results confirmed our greatest fear, the cancer had spread to her brain. She went to the hospital for immediate radiation treatment.

Benji, Cathy and I all called to talk to Mama, but according to Larry, she was in the middle of a massage and unable to come to the phone. Larry explained that she was exhausted from the radiation treatment. I said that I thought Mama would want to speak to us.

We wondered whether Larry was intentionally keeping us from speaking with our mother, whether he was trying to hide something from us. It was not often that the three of us all called together. We continued speaking to each other after Larry hung up the phone. He should have informed her that her children calling, we thought. We knew that Mama wanted to continue with the holistic approach to recovery. Her fear was that radiation and chemotherapy would kill her healthy cells and interfere with the natural healing process. The tension caused from juxtaposing the natural treatment with the traditional treatment was the source of great anxiety for Mama, anxiety which could inhibit the healing process. We hung up the phone resenting the fact that we were unable to directly discuss this issue with our mother.

June 7, 1995. Today was a very good day. This morning Mama called me directly. She sounded great. She had been placed on steroids by the doctors to help minimize the effects of the cancer and radiation on her brain, and felt that they did wonders for her overall disposition. She also said that she finally decided to cut off all of her hair, since the radiation was making it fall out anyway. She already wore her hair in a short style and I wondered if she meant that she would shave her head. I told her that if she shaved her head, I intended to shave mine too. She didn't believe me, nor did I. Suffice it to say, I was grateful when we did not shave our heads.

At 5:30 p.m., Nancy Brown Jamison called. We talked for almost an hour. She said the pain had returned this afternoon. Once again, Mama's condition had drastically declined from only this morning. With each passing hour, we experienced new and unexpected hopes and fears.

June 8, 1995.

Dear Dr. Gonzalez:

I want to talk with you because at the moment I was having what I thought to be lucid thoughts and I'm afraid of losing them. I find late morning to the best time for me to talk with you. But no matter, this fax can be a good substitute. I question where you are with respect to my treatment. I would prefer to have you central to it, to be more in touch with me and I don't know how to make that happen. There are times when I feel that traditional medical approaches push my family toward confusion as to what decisions to make. What they need is either more immediate contact with you or more clearheadedness from me. I don't have a solution, but I'd like to talk with you about it. I suspect that the treatment I am getting locally now strays more from your program more than I would have it, so I'd like to have you more in touch.

Amanda

June 8, 1995. I talked to Yvonne for about an hour, freely for the first time in a while. Larry and my sister Cathy, who flew in yesterday, took Mama to the hospital for her radiation treatment. She only weighs about 126 pounds now. Yvonne took this free time as an opportunity to discuss all of the issues which weighed heavily on her mind.

First and foremost, was Larry's disregard for mom's desire to follow a natural vitamin regimen. The treatment mom selected with Dr. Gonzalez required strict adherence to the program, or else the program would not be effective. Yvonne made sure to fax any and all laboratory reports to Dr. Gonzalez so that he could tailor Mama's program accordingly. The regimen included eating naturally prepared organic foods. Microwaving the organic products was prohibited because it stripped the foods of the proteins, minerals and vitamins. The menus consisted of mostly fresh fruits and vegetables, oatmeal, almonds and brown rice. Larry refused, or constantly forgot, to prepare the oatmeal on the stove. He kept heating it in the microwave. Yvonne and Mama repeatedly asked him to stop nuking the oatmeal. Yvonne even volunteered to prepare it for mom. Larry refused to relinquish the task.

The conflict was a constant source of stress for Mama. She felt that Larry did not respect her choice of recovery. It was not that she would have refused the current radiation treatment. It was that Larry refused to accept her desire to treat the cancer naturally. Yvonne went on further to say that she was very concerned that Larry was keeping Mama from talking to Dr. Gonzalez and from treating her cancer the way she saw fit. He was making communication difficult by refusing to call her to the phone when Dr. Gonzalez called.

I hung up the phone thinking that Larry was compromising mom's ability to recover by causing confusion and turmoil over her course of treatment.

After my conversation with Aunt Yvonne, I stared out of my office window, looking for some sort of sign from God that this dreadful nightmare would soon end. Or a sign that we were pursuing the right course of treatments. I watched the people in the building across the street, wondering about the drama in their lives. I found myself constantly analyzing the Universe at a deeper level. Every word, every action had a deeper meaning. I felt connected to some overall grand scheme. I began to feel that there was more to life than what you see, hear and touch. There were hidden messages and subtle signs. Someone let go of a single yellow balloon and I watched it for a minute as it first lingered outside my window and then floated further and further away until it eventually disappeared into the Universe.

Mama loved yellow roses. After she became ill, we made sure that every week she had a fresh vase of yellow roses by her bedside. Was the yellow balloon a sign? Did it mean that we were going to lose Mama? I felt like I was slowly losing my mind. After all, it was just a yellow balloon.

The day after the yellow balloon, I noticed a squirrel sitting on my windowsill outside my bathroom window. He would not go away. Every time I looked out of the window, he sat there looking back. After several days, it began to concern me. Was he the reincarnation of a spirit trying to tell me something? I began to think that I was losing my mind. On the third day, when the squirrel was momentarily away from its perch, I placed nails and thumbtacks on the ledge to shoo him away. Just in case.

June 9, 1995. Mama called. She wanted to discuss how to handle her estate if she should die first. She was not willing to relinquish entire control of her estate to Larry. She sounded exhausted.

My mother explained that she needed to resolve the internal debate she was experiencing during the past several months. Her sheer exhaustion from fighting the cancer was outweighed by her distrust in Larry's ability to give to others. The life insurance policy, the stock, the bank accounts, all amounted to over a million dollars. Little did my mother know that her children would never see a penny of those proceeds. Money that she had saved for us all of her life, was now going to the man who shared her bed for five or so years. Neither I nor my siblings would ever fight him over the matter. It would have killed my mother. The irony of the situation did not escape me.

Mama then began to babble incoherently. "The great thing is that beyond the mental confusion I am getting greater clarity," she said. "Much clearer this time. It's so much clearer…You know, Larry is so quick, so short tempered. It's really nice that Yvonne is here…She's so good."

I hung up the phone concluding that Larry had pressured my mother into a decision to allow him to keep all of the proceeds from her estate.

June 13, 1995. It's Tuesday and I hadn't spoken to anyone since Friday. I left a message on the machine and Mama called me back. Everything was going well, all things considered. Mama said that in a way this illness had been a blessing in disguise. She said that it had brought her closer to all her loved ones and that was truly is a blessing.

I hung up the phone concluding that my mother was confused in a number of respects, the course of her treatment, the distribution of her estate and the fact that (in my opinion) there was no logic behind her illness.

~ ~ ~

June 14, 1995. Today was Brother Ben's birthday. He turned 39. My sister Cathy called me so that we could telephone him together. She got back from San Diego late last night. She said that it was very difficult to leave this time because Mama's condition had become so tentative. She said that Mama was very weak and lethargic. Benji was scheduled to go out the following week and I was scheduled to go out the last week of June.

We called Benji at his job to wish him happy birthday and we were surprised to learn that he had resigned the day before. Benji had worked for a large computer company in Seattle, Washington. He was not the impulsive type, but he told us that he had been given additional responsibilities with no increase in salary. So what else is new, I thought. He also said that he wanted more flexibility to see Mom during her illness. I envied his ability to make such a drastic move at a moments notice. Single moms rarely had such flexibility.

We decided to call Mama so she could tell Benji happy birthday. When we placed the four way call, Larry picked up the telephone. He said that our mother was meeting with the lawyer about the estate and could not be disturbed. I surmised that he was dotting his I's and crossing his T's to ensure that our inheritance went straight to him.

I turned to the issue at hand. It did not seem fair that Benji would not be able to speak to his own mother on his birthday, although I knew he would not dwell long on the issue. Like the decision to leave his job, he did not waver. He was a very tolerant man who rarely agonized over circumstances. Perhaps it was because he was the oldest child. Perhaps it was because he had always been the man of the house. Perhaps it was just his nature.

Benji was raised almost exclusively around women, first and foremost our mother, then me and my sister Cathy, our aunts Yvonne and Adrienne, our cousins Lynn, Debbie, and Kay, our adopted sisters Carmen and Charlsie, and our stepsisters Kathy and Barbie. The male figures in our lives were fleeting and intermittent. My bother learned from a very early age to go with the flow and not to fret the small stuff. He learned that from his mother.

My brother reminded me of the character Spock from the famous television series *Star Trek*. Like Spock, he was always cool, calm and collected. The house could be burning down around him and my brother would calmly direct us to the nearest exit. Bullets could be whizzing around his head and he would serenely calculate the best angle for cover. To react in any other manner, particularly with an unhelpful emotional response, would be "simply illogical."

When my brother turned thirty-something, he decided to become a vegetarian. He gradually removed red meat from his diet, then chicken, then fish, then milk by-products, then starches and sugars, until eventually his entire diet consisted of only fruits, vegetables and nuts. During this same time period, he began to train in yoga and meditation techniques. I admired his discipline and commitment. He began to lose weight and his complexion became as smooth as silk. Each year when we gathered at Christmas for the holidays, we all were envious of how he managed to look younger and younger.

Benji tried to convert us to his way of eating and his philosophy on life with simple subtle persuasion. But it was difficult for us to resist the foods to which we had grown accustomed, like bacon and eggs with cheese grits, sausage and toast. Mama was the only family member who kept her indulgences to a minimum. In fact, it was she who first suggested to Benji that he consider this life style.

As she grew older, Mama realized how important it was to eat the right foods, foods that kept your system moving. Keeping your system moving was a major issue in our Southern raised family. Living in the South often meant eating heavy or starchy foods which were cooked or fried with plenty of oil and grease. While Mother Dear was the best cook in the world, she would often cook meals like deep fried chicken with collard greens smothered in ham hocks, macaroni and cheese seasoned with mushrooms and onions, and home made biscuits with jelly. Such a meal would be served around noon for "dinner," after a full breakfast of bacon, grits and eggs and before a full supper of ham or pork chops with the customary sides.

Mama realized that eating heavy foods like that would clog up your system leading to the accumulation of harmful cancer-causing toxins, not to mention the accumulation of undesirable fat. When she moved out of her mother's house, she consciously decided to change her cooking and eating habits to a healthier, leaner diet.

Generally, her diet consisted of fruits and vegetables, some chicken and an abundance of fish. She rarely ate red meat. She often cooked freshly caught fish in a shallow frying pan with just a little bit of olive oil or butter. Instead of using salt, she discovered a salt substitute called Mrs. Spike, which contained a mixture of natural seasonings and salt substitutes. She supplemented her diet with a consistent exercise program. Every morning, she walked three miles along the beach around the bay near their apartment.

None of that mattered now. Obviously, these good habits did little if anything to prevent the cancer. Knowing that Mama took such good care of her body made me even angrier that she was afflicted with cancer. It was the irony of all ironies. Why even bother trying to eat right and exercise, I thought? What good does it do? When I asked Dr. Wallach (Mama's oncologist) these questions, she said in a soft, soothing, therapeutic voice, "I know it's easy to think that way Terri, but perhaps Amanda's good habits prevented the cancer from coming sooner." The skeptic in me thought maybe, but then again, maybe not. We will never really know, will we?

~ ~ ~

Cathy and I told Benji to have a happy birthday, even if he didn't get a chance to speak to our mother. I hung up the phone thinking that Mama would probably not live long enough to wish my brother happy birthday again.

June 20, 1995. The cancer index went down from 40 to 32. We were all euphoric. Mama intended to resume the Gonzalez program next week. She finally connected with Dr. Gonzalez who took the time to call her from his house.

"You sure are coming at a good time," Mama told me. "I am feeling better than I have in a long time, plus your brother is in town. He doesn't leave until Saturday. We're going to have a great time together." She went on the say that she had some tingling in the scalp which, according to the doctor, meant that she would lose her hair.

June 21, 1995. The following is a thank you note that I received from Phyllis Brown (my ex-Mother-in-law) who was caring for Nicole and Christopher during my visit with mom in San Diego.

Dear Terri,

You probably won't receive this until you come back. You looked sexy and lovely last night. I received lots of pleasant comments about my daughter-in-law.

The earrings are lovely. It was very thoughtful and kind of you to give them to me. You are too generous to me. I love them and will enjoy wearing them.

I'll take good care of the "chilluns." Our prayers are with you.

Love,

Phyl

June 22, 1995. "Hey Baby," was the way she answered the phone today. She had just returned from her radiation treatment. Small chunks of her hair had fallen out. She will have the last of her 14 treatments tomorrow. She told me that Benji's visit was wonderful. He offered to pay for Aunt Yvonne to see Dr. Gonzalez as a gift for taking such good care of Mama. He figured that the treatments would flush any toxins from her system and thereby prevent future cancers. His offer was incredibly generous.

I thought to myself, live long and prosper, Brother Ben. Live long and prosper.

~ ~ ~

June 23, 1995, Friday. My plan was to visit my mother through the fourth of July. It was hard to leave the children for so long, but I did not know how much longer my mother would survive.

This morning when I took the kids to camp and said goodbye, I could not hold back the tears. I did not want to upset Nicole and Christopher, but no matter how hard I tried, I could not stop the tears. Somehow I felt that this was going to be a difficult trip. The other little girls in Nicole's class kept asking me what was wrong? The little boys did not even notice that I was crying. The differences between the sexes starts at such an early age, I thought.

The airplane ride from New York to San Diego was long. I occupied my mind with thoughts about Mama. I wondered what she would look like at 127 pounds. I hoped that she would be feeling well enough to eat and go for walks. So many things we had taken for granted. So many things I wished for her.

The people on the plane seemed normal enough. There was a man to my right, a woman to my left. I wanted to tell them that I was going to visit my mother who was dying of cancer. This could be one of my last visits. It was important that I come now, before the cancer spread even further. Why doesn't anyone ask me, "How are you doing, how do you feel, how is your mother?" No one said a word to me. How could they have known?

Benji picked me up from the airport. I said a quick thank you prayer to God for sending my brother Benji and not Larry. We quickly found our way to the parked car. He had already taken my bags from my hands, a move he made right after the customary hugs and kisses. We were an affectionate family, especially brother Ben. Greetings and salutations always included hugs and kisses. Sometimes, the whole bunch of us would spend a good twenty minutes at the airport saying goodbye to each other before boarding time.

When you come from a place like Birmingham, Alabama, everyone comes with you to the airport to see you off, including the children and babies. If the timing of the flight allowed, we would all go to the Pancake House or some other breakfast establishment and fill up on pancakes, eggs and grits for a proper send-off meal. We did this even back in the day when airlines were serving meals on planes. Airplane food was no substitute for a good Southern style breakfast. Everyone had to hug and kiss everyone else, from the youngest to the oldest and back around again for good measure. Sometimes people would stare at us as if to say, "Isn't that nice the way they care about each other like that." Sometimes people would just stare. Either way, we were not the slightest bit fazed.

Although Mama and Larry had lived in San Diego for nearly six years, I never learned my way around. A sense of direction was not one of my virtues. I was impatient with no sense of direction. Getting lost, therefore, was not a viable option for me. Fortunately, Brother Ben inherited both patience and a good sense of direction.

~ ~ ~

We arrived at the apartment later than expected. Mama was waiting up for me. The second leg of the flight had been delayed and I was grateful she was able to stay awake for me. She looked exhausted and relieved that I had finally made it. She only stayed up for a few minutes, but it was wonderful to see her and to hold her once again.

June 24, 1995, Saturday. Benji had to go back home today. I hated to see him leave. He has such a soothing affect on everyone, even Larry.

Larry's daughter Barbie came to San Diego with her husband Rick and their two sons. We were all taking our turn, making sure that we visited, not knowing when these opportunities might end.

June 25, 1995, Sunday. Larry, Aunt Yvonne, Mama and I went to see *Bridges of Madison County*. It was the last movie my mother ever saw. For two hours and five minutes, the movie took us away from the stress of our reality. Yvonne and I sat behind Mama and Larry. I saw my mother dab her eyes when Meryl Streep watched as she let Clint Eastwood walk past the front of her car in the pouring rain, out of her life, forever. I wondered had my mother ever found her Clint Eastwood, and if so, had she let him slip out of her life, forever.

June 26, 1995, Monday. Mama was anxious to get a new hair cut. Aunt Yvonne and I agreed that it would do my mother some good to get a new look. She accepted the fact that she would lose most of her hair. Large clumps had already fallen out. As I watched her comb her thinning locks, she rationalized that as long as she was going to lose her hair, it was better to have a short stylish cut. She decided she wanted to get a style similar to the one she got when she visited me in New York in March.

I thought back about the trip to the salon. We noticed a picture in a magazine of a sophisticated lady with a stylish short hair cut. Below the picture of the model, credit for her hair style was given to a salon which was two short blocks from my apartment. I told Mom that we should make an appointment and walk over to the salon. She was worried that she would not have the energy to walk there and back. Not to worry I said. That's what cabs are for. I walked her down the stairs of the little pink apartment, hailed a taxi and authoritatively told him to go two blocks down the street. I held my tongue as the cab driver cursed us under his breath. They were so predictable these guys. What's it to them? I thought. A fare is a fare. By my calculations, multiple short fares meant more money. Had my mother not been there, he would have gotten an ear full of four letter words.

Mama absolutely loved the New York haircut, although she was a little upset when the stylist snipped her ear with his sharp scissors. I was livid. Even the least bit of pain was too much as far as I was concerned. She had enough pain to bear. The astringent he dabbed on the knick only added insult to injury. Later that evening, we took pictures so Mama could show other stylists exactly the cut she wanted.

Of course, as we headed toward the salon in San Diego, we left the pictures of Mom's new haircut at the apartment. No problem. I was happy to drive back to get the pictures while Aunt Yvonne waited with Mama at the salon. It would only take a few minutes and there was nothing I wouldn't do at this point to make Mama happy.

I did my best to follow the directions back to the apartment, but as I slowly backtracked down the streets, my anxiety level increased with each turn. The last thing I wanted to do was to get lost. Mama always told us that as long as we were together, we were never lost. Her sense of direction was almost as bad as mine. When we lived in Newark, New Jersey, she would drive my brother, sister and I around in the big blue Chevy not knowing one highway from the other. All the signs seemed to go in the same direction. Then, before you knew it, the highway you wanted just stopped appearing on the signs and lo and behold you're on some other highway going in the wrong direction. It didn't matter to Mama. She comforted us by singing a familiar song until we were back on the right road. "See," she would say, "We were never lost, just a little turned around. As long as we're together, we'll never be lost."

But now I was alone in the car searching for my mother's apartment. If I got lost, it meant that she would have to sit in the hair salon and wait unnecessarily for my return. That was not an option. Two lefts, right, left, right to get there. That meant, left, right, left and two rights to get back. I never concentrated so hard on tracing directions backwards. It was a small miracle that I did not get lost. I said a thank you prayer as I ran up the steps back into the salon with the pictures in hand.

The trip to the salon was exhausting for Mama. We dropped her back to the apartment to get some much needed rest. Then Aunt Yvonne and I searched all over San Diego for a tube of Orabase B for Mama. Somehow the cancer medication was causing blisters in Mama's mouth. The blisters were not only painful, but they prevented her from brushing and flossing, a task which she assiduously undertook.

After trying three different drug stores, Yvonne and I finally found the elusive Orabase B. We rushed back to the apartment hoping that it would do the trick. But the ointment did little to ease the pain. It was difficult enough to suffer in pain from the cancer. Must she endure these annoying side effects on top of everything else?

June 29, 1995, Thursday. I anxiously awaited the trip to the oncologist's office, feeling like it would somehow bring me closer to terms with this relentless illness. It looked like any ordinary doctor's office, except that the patients and their waiting families bore the same distant and forlorn expressions. There was, after all, the unspoken common adversary, cancer.

Sabina's style and mannerisms were not like the average oncologist one might expect. Although the office was sterile in appearance, her approach with her patients was not. She invited us all into the office, but Larry told me to remain in the waiting room, just as he had done when we visited Dr. Gonzalez in New York. I looked at Mama and without using words she told me to come along. Without using words, she told Larry to relax. Without using words, I told him to fuck off.

Sabina said that, all things considered, my mother looked well. She discussed the possibility of resorting to chemotherapy if necessary. She was not sure whether the cancer had metastasized any further. We would have to wait for the results of recent tests. We should keep an open mind, she told us. I left the office thinking that in her own delicate way, Sabina was suggesting that we undergo chemotherapy, before it was too late.

July 3, 1995, Monday. The call was completely unexpected. Larry brought me the phone and said that it was someone calling from work. It was the head of human resources for the Company. He said, "Terri, I hate to disturb you, I know that your mother is ill. But I have an opportunity as General Counsel to one of our subsidiary companies that I want you to seriously consider. When you return to New York, we can discuss the details."

I could hardly believe my ears. I had been with the Company for five years, but I did not think such a plum position would become available to me. Mama and Aunt Yvonne were sitting on the couch talking. I snuggled between them and told them about the telephone call from HR. They shared my enthusiasm about the possibilities.

Mama said, "I can't believe my baby is going to be the General Counsel of a company."

I told her not to jump to conclusions. It was just a phone call. I did not have the job just yet. But I was going to do everything in my power to secure it.

We were feeling so elated from the morning news that we decided to go shopping. Plus, Mama could use some cosmetics to make her feel attractive again. She had nearly finished her tube of lipstick which was a sheer brown shade of Estee Lauder. We searched a number of stores for the identical lipstick to no avail. We were reluctant to continue for much longer because of Mama's weakened condition. We finally drove her to a small shopping plaza with a department store called The Broadway. To save time, I walked ahead of Aunt Yvonne and Mama inquiring at each counter, showing Mama's empty tube of lipstick to each salesperson.

I finally found the lipstick and purchased the last tube. The saleswoman said that it was a discontinued color explaining why we had difficulty locating it. I retraced my footsteps to locate my mother and her sister. I found them resting on a ledge near the handbag department. They never made it to cosmetics. My mother's face lit up when she saw me take the lipstick out of the bag. The way she looked, you would have thought that I had traveled around the world and back for her.

I opened the plastic cover and pulled out the new tube of lipstick. She handed me the old tube which I compared to the new one. Yup, this was the right one. I handed her the shiny new tube. She twisted it until the chocolate brown lipstick swirled out of the top. She bent her right arm towards her mouth and without the use of a mirror perfectly applied it to her lips. New hair, new lipstick, new sophisticated lady.

I decided to save the old tube of lipstick, just in case we needed to locate another one later on. I still have it, along with the receipt for the new one. I simply could not bring myself to throw them away.

I flew back to New York the next day. When I left San Diego, my mother was still very much alive.

~ ~ ~

July 7, 1995, Friday. Aunt Yvonne said that the past few days had been very difficult. When I was there, we had some difficulty getting Mama to take her pills, but Yvonne said Mama was down right refusing to take her medication because it upset her stomach. Yvonne forced her to take the medicine a few times, but each time Mama would throw up. Mama complained that the medicine was hurting her stomach.

When Sabina, the oncologist, x-rayed Mama's stomach, much to our dismay, the cancer had metastasized to that area as well. Sabina said that this fact explained the pain associated with taking the vitamins. Aunt Yvonne felt guilty for forcing Mama to take the vitamins and yet guilty for allowing Mama to deviate from the program. It was clearly a no-win internal battle which Yvonne constantly fought, and lost.

Sabina urged us to immediately begin chemotherapy. As it turned out, the chemotherapy was the beginning of the end. Mama was conceptually against this type of invasive treatment. She understood that the entire premise behind chemotherapy was to concentrate vast amounts of destructive energy onto a particular site killing both the good cells and the bad cells. Theoretically, the good cells would then regenerate themselves. The obvious defect in this process is that if the patient's body is too weak or torn down, the body will not be able to regenerate itself. Such was the case with Mama.

It was difficult hearing all this from Aunt Yvonne. It was hard to believe that when I left San Diego on July 5th, Mama was doing so well. Now she could hardly lift herself from the bed.

The family seriously debated the pros and cons of chemotherapy. Larry, a proponent of conventional medicine, strongly advocated that Mama undergo the treatment. Cathy, Benji and I didn't know what to do, we simply knew that Mama didn't like the idea, but we wanted what was best for her. In the end, we conceded that perhaps the best course of treatment and the only hope left at this point was the chemotherapy. In her defeated and weakened state, my mother finally agreed to the chemotherapy.

Mama was scheduled to go for a series of treatments, but after the first two sessions her body was so weak that Sabina was hesitant to give her more. So we waited.

When I spoke to Aunt Yvonne, she expressed regret for encouraging the chemotherapy because it was obvious that my mother's condition had drastically deteriorated as a result of the treatment. I tried to console her, explaining that we all encouraged the chemotherapy, thinking it would help. But my words were of little or no consolation to her.

July 11, 1995, Tuesday. I asked Aunt Yvonne if she thought Mama was strong enough to talk. "Hold on baby, let me see," she said in her soft Southern tone. Yvonne and I were accustomed to speaking softly when Larry was around. But this time she was being quiet because she wasn't sure if Mama was awake or not.

I had just accepted the new job as General Counsel of a subsidiary of the company where I worked. I was so excited and I wanted to tell Mama because I knew that the news would excite her too. She didn't respond at all when I told her, in fact I was not even sure she heard what I said. Aunt Yvonne took the phone back and told me she was really proud of me and that she knew Mama would be too. We were both silent. "I love you," she managed to say.

"Me too," I replied. We hung up the phone. I knew she was crying.

July 14, 1995, Friday. I spoke to Mama again today. We talked a little longer today, but she was very groggy. I told her about the new job again, but I wasn't at all sure whether she comprehended a word I said.

July 17, 1995, Monday. When I called San Diego today, my sister Cathy answered the telephone. She had just arrived from the airport. She and Aunt Yvonne, along with Larry, were sharing the responsibilities for taking care of Mama, who was becoming increasingly incoherent.

Yvonne came to the phone. She was upset with Larry. She said that Larry was trying to keep Mama to himself. There were times he would not allow anyone in the room to see her. Yvonne said that every night Larry would fix drinks for the guests who came to see Mama, while my mother lay quietly in her room alone, unable to partake. She asked me, "Why is he always so festive? Why does he do things to draw us away from your mother?"

None of us could understand Larry and his bizarre behavior. In some perverse way he seemed to enjoy the attention of all the friends and family who came to visit Mama during her illness. He never had so many friends, nor had he ever received so much attention.

Yvonne's frustration grew even greater when Cathy arrived on Monday. Cathy was determined to take care of Mama the way she saw fit. Even the simplest issues, like taking a bath, became a bone of contention.

Aunt Yvonne would always say, "I got a bone to pick with you." It was one of those many Southern expressions used by my mother and her sisters. It meant that she was upset about something and it was time to deal with the issue. I did my best to avoid picking bones with the family, especially with Aunt Yvonne. As the oldest girl of thirteen children, she was, in many respects, everyone's mother. When you picked a bone with Aunt Yvonne, she often walked away with the meat, the bone, and the gristle, leaving you wishing you had never messed with her bone in the first place.

This bone was about giving Mama a bath. When Cathy arrived on Monday, Mama repeatedly asked her about taking a bath. Neither Yvonne nor Larry thought it was wise to give her a regular bath in her weakened condition. They preferred instead, to give her sponge baths.

But Mama loved the water. She loved taking baths and Cathy was well aware of this fact. The warm water engulfing her body and soothing her muscles was her daily escape to ecstasy. She spent more time in the bath tub than anyone I knew. Walking along the beach and taking baths. If the day included those two items, it was a good day. Cathy desperately wanted to grant Mama her wish. She argued vehemently with both Larry and Aunt Yvonne. But no one was willing to budge from their position. So Cathy decided to wait for the right opportunity. One way or another, Cathy was determined to give Mama one last bath.

July 19, 1995, Wednesday. When Cathy and Aunt Yvonne checked on Mama this morning, she was extraordinarily lethargic. After a brief discussion with Larry, they all decided to call the doctor to determine the status of her condition. It would be the final house call by the physician from the cancer hospice.

It was during this visit that the physician uttered the now infamous words, "It will be a matter of hours, maybe days, but not weeks."

Then came the long, heated debate. Should they tell Mama what the doctor said or should they wait and see what would happen?

Larry's decision to tell Mama that she was dying upset Aunt Yvonne to no end. She vehemently argued the matter with Larry. Cathy was willing to go along with Larry because she knew that Mama always wanted to know the whole truth.

After the doctors left on Wednesday, Yvonne called her sister Adrienne, exasperated and exhausted from arguing. She asked Adrienne to come for support and to escort her home. So Adrienne took the next available flight from Birmingham to San Diego on Wednesday evening as requested by her eldest sister. For two days Aunt Yvonne and Aunt Adrienne tended to their dying sister. Then, after saying goodbye one last time and promising to return in a few weeks, they left San Diego only hours before I arrived on Friday. We just missed each other. It was the last time they would see their sister alive.

Yvonne later explained her decision to leave. She said that it was difficult to tell Mama she was dying, knowing the adverse effect such news might have upon her sister's will to live. Yvonne thought that knowing less than the whole truth was preferable under these circumstances.

It was even more difficult for me to admit to Aunt Yvonne that after she left, my mother repeatedly called her name looking for her.

The idea of telling someone that she was dying and then preparing for the event was a foreign concept to Aunt Yvonne and Aunt Adrienne. Their Southern Baptist upbringing encouraged them not to give up hope. They were trained to pray for the sick to heal and to ask all your family and friends to pray for a miracle too. Every Sunday in church the names of the "Sick and Shut-in" were religiously added to the church program. The minister individually called out every name so that the congregation would know exactly for whom to pray. "We ask you to pray for the speedy recovery of Mrs. Velma Hawkins who is recovering from hip surgery at St. Joseph's Hospital. We pray for the strength of her children and all of the Hawkins family..."

Fundamentally, not to hope and pray for a miracle was paramount to sacrilege. So Yvonne and Adrienne left for Birmingham, to deal with their sister's passing the only way they knew how.

Meanwhile, Cathy had not forgotten the bath. As soon as Larry left to take Yvonne and Adrienne to the airport, Cathy picked up the phone. She called a friend of Mom's who was a personal trainer at a local gym. She was built like a weight lifter. Together she and Cathy would be able to lift Mama in and out of the tub. If they were fast enough, they would be able to perform the task before Larry returned from the airport. What he didn't know wouldn't hurt him.

The first half of the bath went smoothly. They managed to get Mama into the tub with relative ease. Mama eased her body down into the warm bubbles, smiling with enjoyment. She stayed in the water until her fingers and toes looked like raisins and prunes. Cathy was pleased that she was able to give Mama this simple pleasure. She was fairly certain that she would not be able to accomplish this feat again.

But then Larry returned, before the bath was finished. When he realized what was occurring, he was furious that Cathy had acted against his wishes. To make matters worse, they had difficulty removing Mama from the bath tub, aggravating Larry even further. He screamed at Cathy for taking such risks behind his back. He told her that she had to leave the apartment, that she was no longer welcome in his house.

Larry had no idea to whom he was talking. If he thought that I was strong willed, he was about to find out the true meaning of those words. In a cool, calm and collected fashion, Cathy told him, "I'm not going anywhere. As long as my mother is in this house, I am staying right here." Cathy was never one to mince words. She said what she meant and meant what she said. This was, after all, her mother they were discussing. If anyone was leaving, it wasn't going to be Cathy. Mama finished her bath, unscathed. Larry backed down. And Cathy, she stayed right there, of course.

On July 20th, Thursday morning, I received the infamous call from Larry telling me that my mother was dying. I flew out to San Diego the next day.

14
Final Days

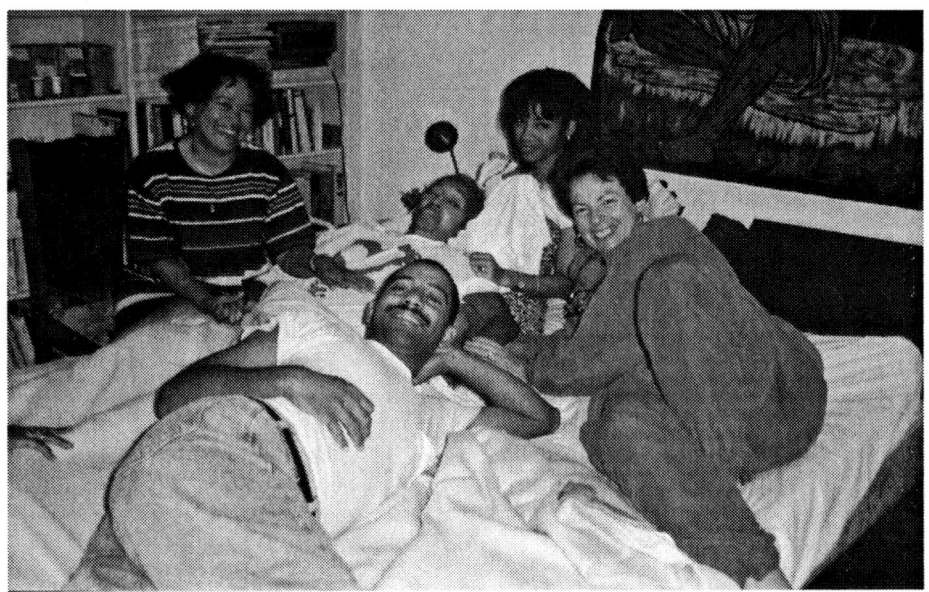

July 21, 1995, Friday afternoon. The cross country flight from New York to San Diego seemed like an eternity. The surreal, out of body feeling continued to recur, especially during the flight. I watched and listened to the other passengers around me, but I was unable to interact constructively. Their words and conversations all ran into each other, sounding like senseless chatter. I sat in my seat, hands folded in my lap, staring out of the window.

I generally disliked flying. It wasn't so much the flying I disliked, rather, the lack of control if something were to go terribly wrong with the plane. Mama always said not to worry about that. "If it's your time," she would say, "it's your time."

"Sure, Mama, that's just great, but what if it's the pilot's time and I just happen to be on the plane," I told her. The remark exemplified the way I felt about flying. Out of control of my own fate. Except not this time. Not this trip. This trip it didn't seem to matter. My fate was in God's hand. I knew I was not destined to perish in a plane crash. I was intended to visit my ailing mother, whose fate, it seemed, was to perish from cancer.

I gazed at the sky and the clouds outside the plane and imagined myself inside the clouds, floating and soaring mindlessly through the air, occasionally snatched back inside the plane when the flight attendant questioned me about more Diet Coke and peanuts. "Sure, I'll take some more," I said, and then back into the clouds I sailed.

I looked at the faces of the other passengers on the plane and wondered where they were going and who they were visiting. I rarely engaged in conversations with other passengers, but for some reason I wanted to tell someone, anyone who would listen, that I was traveling to San Diego to visit my dying mother. Get a grip, I thought, no one wants to listen to you talk about your dying mother. They have problems of their own. So instead of pouring my heart out to the woman next to me, I leaned back and tried hard to sleep and forget about my problems. Maybe if I sleep long enough and hard enough, when I wake up, this terrible nightmare will be over.

I awoke to the sound of the Captain's voice asking us to make sure our seatbelts were securely fastened in preparation for landing. My throat was parched from the dry cabin air. I looked around for a flight attendant in the hopes of obtaining one last Diet Coke, but they were finished with the cabin service and already seated for landing. I looked out of the window to see that the sky and the clouds had been replaced with tall buildings surrounded by streets with tiny cars and even tinier people.

Despite my secure feeling about my fate, the approach to San Diego was somewhat disconcerting because the airport was located in the middle of downtown. I closed my eyes and said the Serenity prayer, "God, grant me the serenity to accept the things I cannot change, the courage to change the things I can and the wisdom to know the difference." I repeated the verses several times and seconds later the plane landed safely in San Diego.

The weather in San Diego was predictably hot and muggy. Had it not been for the cool summer breeze coming off of the ocean, it would have been sweltering. I took off my black sweater and placed it over my left arm. I pulled my hair up with a scrungie to cool my neck and prevent my hair from getting frizzy.

As I walked through the San Diego airport looking for a familiar face, I prayed that it would not be Larry's. The thought of Larry picking me up literally made me nauseous. When I saw my brother I said a quick thank you prayer.

As we drove through downtown San Diego to Mama and Larry's oceanfront apartment, the streets and landmarks grew increasingly familiar. I decided to get straight to the point and ask Brother Ben about Mama before we got to the apartment. "What do you think? Do you really think she is dying?" I decided not to beat around the bush.

"I don't know, hard to say." And then silence. Brother Ben was not big on extraneous verbiage. O.k., Mr. Spock, I thought. I won't push for your real feelings right now. I wanted more information, but for now this would have to do. No need to press Brother Ben for information when I would get all I needed from my sister Cathy, who, like me, was never short on her words. By now, Cathy was probably at the apartment calling the shots, as much as anyone could call the shots when Larry was around.

When I arrived at Mama and Larry's apartment, I headed straight for the bedroom, where Mama was lying in her bed. Their two bedroom condominium was on the second floor of a two story building overlooking the bay off of the Pacific Ocean. It was a relatively new apartment with clean lines and warm colors, decorated with cultural artifacts they had collected from around the world. There was a fireplace in the center of the living room adorned with a large chime they bought during their travels to India.

I was the last to arrive at the apartment, having traveled the farthest. Everyone had gathered in Mama's bedroom. A pale yellow light shone from the two windows facing the no-frills platform bed. A dozen yellow roses brightened the table beneath the window. Because Mama was fond of yellow roses, her closest circle of friends made sure that there was always a fresh arrangement to greet her each week.

The sweet aroma of incense greeted me first. Then I noticed the flowers and the candles, juxtaposed with the pills, the glass of water and the unfinished slice of watermelon. Mama loved watermelon. Winter, spring, summer or fall, it was always watermelon season. She said that watermelon was good for you. It helped to keep your system moving and clear of toxins. She drank water for the same reason. She drank more water than anyone I knew.

Mama's bedroom contained a built-in bookcase covering one entire wall filled with dozens of books, yoga books, psychology books, meditation books, travel books, cook books, self-help books, history books, books about trekking, books about parenting, books about health, all kinds of books. Reading the titles of these books provided the reader with a sketch of Mama's life. She was an independent, progressive thinker which is why California suited her well. She was, by no stretch of the imagination, simply a Southern girl from Birmingham, Alabama.

Life was an adventure to Mama. She sought new experiences, new people. She refused to remain stagnant, preferring instead to jump feet first into the next adventure. Her approach to life explained how she could have married four times (five if you include Walter). It explained how she could have brought so many people into our home who needed help at different times in their lives.

During the course of her extraordinary experiences, she managed to leave a lasting impression upon everyone and everything she touched, which explained why so many friends and family came to visit Mama when they learned of her illness. Just one more visit, just one more opportunity to share time with her, one more opportunity to say, "Thank you for being a part of my life."

Everyone was sitting on the bed surrounding Mama, my sister Cathy, my stepsisters Barbie and Kathy and Mom's best friend, Nancy Brown Jamison. It was a testament to my mother's character that at the age of sixty she still had someone to call her best friend. Larry was there, of course. He loomed large over the gathering, making his presence inescapable.

Before entering the room, I tried to get as much information as possible from my sister Cathy who, as I suspected, had taken charge since her arrival on Monday.

"How is Mama doing?" I asked Cathy. "How much does she know about her condition?"

"The doctors came to see her on Wednesday." Cathy said. "They said that it would not be much longer. Her vital signs are very weak." She paused for a second and then said, "Larry decided to tell Mama everything. I agreed with him because you know how Mama is. She always wants to know the truth." Then she whispered, "But after we told her she was dying, she told me she was afraid."

Larry's decision, for better or for worse, was to tell her the truth, the whole truth, and nothing but the truth.

So help us now God.

The fact that Mama said she was afraid worried me. She did not deserve this type of anguish. No one did. Mama and I shared our deepest concerns with each other. Yet in all my life, I had never heard her say she was afraid of anything, including the concept of death. Her outlook on death was commendable. She always said, "That which you can control, control. The rest, the part you can't control, don't worry about." Death was one of those things that you could not control.

Then I thought about something my sister Cathy said. The doctors came to see my mother on Wednesday. Larry did not call me until Thursday. Why had he waited until Thursday to call me? He knew that I had farther to travel than anyone else. What if my mother had not survived until I arrived? What if the illness had progressed so far that she would not be cognizant and would not recognize me? Was his oversight intentional?

I tried to clear my thoughts before I spoke to Mama, I wanted to focus all of my attention on her. I wanted to comfort and soothe her. I thought hard about what to say and how to ease her fears. Would she be in a joking mood? She always liked to hear my silly jokes and funny stories. But would she be too sick to appreciate any humor? Would she even know it was me?

It seemed to me that Mama had been waiting for me. My stepsister Barbie came out of the bedroom and said, "She is asking for you."

I walked into my mother's bedroom. She looked weak and exhausted. Although the ordeal had taken its toll, she still looked beautiful. Her milk chocolate skin was remarkably smooth and soft with practically no wrinkles, defying her 60 years. Her brown eyes still lit up the room when she smiled, the smile that mesmerized everyone.

My mother's beauty was majestic, she looked like an African Queen. In fact, Larry often referred to her as his Senegalese Queen because when they once traveled together to Senegal she looked like the native women. The children even ran up to her, speaking their native language, thinking she was one of them. Larry was in awe of her natural beauty and the spell she wove on the people she met, not just in Senegal, but wherever they traveled. After that trip to Africa, he affectionately called her his Senegalese Queen.

I leaned over the bed and picked up her right hand. It was soft and warm. I would recognize those hands anywhere. I quietly whispered, "Mama, it's Terri, I just arrived from the airport."

Mama opened her eyes and looked straight at me. She managed to generate a tiny smile in my direction. The smile said, "Hello my darling. I am so glad you are here." She was working up to speaking. After a minute or two she asked me in the weakest voice, "Terri, who did you talk to?"

Her question indicated to me that she was cognizant of her condition. I knew immediately that she was trying to determine just how much I knew. But I couldn't answer her question. The lump growing in my throat blocked my words and the tears forming in my eyes began to blur my vision. I could barely breathe.

Then she said, "Did they tell you what the doctors said?" I still couldn't say anything, as the lump grew larger and the tears, which I could no longer contain, ran down my cheeks onto her pillow. She looked like she was using all of her strength just to utter these few words. She must have known from my silence that I knew everything.

Before I could respond to her questions she said, "Those silly doctors, what do they know?" as she forced a slightly bigger smile. Despite my best efforts, I began sobbing uncontrollably, burying my face gingerly in her bosom to hide my tears.

Even in her weakest condition, her instincts were to protect her children. She was trying to be strong. She did not want me to sense her fear, lest it should frighten me. Her courage moved me as much as her physical condition. I realized that I must say something to soothe her concerns about how I was taking all of this. I finally mustered the strength and mumbled through my tears, "You are right Mama, those doctors don't know a damn thing, not a damn thing." With that, I leaned over, hugged her frail frame and kissed her cheek, still sobbing.

I thought that I better get a grip and control my emotions. I didn't want Mama to start worrying about me on top of everything else.

As I leaned over my mother holding her hand tightly in mine, I said the Serenity prayer. Then I added, "And please dear God, give my mother, your faithful angel, peace of mind for this final journey, if this is to be her final journey." Like Aunt Yvonne and Aunt Adrienne, I also held onto the hope, the hope that the doctors were all wrong, the hope that this would not be her final journey, the hope that Mama would win this battle like every other obstacle she had overcome. We really needed a miracle this time.

July 22, 1995, Saturday morning. I arose from the pull-out sofa in the living room and headed straight for my mother's bedroom. I peeked through the half ajar door. Larry was already up and roaming somewhere. I tip-toed to my mother's side of the bed and gently touched her hand, not knowing what to expect. It was warm. She was resting peacefully. I was relieved. Out of nowhere, Larry' voice pierced the morning air, "Don't wake her up."

"I have no intention of waking her up," I said quietly, as I turned and walked back out of the bedroom. Negative, I thought, always so negative.

We all quietly took turns using the bathroom and getting dressed. The mood was somber as we ate our fruit and cereal for breakfast. Mom eventually woke up and drank a little water.

Mama talked twice on the phone that day, once to my sister's boys (Isaiah, David and Daniel) and later to my friend HW. My mother never met HW, but she liked what she knew about him. He suggested that she rub my head for good luck because she once told him that I brought her luck. I heard her say she was glad I was there. I heard her giggle a couple of times. She was sitting up with her back leaning on my chest. She remained in that position for hours because she said that it was comfortable. Her back had grown weary and achy from lying down so long. I was determined to hold her in that position or any other position that made her comfortable. Long after my own back began to ache, I held her up. It was the least I could do.

Larry took a picture of us sitting in that position. He later mailed the picture to me. I felt as though Mama was somehow there with me again. Her conversation with HW began to wane in and out. I wasn't sure if she was fully participating in the conversation. But, when I tried to take the phone away from her because I thought she was getting tired, she joked and said, "Is that all I get to say?" The last thing Mama told HW before she hung up the phone was that she would talk to him tomorrow. She never did.

As the afternoon progressed, my mother began to ramble somewhat incoherently. I hung onto every word. It seemed that she was talking from beyond, with wisdom greater than ours. Although she was initially afraid, by the time Saturday's dusk crept upon us, she said that it was going to be all right, that it was beautiful. I wanted to know what she meant and to understand what she saw. She kept repeating, "You know what?" "Oh boy." "That's beautiful." Then she would chuckle lightly. We were relieved that she was content. I imagined that she was envisioning bright colorful lights. I thought she must have been talking to someone. Was she talking to Angels, to God, to us?

Later that afternoon, I was lying on the bed holding my mother's hand and talking to Barbie. Barbie asked about my new position as General Counsel.

As we sat on the bed next to Mama, I told Barbie as much as I knew about the new job which I was scheduled to start on Monday, August 7th. I would have a staff of my own. I would prepare my own budget. I would report directly to the President of the company. It was an exciting opportunity. I didn't think Mama was listening, I didn't even know she was awake. She opened her eyes and looked straight at me and said in a raspy voice, "Terri, I'm so proud of you."

I stared at Mama and then turned to Barbie in disbelief. I was astounded that Mama heard and understood our conversation. The words came from far away and took every ounce of energy she could summon to articulate. The utterance left her weak and exhausted. She closed her eyes again and took a deep breath. I parted my lips to say, "Thank you Mama," but she was gone again. I wanted to tell her how much her words meant to me, but I think she must have known.

I am forever grateful that she was able to tell me how she felt. Those words are indelibly etched in my mind. Those words were the last coherent utterances she ever said to me.

By Saturday evening, Mama became increasingly agitated. She kept tossing and turning and she moaned continuously. These were clear indications that the pain was worsening. She seemed somewhat delusional at times, unable to focus, unable to speak. Nancy and I tried to pinpoint the origin and nature of the pain, but it was difficult. When we called the hospice nurse, she said that, "it won't be long now." I asked the nurse about easing the pain and she suggested that we start a morphine drip because the pain patches were obviously not working sufficiently. We told the nurse to head over to the apartment to set up the intravenous drip, knowing that in all likelihood, Mama would loose consciousness, slip into a coma and die.

Until the nurse arrived, Nancy and I tried desperately to ease the pain. We crushed a Vicodin pill into small pieces and placed them on her tongue, hoping they would melt. She gagged and shook her head as if to say, "No, stop." I took a damp paper towel and wiped the remnants of the pill from her tongue. Nancy and I discussed the merits of adding one or two additional pain patches to Mama's chest until the nurse arrived. The nurse had already informed us that the maximum benefit would be gained from three patches and that any additional patches would be superfluous. It didn't matter. As long as the additional patches were not harmful. Our view was that we should do everything humanly possible to make her comfortable.

Of course, Larry saw it differently. Frankly, he was upset that I even spoke to the nurse. As the person in charge, no one should speak to the nurse or the doctor or the delivery guy, or anybody except Larry.

And that's when it happened. The fight with Larry. Had it not been for his daughters, Barbie and Kathy, who I loved and respected, I would have killed him. I never felt such anger, such extreme emotion. I wanted him out of our lives. He confronted me and Nancy and accused us of interfering with my mother's care. He said we were wasting our time applying the pain patches. I told him that I didn't care if it was a waste of time. I wanted to do everything possible to help ease her pain. I was appalled that he did not want to do the same. Did he want her to suffer? Was he upset because it was not his decision? Whatever the cause of his aggravation, it was unprovoked and completely irrational. I had no tolerance for his insanity. I told him to get out of my way. This was my mother. Sleeping with her for the past five or so years did not entitle him to make the final decision regarding her pain medication.

Barbie and Kathy had to restrain me and remove me from the premises. I knew the level of my anger had surpassed his, which is why I allowed them to take me outside. Barbie walked with me, at first outside the apartment and then down to the beach. We walked along the water's edge, the sand beneath our feet and the setting sun on our backs. Barbie did most of the talking, trying to calm me, explaining that she too was often at odds with him. Don't let him get to you, she said. Think about Dah. What would she want us to do right now?

She was right.

The nerve of Larry, to start an argument in front of my mother. What kind of sick bastard was so insecure, so self-centered that he could only focus on his role, his needs, his decision-making capabilities? I resented the lost time with Mama, time which was now being spent on dealing with Larry and his idiotic neuroses.

~ ~ ~

Murder. I hesitate to write the word. It looks so very harsh in black and white. I have verbalized it before. Whispered it in secret telephone conversations with Aunt Yvonne. To Mom's best friend, Nancy Brown Jamison. To my girlfriend, Theresa. To my cousin Ari, especially to my cousin Ari, who could talk to me about anything, no matter how taboo the subject.

The truth of the matter is that I felt Larry helped to kill my mother. There, I've said it. Alas, I do not feel better, and certainly there are those who will now feel worse.

His weapon was a heinous, slow poison of words. Hateful words mixed with loving words to keep her coming back for more. And back she would always come. She was drawn to him, craving his total devotion, his all encompassing adulation. When he succeeded in getting her full attention, the poison seeped slowly from his lips to her heart, making it ache. Then the poison cancer managed its way to her lungs, gradually blocking her air passages, slowing suffocating her, to death.

From the very beginning of their marriage in October of 1989, through the depths of her illness, he tortured her with his cruel rantings and ravings. Some attributed his horrible behavior to his miserable childhood. They blamed his mother, who lingered in and out of sanity in a nursing home, for constantly berating and criticizing him. These childhood experiences presumably caused his erratic and oppressive behavior. I wasn't buying it. There was no excuse for his behavior as far as I was concerned. He was an intelligent adult and should have known better.

Larry's cruel behavior surfaced not long after the wedding. Mama called me sounding distraught. She had been crying. I tried in vain to console her. I couldn't remember the last time I heard my mother cry. This fact alone, the fact that he caused her to cry, upset me to no end. Any man who could do this to my mother was no friend of mine. She was having some financial difficulties with the IRS as a result of the divorce from Bob (her previous spouse). Right after the divorce, Bob decided to file for bankruptcy, leaving Mama solely liable for any and all tax obligations incurred during their marriage. Unfortunately, she knew very little about the situation because much of it involved amounts owed for income earned from Bob's medical practice. Her own practice as a management consultant had barely taken off the ground.

I helped her hire an attorney to untangle the mess, but the IRS was incessant. They went after my mother with a vengeance. I felt helpless as I watched this agency attempt to degrade and demoralize my mother. All I could do was offer verbal support. Eventually, Mama's attorney helped her to reach a settlement with the IRS, but it left her financially ruined. She ultimately had to file for bankruptcy to save herself from complete financial ruin.

Shortly after my mother's encounter with the IRS, the national media reported similar experiences involving other law abiding citizens. The media attention soon caused the federal government to investigate the practices of the IRS. Ultimately, reforms were made to control the agency's ability to harass and terrorize honest and decent people.

Larry knew full well beforehand about Mama's financial problems. Both of them had been married three times before. They shared their former experiences in great detail, long before they decided to marry. But instead of being supportive, he repeatedly accused her of being unable to adequately handle her affairs. The verbal battering was incessant. She said it made her feel like an incompetent fool. The irony of the situation was that he was no financial genius either, as evidenced by his paltry coffers.

He had no right to criticize my mother. He could not possibly understand the hardships she had overcome just to reach this point. In spite of his constant criticisms, within two years of their marriage, she would develop a successful management consultant practice in San Diego. In fact, her success far exceeded his accomplishments. They both worked as management consultants, but because of his inability to relate to people, his practice did not flourish. He may have been credentialed, but she made it happen.

I remember when she landed her first major contract with a large manufacturing concern. She faxed a draft of the agreement to me for review. She didn't want

Larry to know she was sending it because she knew he would be upset. He wouldn't understand why I needed to review documents he had already reviewed. The fact that I was an attorney, a writer and her daughter was irrelevant to him. He needed to control everything.

His possessive and controlling behavior manifested itself in other ways too. Ten months after my mother and Larry were married, mom invited my cousin Ari to San Diego to prepare for her upcoming uterine fibroid surgery by cleansing her body and clearing her mind. Several months later, Ari visited mom again to receive skin treatments from a well-known dermatologist in San Diego whom my mom read about. Larry vehemently complained that in the 300 or so days they had been married, they had only spent 162 days alone at home. He actually counted the days. He neglected to consider that my mother spent many of those days on the road earning a living for the benefit of both of them.

Controlling. Irascible. Murderer.

~ ~ ~

July 23, 1995, Sunday. I woke up this morning at 7:00 a.m. and headed towards my mother's room. I tapped lightly on the door. After hearing no response, I walked into the bedroom. Larry was half awake, but he didn't say anything when I walked over to Mama's side of the bed. I picked up her right hand. It was cold as ice. My heart began to race. The coldness frightened me. I gently rubbed her hands to warm them, thinking this would help. I glanced back at Larry who was lying next to her, staring blankly at the ceiling. He did not even bother to look in my direction. I said nothing to him, he said nothing to me.

I placed my mother's hand down by her side and put my hand on her chest. Her chest moved up and down beneath my hand. I felt a small sense of relief. I walked out of the room into the hall bathroom, shut the door and buried my head in a towel to muffle the sounds of my tears. I did not want to wake the rest of the household. Let them rest I thought. It was going to be a difficult day. I knew that this would be the day my mother would die.

I left the bathroom and walked down the hall to see who was awake. Cathy had gone to the airport to pick up the boys. She wanted them to be there when Dah passed. We told her that they should remember Dah as she was when she was vibrant and alive, not like this, weak and dying in her bed. The boys had their memories of Dah taking long walks along the beach or talking on the phone with the headsets in her office or preparing Christmas dinner with everyone gathered around. But once Cathy made a decision, there was no turning back. She kissed Mama goodbye and told her, "I'll be back with the boys." That was the last time she saw Mama alive.

I found Benji sprawled out on a blanket sound asleep on the floor in the living room, his clothes neatly folded on his bag in a corner. Good old Brother Ben. So easy to accommodate.

My stepsisters and Nancy had not yet arrived for the day's vigil. Unable to find someone to talk to, I walked out onto the patio and sat down on the chair, staring out at the bay. It was a beautiful sunny day. The fog had already lifted from the water, making a way for clear blue skies. I wished my mother could share the view with me. It was a perfect day to be alive.

When I walked back into the room to check on my mother again, I noticed that she had a piece of watermelon stuck in one of her front teeth. It seemed like she was trying to remove it with her tongue. Even though she was near death, I wanted to make sure she was as comfortable as possible. I asked her if she wanted me to brush her teeth and she just moaned. I interpreted that as a "yes." I flossed and brushed her teeth while fighting back the tears, knowing that Larry was watching and thinking that it was all so unnecessary. From the corner of the bed, he grumbled, "I don't know why you even bother at this point, she has no idea what you're doing." I did not bother to respond.

I knew better. My mother seemed much more content when I finished brushing and flossing her teeth. At least she stopped sucking at them.

Larry couldn't possibly understand. This was something shared between a mother and daughter. I remember once long ago when my grandmother was ill, it prompted my mother and I to make a bargain. If one of us became incapacitated, we promised to take care of all the little personal things, like tweezing the little hairs from our chin. I kept my promise to Mama and remembered to tweeze the three little hairs from her chin.

July 23, 1995, Sunday afternoon. I went back into the room to sit next to Mama for a while. She looked so peaceful. I picked up her hand and began to sing a few verses from the song "Amazing Grace." I knew she liked the song as much as I did. My children said I was "relaxing" whenever I sang it. To my utter amazement, my mother began to moan in rhythm with my singing. It was as though she was singing along with me.

> *Amazing Grace, how sweet the sound*
> *That saved a wretch like me*
> *I once was lost*

But now am found
Was blind but now I see.

Twas Grace that taught my heart to fear
And Grace my fears relieved
How precious did that Grace appear
The hour I first believed.

Amazing Grace has set me free
To touch, to taste, to feel
The wonders of accepting love
Have made me whole and real.

Amazing Grace, Negro Spiritual

It was just a matter of time now. The morphine drip did as promised and eased the pain. The nurse said that my mother had slipped into a coma shortly after we administered the drip last night. She surmised that Mama would probably die today. I wondered exactly when she had slipped into a coma? Did I miss the moment? Was I in the room? Did she know she was going?

Still in partial denial, I thought the nurse was wrong about this. I assumed that comatose patients did not respond to external stimuli. Didn't my mother moan contentedly when I cleaned her teeth this morning? She couldn't be in a coma. And she moaned the tune of Amazing Grace when I sang for her this afternoon. If she had been in a coma, she would not have been able to hum along to the song.

But the nurse was right. Mama slipped into a coma and died on July 23, 1995, Sunday night at 9:17 p.m.

As she took her parting breath, the cool ocean breeze sent the sweet aroma of the incense from the nightstand through the bedroom air and into the peaceful night. We all sat on Mama's bed. Larry, his daughters Kathy and Barbie, Benji, Nancy Brown Jamison and me. My sister Cathy was the only one missing. She was on the highway driving back from the airport with her three boys.

Mama's final gaze locked upon my stepsister Kathy the moment she took her last breath. It seemed as though Mama was trying to tell her something. My mother knew that Kathy had a keen sense of perception, even beyond the physical present. Kathy later told me that my mother felt she could not let go until she knew that I was all right. Kathy promised Mama that she would make sure I was all right and that Mama should feel free to go.

I felt guilty that Mom's parting thoughts were concerns about me. But I had difficulty letting her go and she obviously sensed it. The loss of a parent is a very deep wound, a wound that heals but leaves lasting scars. A wound that breaks open when you least expect it. At the sight of yellow roses, or when your daughter falls and scars her knees, or when you look in the mirror.

I also felt guilty for missing so much of my mother's life. I didn't see her enough when she was alive. I should have taken the time to see her more often. Now it was too late. I had taken so much for granted.

Sorry I never told you
all I wanted to say.
Now it's too late to hold you
cause you've flown away,
So far away.

Never had I imagined
living without your smile.
Feeling and knowing you hear me
it keeps me alive,
Alive.

And I know you're shining down on me
from heaven.
Like so many friends we've lost along
the way.
And I know eventually we'll be together
One sweet day.

One Sweet Day, by Mariah Carey

I felt like screaming, like running away and screaming. The apartment seemed empty without Mom's life force, even though the family was still there. I slept out in the living room on the convertible couch. Cathy slept on the floor in the back den, busying herself by organizing Mom's things. Benji slept on the floor in the living room. I don't know where the boys slept, though they were probably on the floor in the den with their mother.

We all stayed around for a day or two, no one wanting to abandon Larry at this difficult time. We had a family meeting to decide how, when, and where to do the memorial service. We knew Mom wanted to be cremated. That was the only easy decision. Larry wanted to have the service in San Diego, where they lived together for the past six years. My brother, sister and I wanted to have the service in Birmingham, Alabama, where our entire family was located.

We also needed to decide who was going to plan and organize the service. My brother, sister and I thought that that Aunt Yvonne should take care of the arrangements. Larry thought he should make the final arrangements because he was the surviving spouse. I didn't think that Larry should dictate how to handle our family affairs just because he slept with my mother for the past five years.

We finally decided to hold two services, one in Birmingham within the next two weeks which Aunt Yvonne would organize and one in San Diego around Christmas for those of us who could afford to fly back. Of course, Larry would organize that service.

I didn't know exactly how, but I had to get away. During one of our conversations, HW suggested that I get away for a few days with him to his beach house in the Hamptons. I told no one where I was going. We spent four days walking along the beach and talking. He took my mind far away. When I thought of my mother's death, he helped me manage the harsh reality of her absence. It soon became evident that HW's purpose in my life was to get me though this difficult time.

When I returned to my own apartment, the impact of the situation finally hit me. I looked at the phone and realized that I would no longer hear my mother's voice on the other end of the line. To think that I could no longer share my thoughts with her flung me into a mild depression. But there was little time to wallow in self pity. I had to focus and prepare myself and the children for the funeral. I systematically began to attack my list of things to do. It was an automatic defense mechanism. I called my office to let them know I would be returning to work on Monday, the day after my mother's service. I needed the distraction. I was determined to get through this.

Shortly before Mama died, I was scheduled to reunite with my best friend from high school, Nancy. I had not seen Nancy for years until recently. We were scheduled to get together on August 5th, the same day as my mother's memorial service. When I contacted her to let her know that I would not be able to get together, she wrote me a letter. Enclosed in the letter was a poem she had previously written during her own struggle with cancer. She gave me permission to use the poem in mom's eulogy. Her words of support gave me the faith to carry me through those most difficult days. Her letter read as follows.

August 3, 1995,

Dear Terri,

My heartfelt sympathy goes to you and all your family. Although I haven't seen your mother in 20 years, I remember her gentleness and caring nature. Even at age 17, a time of precarious parent-child relationships, she trusted you and believed in you. I remember how she would always ask me how things were and she always had time to listen, to smile and add words of support and encouragement. But most of all, I remember how much you loved her. I can only imagine the sadness and pain you are carrying with you now as you bid her goodbye. I hope that the poem brings you a bit of comfort. The words are mine, but the message of faith and hope belongs to everyone. The same angels who saved me from my own cancer have surely swept her lovely spirit up on their wings to a world where she will continue to touch the lives of those in need. She's with you now as she always has been.

All my love,

Nancy

August 4, 1995. My mother always said she would come back. She kept her promise. I had my first dream the night before the memorial service. The images in the dream were very clear. Cathy, Benji and I were driving in a small car on our way to see Mother Dear, my maternal grandmother. When we arrived at the house she was standing in the doorway wearing her Sunday best. She beckoned me into the house. Cathy and Benji waited in the car for me.

When I went inside the house, Mother Dear pointed to the table and said, "Your mother left these scrolls for you. She wanted you to open them and read them for the rest of the children." I opened the first scroll which was addressed to my brother Benji. It said, "Dear Benji, I want you to know that I love you very much. I will carry you with me in my heart forever."

The second scroll was addressed to Cathy and the message was identical. The third scroll bore Larry's name. When I opened the scroll it was blank. All of a sudden, Larry appeared out of nowhere and shouted that I had erased his scroll.

He raised his hand to hit me and I blocked the hit. When we made contact, he disappeared.

Mother Dear told me in a sweet calming voice, "Never you mind honey, go ahead and open the last scroll." The last scroll had my name on it, but I couldn't open it without destroying it. Mother Dear told me not to force it open. "Don't worry baby," she said, "we don't need to open it. Your message will come later." I woke up feeling lost.

My mother also came to Cathy the night before the memorial service. Cathy dreamt that she was sorting through Mom's clothes and suddenly Mom appeared. Cathy asked her if she needed her clothes and Mama told her, "Silly girl, I don't need those clothes where I'm going." Cathy asked her where she was going and Mama told her that she had some people to take care of and some things to do.

"But Mama," Cathy said, "does this mean that you are not coming back? We need you here. Are you sure it's time for you to go? Why are you leaving so soon?"

In her dream, Cathy put her head down on her pillow and started to cry. She asked Mama how to find her in case she needed her. "I'll always be right here next to you," Mama said, "lying right here next to you."

August 5, 1995, Saturday. Today is my mother's memorial service. If ever I needed the Lord to carry me, it was now. So many thoughts swirling around my head.

Mama is gone. I need to finish the Eulogy. The kids are confused and emotional. Chris wet the bed for the first time since he was trained two years ago. Nicole's birthday party is next Saturday in Central Park. I start my new job as General Counsel on Monday. The bills are starting to pile up. My apartment lease expires at the end of the month. I can't sleep. Mama is gone.

Cathy and I walked up to the front pew of the Church with our five children and quietly took our place with the rest of the family. We were five minutes late. Someone had given us the wrong directions and we drove around in circles looking for the church. I was going crazy inside the hot steamy car. Impatient with no sense of direction.

We were only five minutes late and yet Aunt Yvonne had already instructed Reverend Wilson to begin the service. As a school teacher, Yvonne was accustomed to sticking to schedules. The clock struck 8:30 a.m. and it was time to start the service, no ifs, ands or buts about it. Cathy did not seem at all concerned. She led us to the front of the church as though she owned the place.

Now, on top of all my other concerns, I fretted that we were late for our own mother's funeral.

I was honored to deliver Mom's eulogy. After input from both Nancy, my best friend from high school and Theresa, my best friend from law school, my speech was ready. I wore a simple black dress with an empire waist and black sandals with a one inch heel. I wore my hair down and pulled back away from my face.

Reverend Wilson nodded for me to take my place at the podium in front of the church. I was the first person to speak. All my public speaking experience, before judges and juries, before executives and colleagues, did not prepare me for this moment. Everyone watched as I walked up to the podium and adjusted the microphone. I said the Serenity prayer, "God, grant me the serenity to accept the things I can not change, the courage to change the things I can, and the wisdom to know the difference." Then I took three deep breaths. These rituals normally carried me through, but this time I had trouble calming my nerves. One more deep breath. Look up. Now speak.

I did not want to lose my composure in the middle of the eulogy. After all, Aunt Yvonne expected poise and eloquence, even during this difficult moment. I did my best, but paused on more than one occasion to regain my composure. As I looked around the church, I found the faces of my sister and brother, both of them were crying with me. Cathy made a gesture as though she was going to come up to the podium to help me regain my strength. But I waved in her direction as if to say it would be all right. Then I heard my cousin James say, "Give her strength Lord, help her through." And so He did. The rest of the congregation said "Amen." Then I knew it would be all right. Somehow I managed to deliver the rest of my words. Benji later told me that it was the first time he had cried since Mama was diagnosed with Cancer. I was grateful that my words touched him.

I looked in the pew behind the family and saw Theresa, my best friend from law school. We met on the first day of law school standing in line to register for classes. Her last name started with a "B" and mine with an "A," so we ending up standing together in many of the same lines. We were instantly drawn to each other. We were both talkative. We were both outgoing. We even looked alike.

After we completed the registration process, we spent the afternoon shopping for notebooks, pens, paper, toiletries and other items we deemed essential for survival. As it turned out, not only were we in all of the same classes, but our rooms were located near each other in the same dormitory building, Johnson Hall, where most of the "One L" students were housed. I knew from the beginning that this would be a life long friendship, no matter where our lives took us.

Theresa's life led her to her husband Vernon who she married in August of 1982. I was one of the bridesmaids, along with three of her sisters and two other close friends.

The morning of her wedding she and I got our nails done together. After we left the salon, we decided to sit and relax over a glass of wine, for just a minute. We sat down and started talking and before we knew it, two o'clock had come and gone. The wedding was at four. We were scheduled to return to the house no later than two. We ran to the car and pulled up to the house where Theresa's mom was standing on the stoop waiting for us. "Girls, where have you been?" she said in a high pitched voice, waving us into the house. She was a tiny little woman and she made quite a sight standing on the stoop waving and screaming.

Miraculously, we made it to the church on time for the wedding which went off without a hitch. A chance encounter at her wedding would completely change my life fifteen years later.

Somehow, Theresa found a way to attend my mother's funeral, even though she was working full time and married with two children. She had another commitment on the same day, but she was determined to come to the funeral to give me moral support.

She helped me finish writing Mom's eulogy, she listened as I practiced delivering the words and she came to the church to support me. She stayed as long as she could, then slipped out of the church, waving farewell as she left.

~ ~ ~

The Eulogy

> On behalf of the entire family, I would like to thank you all for coming to celebrate the life of a woman I am fortunate enough to call my mother. She was no ordinary woman by any stretch of the imagination. From the moment of her birth, Amanda touched the lives of all those who knew her. Beyond her physical beauty and her intellectual brilliance, she possessed a spiritual love that she shared without hesitation, without qualifications, without limitations. Whether you knew her as Mama, Amanda, Dah, Auntie Lala, Baby, Lover, Wife, Colleague or Friend, she gave you her all.
>
> The essence of her being could not be contained, it could not be held back, for she shared her love regardless of who you were. You did not have to be a blood relative or an important political figure or a wealthy individual to gain her love. You just had to <u>be</u>. Our memories of Amanda are filled with the people she loved,

weaving in and out of our lives. Sometimes they needed a place to live, a shoulder to lean on. Mama would always extend herself-willingly. God knows she was our rock, she was our strength, she was our guiding light. It is not easy to accept the passing of one so dear. But a dear friend wrote a poem about an angel like Amanda which I'd like to share with you.

*I'll tell you a secret
to all who care to hear
Was whispered by an angel
Fell like stardust in my ear*

*She spoke of loving moments
The ones you let slip by
And taught me how to hold them
in your heart so they don't die*

*She spoke of counting blessings
how simple it could be
Happiness is nothing more than
all God's given me*

*Her message came as beauty
wrapped in ribbon that was love
She sang an operetta
she danced and kissed a dove*

*I listened so intently
never wanting it to end
But she was needed elsewhere
to help a certain friend*

*She had just one last secret
to me she would impart
It will stay with me forever
it has lightened so my heart*

She told me of the angels
that live amongst us here
To guide and guard and keep us
to calm our deepest fear

So perhaps you'll say I've dreamed it
some imaginations run
Well as far as my uncertainty
I'll tell you I have none

These angels are amongst us
God's cherubs from above
And they spend their days,
finding ways
of weaving life with love.

N.S.B. 1995

Thank you Mama for weaving all of our lives with your love.

* * *

A Poem for Amanda by Brenda Gipson

Regal,
Beautiful, sensual, thinking Amanda,
Modeling true Black womanhood,
Moving gracefully,
Quietly ruffling leaves, flowers and spirits as she
passes,
Spirit woman,
Commanding her space as she moves through this
world,

Bringing delight, warm summer night breezes, and amber light.

Amanda,
Touching my soul,
Embracing, affirming, soothing, consoling my being.
Wise African woman,
Teaching, healing, nurturing in the Old Way.

Amanda,
In two pony-tails, Black southern girl,
Innocent and yet knowing, knowing,
Knowing about time and space,
About purpose and being,
About how it all works.
Analytical, deep, deep sistafriend.

Amanda,
Beckoning me:
"Come on over, child,
Sit down and have a cup of tea,
Got somthin' to tell you about life, livin' and lovin"
Reaching out and gently grabbing my hand,
Whispering unknown truths in my ear,
Sharing her secrets,
Letting me cop a peek into her world,
Connecting me back,
Hooking me up,
Guiding me into my own
Womanist essence.

Amanda,
Pushing the limits,
Causing me to think, to reflect, to be conscious—
"Please don't let her catch me sleeping."
Watchful eye,
Watchful eye Amanda,
Watching me, watching her, watching me,
Making me feel humbled to be in her presence,
Feeling unworthy of her loving attention,
But grateful none-the-less.
Making me want to be like her,
Like Harriet, like Sojourner, Nefertiti and Isis.

Amanda
 Ancient
  African
   Warrior-Queen
    Goddess.

I recognize you, and
Blessed am I
To be in your presence.

* * *

A Memorial Resolution by the Honorable Juanita M. McDonald
<u>Fifty-fifth Assembly District</u>

WHEREAS, The passing of a distinguished California resident and doctor of clinical psychology, Amanda Fouther, whose good deeds earned her the respect and admiration of her colleagues and the countless individuals whose lives she touched, brought immense sorrow and loss to people throughout the State of California; and

WHEREAS, Dr. Amanda Fouther, a native of Birmingham, passed away at her home in San Diego on July 23, 1995, following a brief illness; and

WHEREAS, She was educated in the public schools of Birmingham and went on to receive Registered Nurse and Bachelor of Science degrees in nursing from St. Francis School of Nursing in Ohio and Tuskegee University, respectively; and

WHEREAS, She later received Bachelor of Science and Master of Science degrees in psychology from St. Lawrence University in New York and obtained a Doctor of Philosophy degree in clinical psychology from Syracuse University; and

WHEREAS, Dr. Fouther's primary professional experiences included her services as a consultant to organizations, and her major focuses were diversity and group dynamics; and

WHEREAS, Her clientele included organizations in the United States, Europe, Central America, and Africa; and

WHEREAS, The memory of Dr. Amanda Fouther will live not only through her personal, professional, public and civic achievements and her contributions to the State of California and the world, but also for the inspiration that she provided to those individuals who were fortunate enough to know her; and

WHEREAS, Dr. Fouther leaves to cherish her memory, her husband, Dr. Lawrence Porter; her son, Arthur Benjamin Tiddle, her four daughters, Terri D. Austin, Catheryn Longino, Barbara Springthorpe, and Katherine Dimambro; her nine grandchildren, Isaiah, David and Daniel Longino; Liam and Josh Springthorpe; Heather and Alexander Dimambro; and Nicole and Christopher Brown; her brother, Willie Fouther; and her two sisters, Yvonne Green and Adrienne Lee; now, therefore, be it

RESOLVED BY ASSEMBLY MEMBER JUANITA M. McDONALD, That she expresses her deepest regret at the passing of Dr. Amanda Fouther, and extends her heartfelt sympathy to her bereaved family and friends.

~ ~ ~

After my mother's memorial service, the recovery process slowly began to take place. The sympathy cards and letters were particularly helpful in the healing process. One by one, over and over, I read them. The words carried me through the difficult days and nights.

August 1995,

Terri,

On behalf of the Bailey family, know that our prayers are with you at this difficult time. Believe me we know how you're feeling, there is not a day that passes that we don't all think about mom!
Just steer your thoughts to what's positive and loving.
Drake and Karen Harrison
(Theresa's sister)

~ ~ ~

August 1995,

Dearest Terri (Nicole & Christopher too),

You'll never know how truly sorry I am and how deeply I feel for you at this very difficult time in your life. I know I cannot possibly imagine what you are going through, but one thing I do know is how very special you are to me as one of my truest friends and how very much I care about you and your wonderful children, and that if there is anything at all I can do for you at this time or any time, please let me help you through. I love you Terri and I'm here if you need me.

With much love,

Angie (My closest friend in New York)
(Eric and Renny too)
XXX

~ ~ ~

Dear Terri,

We were so sorry to hear about your mom. You are in our hearts and prayers. We can't even bear the thought of losing our moms. Please be strong and find a way to understand.

We love you Terri. You're family. You and the kids. We are here for you if you need us, whenever you need us.

Love, Hugs and Kisses,

Sam and Dana (Angie's sister)
xxoo

~ ~ ~

August 22, 1995

Dear Terri,

Dana told me about your mother—and I want you to know my heart goes out to you. I know it is not easy—especially at your age with your young children.

I admire you so much, and your mother must have been and continues to be so proud of you. She must have been a wonderful mother to have you as a daughter.

Your spirit is so generous and evidenced in your smile, your eyes, your way with others—and when I think of the courage you've already shown in your life and your determination—I know how she must have and continues to feel about you.

I say "continues" because I don't really believe that death is the end of anyone—Her being and her love for you and your children continues.

I know your grief and mourning for her are a natural and necessary response to this separation—I still carry my mother in my heart—I think of her many times a day and talk to her and feel her love. In the Egyptian Book of the Dead, which is really the Book of Coming Forth By Day—one of the oldest healing texts known, it says "What is remembered lives."

I am enclosing an imagery exercise which many have loved—which sometime further down the road, might be helpful to you. It is from the book Healing Visualizations, Reaching Health through Imagery, by Gerald Epstein. He is the man I have studied with for 4 years.

It is called <u>Change of Heart</u>. It's intention is to remove grief. You simply sit in a chair, close your eyes and breathe out slowly three times. See your heart. Zip open your chest, and take out your heart. Clean it gently and afterwards, throw it into the cosmos. Retrieve it from the cosmos and see that it is a crystal heart. Invite all the people you love to enter it, smiling and bright, be aware that you *can see them there always. Put your crystal heart back into place, zip up your chest and then open your eyes, knowing that you grief is relieved.*

It may be too soon for this—but someday it might be helpful. But for now, Craig joins me, in just letting you know that our love goes out to you and your dear family.

Much Love,

Suzanne Greason (Angie's sister-in-law)

~ ~ ~

The day after mom's memorial service I dreamt that I was floating on my back out into the ocean. There were lots of people on the beach, but Mama stood out in the crowd. She was waving to me. Not to come back. Just waving to me. I waved back and floated into the arms of someone who was waiting there for me, in the middle of the ocean. I could not see the face of the person holding me afloat. The water was warm and shallow. I felt safe and warm.

August 7, 1995, Monday. Two days after my mother's memorial service, I started my new job as General Counsel of a large subsidiary of the Company where I worked. It was a big promotion for me, Mama would have been very proud. I was virtually certain that before she died she understood that I had gotten the job, although lingering doubts crossed my mind. When I walked into the reception area of the new office my first thought was, "If only Mama could see me now."

I assumed that she knew I got the promotion because I mentioned it to her a couple of times over the phone when I first received the offer. And she overheard my discussion with my stepsister Barbie when I told Barbie that I accepted the position. Not to mention the fact that her last coherent words to me were, "Terri, I'm so proud of you."

But in case I had any lingering doubts about her knowledge, she provided me with a clear sign, thoroughly convincing me that she knew I got the job and thoroughly convincing me that it is possible to communicate after death. I walked into my new office on the 21st floor of the Wall Street office. It was the largest office I had ever occupied, with four large windows. The carpet colors matched the curtains, the plush green ones with the matching tie back sashes. When I saw the curtains I remembered telling Mama that you knew you had arrived at the

Company when you got an office decorated with plush green curtains, with the matching tie back sashes.

The desk was grade A issue, solid wood with a glass top for protection. The office also contained a couch, coffee table, three guest chairs and a book case. My eyes were immediately drawn to the top of the bookcase. Perched on the top of the book case was a vase of a dozen yellow roses. I could not believe my eyes. My mother's favorite flowers were yellow roses. We had purchased a dozen yellow roses for her every week since she became ill. I never mentioned this to anyone at the Company. Who could have sent me yellow roses? Did they know that these were my mother's favorite flower?

I slowly walked into the office and placed my purse on the desk. I walked over to the vase of roses and admired their beauty. I located the little card placed in the middle of the arrangement and carefully removed it. The card read, "Congratulations on your new position. I know you will be a great success. Ed." Ed was the outside attorney who I used to handle my litigation matters at the Company. He and I had worked together for five years and in the process I had grown close to him and his family. His wife contracted cancer a few years earlier and he understood the struggles I recently experienced. But Ed had no idea that my mother loved yellow roses. There is no doubt in my mind that my mother, in her own way, sent a message to me through those yellow roses. The message was, "Yes, Terri. I know about your promotion and I am very, very proud of you. Congratulations on your new position."

One month later, I dreamt that Aunt Yvonne, Mama and I were at a party with mostly children. We were sitting out on the porch at a small table playing a card game. Mama was teasing us and telling us that she had a good hand, but she wouldn't let us see her cards. I was smiling and begging Mama to show her hand. Aunt Yvonne sat quietly with her arms folded, just watching. Different children kept coming up to Mama to talk to her. She would say a few words, laugh a little bit and then the children would run back and play. Then my mother said, "It's time for me to go."

I asked my mother if it was all right to hug her goodbye. Somehow, I realized that if I hugged her she would disappear. She smiled and said, "Of course you can hug me, honey."

When I reached out to embrace Mama, Aunt Yvonne sat up straight and said, "No, if you do that she will disappear."

"But Aunt Yvonne," I said, "she already told us that she was leaving, I need to hold her." When I hugged her, the embrace was real, so real that it woke me up from my sleep. I had no doubt that my mother had been there with me that night. But with the embrace she vanished into thin air. I turned around to see that Aunt Yvonne had disappeared too.

~ ~ ~

October 8, 1995, Sunday. The phone rang. I had an eerie feeling about the call. After so many calls about my mother, I had learned to hate answering late night phone calls. The thought of bad news was too much to bear.

The kids and I had just returned from an apple picking trip in Westchester County, just north of New York City. Every October millions of New York City residents were compelled to make the trek north so that their children could enjoy the great outdoors, the spectacular array of colors of red, yellow, orange and green leaves painted across the skyline and the smell of fresh donuts and hot apple cider. Not to mention the incredibly long lines, the lack of parking and the incessant wasps hovering everywhere.

"Did everyone have a good time?" I asked as we walked through the door. I knew the answer, but it was reassuring to hear. As long as their answer was, "yes," and it always was, I didn't mind the hassles associated with the trip. I cherished taking them on these types of excursions. It's what made life memorable. I loved watching Christopher pick up apple after apple, taking one bite out of each apple and throwing them all back on the ground. I knew that at the end of the day he would wind up with a bloated tummy from taking one too many bites. It was just as amusing to watch Nicole pick up apple after apple, discarding most of them because of some minor imperfection. Later, at the end of the day, Nicole would show off her perfect basket of perfect apples. I tried to keep up with them. By the end of the day I was exhausted beyond belief. The utter joy of watching them embrace their world.

I thought about my mother as I watched Nicole and Chris running through the apple orchards. During one of my visits near the end, she told me that she would miss seeing the children grow up. Until then, I had thought mostly about how I would miss her presence. I had not considered her perspective, how much she would miss of the children's lives, all of our lives. It was a painful thought. Through a stream of tears, I told her that she would be able to watch over them, no matter where she was. I trusted that she was watching over them as they ran through the apple orchards scrupulously picking apples.

Sometimes I imagined her with me when the wind blew the leaves into a mini tornado, right before my very eyes, or a flower peaked out of tall grass from nowhere, all alone, or a bird stopped on a perch right next to me, to sing a song just for me. Mama always told me to slow down and enjoy the journey along the way, for the journey is way too brief. Maybe these signs were her ways of communicating that message to me.

By the time we got home from the apple orchards, the kids were exhausted. Christopher didn't even wake up when I first took him from the car and carried him up to the apartment. Nicole, on the other hand, woke up and wouldn't go back to sleep. Just as well, I thought, carrying two sleeping children would have been difficult, though I have done it when my supernatural single mom power kicked in. But after the phone rang, I needed her to lie down and go to sleep so that I could concentrate on the phone call.

The call was from my cousin Michael. I was right, the news was very, very bad. He said, "Terri, I don't know how else to say this except to come right out and say it. Aunt Yvonne died today."

I was dumbfounded. I didn't know what to say. "Michael please, don't tell me that. What happened?"

"She died of a massive heart attack while she was sitting on her bed doing some school work. She just died. They found her lying on her bed with her fists clenched. They said that it happened quickly."

Michael and I talked a few minutes more. He said he would call me back to give me details about the funeral arrangements. He thought that the service would probably be held the following weekend. I wanted to talk to my cousin Ari. She would know everything. Something did not seem right. Michael was holding back. I could tell that he felt there was more to Aunt Yvonne's death than it appeared. Once I speak to Ari, I thought, this whole thing would make more sense.

I quickly bathed Nicole and Christopher and put them to bed so that I could speak freely with Ari. I tracked her down on her cell phone, which she carried with her at all times. "What happened Ari?" I asked.

Ari began to tell the story, backtracking in time. Uncle Bernard called at 7:00 p.m. to inform Aunt Adrienne about her sister Yvonne's death. Andre and Ava (Yvonne's grandchildren) had tried to get into the house at 3:00 p.m. Every Sunday afternoon, they stopped by to visit their grandmother. Uncle Bernard (Yvonne's husband) said that he was in the den and that Aunt Yvonne was in her bedroom for the entire afternoon. Yet, when Andre and Ava came by the house at 3:00, Uncle Bernard claimed he did not hear the door bell ring. His car was parked in the driveway the whole time, so they knew he was there. When no one answered the door, Andre and Ava left.

By the time the ambulance arrived that evening, Yvonne had been dead for hours. No one understood why Bernard waited so long to call the ambulance.

We questioned when he first learned of the heart attack. It seemed unusual that he could be in the same house with his wife for hours and not interact with her all afternoon. If he had taken faster action, perhaps Aunt Yvonne's death could have been avoided. Was his neglect intentional? Aunt Adrienne suggested that the coroner perform an autopsy, but Uncle Bernard vehemently objected. In the end, there was no autopsy performed.

I thought to myself, our Angel of Mercy has literally died of a broken heart. No one could tell us otherwise. Aunt Yvonne's heart was weak, but had it not been for my mother's illness and death, Aunt Yvonne would still be with us today. It was simply too much grief for her to bear. Her baby sister, the one she had nurtured from the moment she was born through her dying days, was gone. Now they were both gone, vanished into thin air, just as my dream foretold.

I talked to Aunt Yvonne half a dozen times in the weeks following my mother's death. She was not quite the same. In an effort to comfort her, I told Aunt Yvonne that no one had sacrificed as much as she had to take care of Mama. I was unable to console her. Aunt Yvonne's death certificate said massive coronary, but in my humble opinion, she died of a broken heart.

~ ~ ~

Except from Aunt Yvonne's Funeral Program

>Green, Yvonne Fouther, age 64, passed away October 8, 1995. Yvonne Fouther was the oldest of three daughters with five brothers who blessed the union of the late Willie, Sr. and Annie Mae Ellis Fouther. She attended Birmingham Public Schools and graduated from A.H. Parker High School. She received the B.A. degree from Talladega College, the M.A. degree in Reading from the University of Chicago, and the Certificate of Advance Graduate Studies from Johns Hopkins University. She worked for 15 years in the Birmingham Public Schools, Council Elementary and Graymont Elementary, 18 years in Vestavia Hills Public Schools, Pizitz Middle School. She had begun her 4th year at Miles College. Throughout her professional career, she was involved in all facets of reading instruction. A loving family survives to honor and cherish her memory: husband, Bernard Green; son, Andre L. McShan; sister, Adrienne F. Lee; brother, Willie Fouther, Jr. (II); grandchildren, Andre L. McShan, II and Ava Yvonne McShan; several nieces, nephews and grand-nieces and grand-nephews, along with many other relatives and friends. Memorial service will be on Friday, October 13, at 1:00 p.m. at St. Mark's Episcopal Church, 228 Dennison Ave. S.W., Birmingham. Father Edward Wilson officiating. In lieu of flowers, please make contributions to "The American Heart Association."

Aunt Yvonne wrote at least three letters the day before she died, one to Nancy Brown Jamison (my mother's best friend), one to my daughter Nicole and one to my son Christopher. Each of them was postmarked on Monday, October 9th, the day after she died. She must have taken them to the mailbox late Saturday or early Sunday morning. One week earlier, Nicole had written a letter to Aunt Yvonne to "cheer her up." Aunt Yvonne encouraged the children to write letters. She always wrote back.

On Monday, the day after Aunt Yvonne died, Nicole begged me to look into the mailbox for a return letter. I assumed that if Aunt Yvonne had written a letter, it would have already arrived. To placate Nicole, everyday that week I checked the mailbox for a letter from Aunt Yvonne. As each day passed, I didn't know how to explain to Nicole that Aunt Yvonne probably did not have a chance to write back before she died.

On Thursday, as we left the apartment headed for the airport to attend Aunt Yvonne's funeral, Nicole said, "Look in the mailbox Mommy, I know Aunt Yvonne wrote me back, I just know she did." We looked in the mailbox and, as I expected, there was no letter. I tried hard to put the thought out of Nicole's mind, but she continued to believe that her letter would come.

When we returned from the funeral on Sunday, again Nicole asked me to look in the mailbox for a letter from Aunt Yvonne. Again, I did not know what to say. I grabbed the huge pile of mail out of the box and began thumbing through the junk mail and the bills. My fingers paused, my heart stopped. There, in the midst of the pile, were two letters from Aunt Yvonne, one addressed to Nicole and one addressed to Christopher. The back of the envelopes had little red and white teddy bear stickers. The letters were postmarked the day after she died.

Dear Nicole,

I was so happy to hear from you! Thank you so much for thinking about me.

We have had some bad weather here. Opal, a hurricane, hit our area and schools have been closed for two days—that's the bad thing. The good thing is that all the growing things are green again. My roses are beautiful and each time I cut one I think of you. I will be so happy when you can come back again!

Please say hello to Mommy for me and give her a big hug and kiss.

I want you to write me again as soon as you have the time. Tell me everything about school, your teacher, your new friends and what you are doing away from school that you like a lot. I will be looking to hear from you.

Hope you like the new house! Be sweet and remember that I miss you and I love you very much!

Hugs and Kisses

Aunt Yvonne

~ ~ ~

Christopher,

You will have to ask Mommy to read this card to you, but that is o.k. Now that you are a big boy and in school you will very soon be able to read for yourself. Won't that be fun!

I hope you are having fun at school each and every day! I miss you and plan to see you, Mommy and Nicole very soon.

Please write to me when you have time and remember to be a good boy.

Love and Kisses

Aunt Yvonne

~ ~ ~

Aunt Yvonne also mailed a letter to my mother's best friend Nancy on the same day. The letter to Nancy was revealing, but it could not have foretold the tragic event that followed the next day.

Nancy,

Please know how much I sincerely appreciate your consistent thoughtfulness. I love all the picture-cards, and especially the one of HW and Terri…thank you!

The school year is progressing much too fast for me, midterms are only a week away. It seems the students were just entering my classroom a few days ago. They are by far the best students I've had since beginning my work at Miles. The work ethic appears in place, there is a more positive attitude towards school/learning and they seem more goal-directed.

I should be very excited, but quite frankly I'm not. This year, so far, has been very hard. Everything requires more effort than I've been willing to give. The lonely emptiness I feel at times is most unbearable. I always realized life without Amanda would be difficult...it is even worse than I imagined. Trying to adjust to the loss presented by her death will be a long, drawn-out struggle.

Opal was devastating to many parts of our area including some here in B'ham. You know, Southerners can't cope very with severe weather changes. Everything slows to a stop and our schools have been closed for two days. Electric power is still out in many homes including Ava's. Since she is unable to do without her curling wand and other "necessities," she has been with us the past two days. It is different to say the least, to have a girl around.

Please say hello to Bill for me. I do very much look forward to meeting him. Always remember, in spite of my apparent negligence, that you and your friendship are very important to me. Besides, hug withdrawal is not at all easy! I think of you a lot!

Love and hugs,

Yvonne

Aunt Yvonne died the next day.

~ ~ ~

October 20, 1995. HW and I walked into Mount Sinai Hospital, into the Andrews Pavilion entrance as directed. We asked the attendant at the door for directions to the out-patient clinic. "Go down the hall and take the elevators on the left to the third floor," he told us. I held tightly onto HW's arm. I was feeling nauseous, week and apprehensive.

When we arrived to the third floor, we were directed to a small room to complete the paperwork. There was a woman behind the desk sitting in front of a computer. There were two chairs in front of the desk where she directed us to sit. She handed me a barrage of forms to complete and began asking us questions. At first her demeanor was rigid, but she immediately warmed up to me.

"Is this your first time here honey?" she asked forming a little smile at the corners of her mouth, clearly sensing my anxiety.

"Yes," I said, finding it difficult to utter even the smallest words.

"Don't worry, the procedure is swift and painless. You will be out of here and back on your feet in no time," the lady behind the desk told me.

I managed to force a tiny smile and continued to complete the paperwork in front of me. Name, Address, Phone Number, Next of Kin…I read the words aloud, "Next of Kin," I stopped for a second to contemplate the answer. My father had just died of a heart attack in May the year before. My mother had just died of cancer in July. My mother's oldest sister had just died of a heart attack two weeks earlier. For the life of me, I could not think who to list as my next of kin.

As I stared at the piece of paper in front of me, my eyes began to fill with water and overflow onto the form. I dreaded crying in front of a complete stranger, it made me feel vulnerable. But it was too late now, the tears had already formed a wrinkled wet spot on the piece of paper below me. It seemed to me that all I did anymore was cry.

The women behind the desk extended her hand over the desk and placed it on top of mine. HW sat up in his chair and leaned over to wrap his arms around me. For the first time in my life I felt alone, entirely and utterly alone.

After an awkward moment, HW finally said, "Just put down my name, honey." I wrote his name in the blank space provided, all the while knowing he would not be with me forever.

After we completed the paperwork, the lady behind the desk directed us down the hall to the changing room and then to the waiting room. I opened the locker they furnished me, took off all my clothes, hung them carefully in the locker and slipped into one of the flimsy blue gowns piled neatly in the corner. The first one tied to the back and the second one tied to the front, I was told. Or was it the other way round? I wondered who invented this system of dress and why. Was it easier to operate on patients wearing two gowns at a time? Couldn't you just wear one gown that opened in the front and the back? I obediently put the first gown on backwards and awkwardly tried to tie the sash in the back. I put the second gown over it and tied the second sash in the front. I felt naked.

After I finished changing, I placed the flimsy little blue slippers they provided on my feet. I thought if the object of wearing these slippers was to keep the outside dirt from getting inside, then why didn't everyone have to wear them? Everyone else on the floor was tracking dirt into the hospital with their dirty shoes. If Mama had been there, she would have told me to stop fretting the small stuff. So I placed the rest of my belongings in the locker, turned the key to lock the door and silently returned the key to the attendant.

I left the changing room and looked down the hall. The lady behind the desk was speaking to other hospital personnel, occasionally glancing over in my direction. She told us that I was next and that the procedure would take no more than three hours, including recovery. She told HW to come back in about two and one-half hours to pick me up and take me home. We stood there in the corner of the waiting room, the other patients staring and wondering why I did not have to wait as long as everyone else. I heard the lady behind the desk telling someone that I was a patient of Dr. G and that he was ready for me now. I felt small and vulnerable standing there in the blue hospital gown and matching blue slippers. HW leaned over and kissed me on the forehead, "Everything will be all right," he said, "I'll be back by 10:30 to pick you up. Stop worrying."

After he left, I moved from one area to the next, first the rest room, then another waiting room, then the operating room. Everyone who assisted me was attentive and kind. Part of me assumed that they were being nice to me because unlike many of the indigent patients, I had insurance to cover the procedure. Part of me assumed that they were being nice just for the sake of being nice, like the lady behind the desk. Part of me really didn't care. I just wanted to go home.

As the anesthesiologist started to put me under, I began to panic. I did not want to go through with the procedure. The anesthesiologist noticed that I was breathing erratically. I remember telling him that I couldn't breathe. The last thing I heard him say was, "Just relax now Terri, take a deep breath." As I slowly drifted into unconsciousness, I remember thinking, you know how to relax Terri, Mama showed you how. Just breathe.

I left the hospital feeling depressed. The surgery eliminated my physical pain, but it could not alleviate the anguish I endured from the loss of my mother.

~ ~ ~

October 25, 1995. Journal Entry
I haven't been able to write since Mama died. July 23rd, 9:18. The world stopped and an Angel named Amanda went on to help others who need her. God, I miss you so much it aches. I keep thinking about our last days, months. And now Aunt Yvonne on October 8th. What does it mean? Why has God allowed this to happen? I'm trying Mama, but it hurts so much. I just want to see you and hold you and fix all the times I wasn't there for you. Please forgive me. I know you said I gave a lot, but not nearly so much, not nearly enough Mama.

What was Mother Dear trying to tell me in my dream? She came to the door. Cathy, Benji and I were in the car. I drove. Mother Dear was dressed in her Sunday church clothes with a beautiful pink hat like the picture of her. She showed me the scrolls you left. Cathy's and Benji's spoke of love. Larry's was empty and he hit me, claiming if was my fault. I couldn't open my scroll, but Mother Dear said to wait so it wouldn't tear. I waited. I still await word from you. Mama, have I missed the signs? What was the beautiful bird on the ledge in my office trying to tell me? What of the dream about the party and the cards and the children and Aunt Yvonne? I woke up feeling your presence. I want more...Happy Birthday Terri. I know that's what you would tell me. And how proud you are about my promotion. You were always so proud of me...

October 29, 1995. Journal Entry
Nights are the hardest. Sunday nights the hardest of all. Is Aunt Yvonne really gone too? I hope the two of you are sharing time together in a more perfect form. I must remain and stay strong...

November 20, 1995, Monday. I woke up thinking that my mother wanted me to continue writing her story. It was just a feeling I had. When Nicole arose later that morning, she told me that she had a dream about Dah. I listened carefully to her recitation. Dah said that she lived not just in heaven, but also inside of her. My mother told Nicole that if she remembered her, she would live on forever.

That sealed it. Someway, somehow, the book would be written.

Mama always said that she would find a way to come back to us. She found her way in our dreams, at night in our sleep when our minds were free from the thoughts of daily life and open to messages from beyond.

15
The Legacy

January 11, 1996. I received a Spousal Petition in the mail from Larry. It was the first communication from him regarding my mother's estate. I was not sure how to respond, so I decided to seek advice regarding my options.

When Mama initially considered changing her will, she suggested that I speak to their joint attorney, Evelyn W. So I contacted her first. But Evelyn refused to talk to me citing conflict of interest. So Mama told me to contact Marsha L., another San Diego attorney whom she had used in the past. Marsha had told us to either change the will or withdraw the money from the bank and set it aside for the children. But with Larry constantly present, my mother never had the chance to do either.

I looked through my Rolodex to locate Marsha's address and phone number. I knew that it would be virtually impossible to object to the will now. But I had to try. I wrote Marsha a letter asking her whether it would be possible to object to the will. She wrote back as follows.

Dear Terri:

Your letter and other documents were received and reviewed. I do not see any defects in the will to prevent probate…

Basically, the will passes personal property to her husband and any residuary to the trust. Apparently there was no residuary of significance to pass to the trust. The trust income and principal are to be used for the survivor of the two and on the survivor's death to his children and your mother's children.

As we discussed, there is no basis for opposition to community property passing to the spouse and in this case it was willed to him.

If you have any other questions or concerns please feel free to call.

Sincerely,

Marsha L.

It was as I thought. Now it was official. There was no sense in objecting to the terms of the will during probate. The only option remaining was to attempt to appeal to Larry's sense of morality and decency. I needed to write down my thoughts. It was the only way I could effectively communicate with him. I sought guidance from my brother and sisters. I also prayed that the right words would flow through me to my pen and my paper. After much debate and many edits, I sent the following letter to Larry.

January 16, 1996

Dear Larry,

I am writing in response to the Spousal Property Petition which I received from your attorney. I was somewhat surprised to receive the papers in the mail without any prior communication from you. It has been nearly six months since

Mama passed and you have said nothing about her estate. I realize that much of this time you have been grieving the loss and probably trying to cope with life without her. I am certain it has been difficult. I did not broach the subject myself because I felt it would be insensitive on my part to inquire first about the state of Mama's affairs. But I think in order to proceed with clarity in these matters, we should have open communication.

I am not certain if you are aware, but when it became clear that Mama may not survive her illness, she asked me to help her straighten out her affairs. First, let me start out by saying that Mama clearly loved you more than life itself. She expressed concern over your ability to handle payment for the condominium in her absence. She wanted to make sure that there was enough money in the estate so that you would not be left unable to pay the mortgage.

But she distinctly expressed concern that if she died first and her entire estate was released to you, you may not provide for her children the way she intended. She was concerned about all five children, but understandably she was more concerned that you may express some hesitancy regarding her three children.

My mother's entire life was dedicated to achieving excellence within her profession and to making a better life for her children. There were often times when she could not provide for us the way she wished she could. I recall when I returned to Columbia University my second year, we could not pay the tuition and I was asked to leave my classes. It broke her heart. Together she and I decided that I should not drop out of school for financial reasons and consequently I got a part-time job and obtained substantial school loans.

Giving was an expression of love for Mama. She often gave to all five of her (and your) children, sometimes without your knowledge. She never gave away anything substantial without your knowledge, but Mama understood that if your life had been different, you would also give freely to the ones you loved. She wanted to help you let go of material things in the same way that she did, but it was not an overnight process and she did not believe that you had reached that point.

I obtained various recommendations for her regarding her concerns, but at the end she was too sick to carry out any concrete actions. She specifically stated that she wanted to give each of us an amount which would relieve us of our financial burdens. She even quantified an amount which would enable each of us to make a fresh start. Cathy would be able to quit her job and finish her Master's degree without worrying about income. I would be able to pay my school loans and my leftover house and co-op loan. Benji would be able to reduce the mortgage on his new house so that he could begin to save real money. Kathy could establish herself independently. Barbie could go back to school. Mama and I had these discussions when she was quite lucid.

I have carefully reviewed the Petition, the Wills and the Trust Document (which you and Mama previously forwarded to me). Generally the Wills both provide that personal items and household furnishings will be released to the surviving spouse and then equally to the surviving children. The language and various provisions contained in the Wills are fairly standard. The Trust is set up in much the same way, in other words, all of the assets designated in the Trust will go first to the surviving spouse and then equally to the surviving children. Thus far, however, the Trust only lists the Washington State property as the sole asset. The Petition, as I understand it, requests that the nine designated items (i.e., the car and the Merrill Lynch accounts) be released to you as the surviving spouse without the need for probate administration.

Most of what I have reviewed makes complete sense. I have a number of questions, however, which I hope you can address. I hesitate to contact Evelyn W. directly because the one time I approached her for clarification of a question from Mama regarding the estate, she told me that she could not talk to me because it would be a conflict of interest.

1. *As stated above, both Wills are fairly standard in that they make reference to personal items and household furnishings. Although we have not discussed it, Kathy and I (along with the rest of the children) will be able to equally distribute the remaining property without any problems, similar to the way we handled Mama's personal items. But if you have any specific desires for someone to receive any item in particular, you should express those intentions to us now.*

2. *At present it appears that the only asset listed in the Trust is the Washington State property. What assets have been transferred into the Trust other than the property in Washington? Your current residence and any other property, held jointly or individually, should be placed in the Trust to avoid probate or interference from creditors.*

3. *What happens to the nine items (including the Merrill Lynch accounts) which you have requested turned over to you in the Petition? I have been advised that those items should also be placed in the Trust to avoid a lengthy probate, probate fees or creditor interference. You should definitely clarify this issue if you have not already done so. My impression from discussions with Mama was that there was nearly $600,000 in the assets, contained primarily in the Merrill Lynch accounts.*

4. *Finally, I would like for you to consider distributing some of the assets of the estate to all five of your children. I am certain that Mama would want you to open yourself to that possibility. Through you, I believe that Mama can accomplish in death, what she could not attain in life.*

I trust that you will receive these comments in a loving and positive way. I apologize for communicating by letter, but because of the complexity and sensitivity of the matter, I thought it was best to write down my thoughts. I look forward to hearing from you.

With love,

Terri
cc: Kathy D.
Cathy L
Barbie S.
Benji T.

January 22, 1996. Larry did not have the decency to directly respond to my letter. Instead, he forwarded my letter to his attorney, the one who refused to talk to me in the first place. The following was her response.

Dear Terri Austin:

Larry has passed your letter on to me so that I could respond to you on his behalf.

In an effort to continue the close family relationships that have been held by both your mother and Larry throughout their relationship, Larry has authorized me to respond to your questions in some detail so that you can rest assured your mother's wishes are being carried out as planned. Let me assure you that I was in fairly constant contact with your mother and it was her final decision to leave everything to Larry upon her death. If Larry wants specific items of personal property to go to any of the children he can so designate at a future time by way of a codicil to his will.

The only asset that was transferred to the trust prior to your mother's death was the Washington property. The current residence was held as community property and can pass to Larry outright via an affidavit, thereby avoiding probate at this time. It should be put into the trust to avoid probate at his death. The items you list in your number 3 should also be placed in the trust to avoid probate at Larry's death. I will address each item separately so that you can have an accurate picture as to how they have passed to Larry as follows:

1. *Amanda's business is essentially nonexistent without her at the helm. Larry does not have the skills necessary to carry that business on. The equipment and furnishings of the business were de minimis. The debts*

have been paid and the balance of the receivables are Larry's by virtue of its being a community property asset.

2. This account was held as a joint tenancy account with automatic rights of survivorship. It all became Larry's at the moment of Amanda's death.

3. The above is true for this personal checking account also.

4. The home furnishings as community property become Larry's.

5. The car as a community property asset also becomes Larry's via an affidavit procedure with the Department of Motor Vehicles.

6. The cash account was held in joint tenancy.

7. The Business account, since acquired as community property is Larry's and becomes his.

8. This business account is the same as in item 7.

9. Obviously Larry's account, as to her interest, is Larry's also as community property.

Your impression as to the value of the entire estate was incorrect. There was considerably less than that in the estate. Anything held in joint tenancy form passes outside of the probate estate and is not subject to the will. Those assets that might have been subject to probate, are not subject to probate since their value was under $60,000. The Washington property was already in the trust.

I have taken the Spousal Property Petition matter off calendar, since the affidavit procedure is available as to the condominium and all other assets can pass either automatically or via an affidavit procedure to Department of Motor Vehicles or by presenting a certified death certificate as proof of Amanda's passing and via the trust.

If you have further questions please feel free to write me.

As I am sure you are aware, the trust provides that Larry can remove assets from the trust at any time, as well as change beneficiaries. Please see Article III, paragraph 2. It was clear from the trust that the parties wanted one another to be secure in their remaining years and to be able to have the monies available for the use of the survivor. After the death of the survivor, if any money was left it should be passed via Larry's will and any codicils to that will, and via the trust provisions and any amendments thereto. There may in fact be no money left for the children at the time of Larry's death, depending on Larry's health needs in

> his declining years, among other things. Fortunately for now he is quite healthy and can look forward to many years of vigorous life.
>
> Larry is not desirous at this time of distributing any assets prematurely, due to the vagaries of the future. I am sure you can appreciate his position in that regard.
>
> I hope you receive this letter in the spirit in which it has been sent which embodies an effort to maintain the always good relationship among the two families. Feelings are very tender at these times as you pointed out in your letter and it is Larry's desire to be allowed to carry out Amanda's wishes in the manner that the two of them mutually decided.
>
> Sincerely,
>
> Evelyn W.
> cc.: Kathy D.
>   Cathy L.
>   Barbie S.
>   Benji T.

As I held the letter in my hands, they began to shake uncontrollably. It took all the control I could muster not to rip the letter to shreds. I was tempted to call Larry and tell him to go to hell. His response to my letter was as I thought. It was even worse than I thought. I interpreted the letter as Larry saying, "You will never see a penny of your mother's estate, not now, not ever." At that moment, I wished him dead.

I carefully folded the letter and placed it in a folder in my file cabinet. I had no plans to ever look at the letter again. I folded my legs in a squatting position, hands on my knees, index fingers to thumbs. I took a deep breath and tried to clear my mind. I had to get rid of the intensely negative feelings I was harboring. The word "hate" had taken on a brand new meaning. Mama always said that hate was a harmful emotion, more harmful to the hater than the hated. We were not even allowed to use the word in our house. "You don't hate anything," Mama would say, "If you don't like something, just say you dislike it." It was one of those emotions like greed and envy that could tear you apart. Forget about the letter, I thought. Forget about Larry. Forget about the estate. Just remember Mama.

The letter from Larry's lawyer failed to accurately describe the total value of the estate. Essentially, Mama and Larry had: 1) the Washington State property which was safely held in the Trust; 2) a number of Merrill Lynch accounts held in joint tenancy and therefore not subject to probate; and 3) a few items which may have been subject to probate but were spared because the total value was less than $60,000.

The lawyer conveniently neglected to place a value on one crucial item—The Merrill Lynch accounts. Mama showed me the Merrill Lynch bank account statements before she died. As we reviewed the statements and added the numbers together, she told me that the bulk of their fortune was in these bank accounts. She said she wanted to make sure the children had access to those funds. She specifically stated that she wanted the children to take half the value of the funds and to split the proceeds equally.

She tried to go to the bank to personally withdraw the funds and distribute them to us before she died. But every time she attempted to go, Larry literally stopped her. He interrogated her about where she was going. He told her he wanted to handle any errands she needed outside of the house. He claimed she was too sick to leave the house.

Even when I visited and attempted to take Mama out alone, he would insist upon coming. It was very difficult to maneuver without him. His presence was overbearing. He literally wore her down, exhausted her spirit.

During my visit in early July, Aunt Yvonne, Nancy Brown Jamison and I finally got Mama out of the house alone. Mama helped us to concoct a list of errands which would occupy Larry for several hours. It was absurd that we had to scheme and connive just to get Mama alone. We got Mama dressed and took her to the beach to sit and talk once and for all to determine how to handle the money in the accounts. I could tell that Mama was exhausted. All this talk about money was depressing her. She looked at the three of us and said, "I can't fight it any longer. I don't have the energy to change things now. Let's just keep things the way they are. It will be much simpler that way."

And that was that. Mama had finally put the issue of the money to rest. That day on the beach, shortly before she died, she finally made a decision. It may not have been the right decision, but it was a decision just the same. We could see that a weight had been lifted now that the money issue was resolved. She took a deep breath, stood up from the bench and said, "Let's go home now, I'm tired."

Yvonne, Nancy and I looked at each other. We were all thinking the same thing. The money was not that important. The only thing that mattered to us was Mama's well being. We took Mama arm in arm and walked slowly along the beach back to the apartment, commenting along the way on the beauty of the world around us.

Based upon my review of the Merrill Lynch statements, the total value of those accounts was a little under $600,000. And so it came to pass, that my mother's entire life's work transferred not to her children as she had intended, but to the man she had known for the last six years of her life.

~ ~ ~

January 25, 1996, Thursday. I had a dream about my mother last night. As it turned out, today was the scheduled court date for the probate of her will.

I was sitting beneath a large tree in the back yard of a huge white house. Larry was there. He was giving a group of about ten people a tour of the house. This was upsetting to me and I started to cry. He was trying to explain something to me, but I couldn't understand him. I couldn't hear him. He was moving his mouth but there were no words. Then Mama appeared next to me from out of nowhere. She stood next to me and took me by the hand. No one else could see her. She was whispering to me. She told me not to worry, that everything would be all right. She held my hand and we walked right past Larry, past the crowd of people, past the huge white house. The last thing she said to me as she disappeared was, "Remember, I love you."

Then it dawned on me. My mother had already given me all that I would ever need in life. She gave me her strength, her love and her compassion. That was her message. These were my scrolls. This was her legacy.

~ ~ ~

August 17, 1996. The phone rang. I heard my secretary say, "I'm sorry, she's on the other line. Can I take a message?" Then the intercom buzzed. Marcia knew not to disturb me on the phone unless it was urgent. Patience was not one of my virtues.

I placed the first call on hold and picked up the intercom. "Who is it?" I asked curtly.

Without hesitation Marcia said, "It's your cousin Ari."

I knew then that the call must have been urgent because Marcia would not interrupt a business call for family matters. Marcia began working for me right after my mother died. Janie, my prior secretary, quit the day after the infamous phone call from Larry. I begged her not to leave. I told her that she and I would make a great team. I explained that working for the General Counsel of a subsidiary of a Fortune 500 company was a prestigious position. But nothing I said to her made a difference. She told me flat out, "You are a very nice person, but you're a perfectionist. I can't work like that."

I pondered her words for two seconds and said, "O.k., you're right, you probably would be better off someplace else." No sense in straining your pretty little head, I thought.

As it turned out, Marcia was much better suited for the position. She started working for me on August 7, 1995, two days after my mother's funeral, my first day on the new job.

Ari rarely called me at the office. Like everyone else, she thought that I was too busy to interrupt at work. I was never too busy to talk to Ari, but I must have sounded harried.

Ari was unusually quiet as I rambled for the first minute about how busy I'd been, how I cherished her recent letter and how I meant to call. I knew from the silence that something was wrong, terribly wrong. Part of me did not want to stop rambling because I dreaded hearing any more bad news. I worried about Aunt Adrienne, Ari's mom. I realized how difficult it must be to lose both of your sisters three months apart. I prayed that she would remain strong.

Instead, Ari said, "Dad died this morning. We don't know exactly what happened. They said that it was a heart attack but nothing was wrong with his heart. Last week Dad fell and broke his hip. We didn't even bother calling because it was not life threatening. So we took him to the hospital and he was doing fine. Then we transferred him to the rehab center and two days later he died. It just doesn't make sense. Mom's having an autopsy done."

Ari was right. It didn't make sense. I tried to take it all in, but I didn't know what to think or what to say. "Oh God, Ari, I'm so sorry. How is Aunt Adrienne?" I asked, thinking that losing two sisters and now her husband is more than any one person should have to bear.

"She's hanging in there. You know Mom, from the outside she always looks so strong, but I'm worried about her. She doesn't really have any very close friends. You know, Nancy (Brown Jamison) has been great, and she keeps up with Mom even though it's been a year since Auntie La La died. She really is a remarkable woman. It's like she's made our family part of her own family. She gives and gives and never expects anything in return."

"I know. She's a Godsend," I said. "No doubt about it, she's simply an angel. Mom and Aunt Yvonne must be looking down and smiling on us because they know that Nancy Brown Jamison will be our source of comfort."

"I don't know anyone else who even comes close to her," Ari said.

"Me neither," I replied.

Ari and I discussed the funeral arrangements and I assured her that I would be there. Uncle Afton said that he wanted to be cremated. It surprised me that a conservative old man like Uncle Afton would want to be cremated. But after my mother was cremated, Uncle Afton decided that would be best for him too.

According to the memorial service program, Uncle Afton was born in Birmingham, Alabama on February 25, 1922. He served in the Air Force and received his Bachelors degree in Business Administration at Wilberforce University in Ohio in 1948. Afton later worked side by side with his father as owner of Lee Grocery store located in the Homewood section of Birmingham. He also invested in real estate and other properties which he developed, leased and sold. He was well known in the community and always "on the go." He and Adrienne were married in 1955. He was survived by his wife and three lovely children, Ari, Michael and Adrienne.

My cousin James, who is a Southern Baptist minister, said a few words at the service, as he had done for my mother and for Aunt Yvonne only months earlier. "And the Lord gave Afton a purpose, to show us the importance of being entrepreneurial, of giving back to our community, of being a strong family man. And like Amanda and Yvonne before him, Afton has returned to the Promised Land where he awaits the arrival of his beloved family."

James' delivery could only be described as eloquent. He had grown into an admirable young man. At the age of twenty-four, he had acquired his own congregation in Miami, Florida. A congregation which admired him so much, it purchased a home for him and his young family. Preaching came naturally to cousin James, the first born child of James Fouther, Aunt Yvonne's twin brother.

When James finished speaking, the church choir sang two gospel selections, bringing tears to my eyes. I noticed tears streaming down my brother's cheek as well. It was uncharacteristic for him. I found a tissue and wiped his face. He reached across my leg and squeezed my hand. I knew he was thinking about Mama. So was I. There were many friends and family members who shed tears of sadness that day. Too many had perished in too short a time. Let it stop now, please let it stop.

When the service concluded, we proceeded from the church in an orderly fashion, greeting all those who had come to pay their last respects. We gathered outside in the summer heat and stood around talking and hugging and kissing, until Father Wilson came out and said that it was time to come back in and be seated in the church's dining room. The family sat together as others clamored to sit as close to us as possible.

Members of the church, who I recognized from the two previous funerals that year, prepared each of our plates. Everyone received respectable portions of smoked ham, rice, green beans, macaroni and cheese, and cornbread. For dessert, we had a selection of apple pie, sweet potato pie and pound cake. All of the food was home made. It was a Southern tradition to mark the passing of a loved one through prayer and food. Through hushed tones, Ari and Aunt Adrienne remarked that they were pleased to see real china and fresh flowers on each of the tables. It was a small gesture that did not go unnoticed. It was a sign of respect from the congregation to Uncle Afton for his contributions to the community as one of only a few African American entrepreneurs.

~ ~ ~

September 1996, Essay written by my daughter Nicole in second grade at P.S. 87

"My Grandma"

Me and my family had a good time at poppy's, everybody except my grandma. Me and my family went out on boat, everybody but my grandma.

My grandma had passed away not so long ago. And my mom is making a long story about her. My grandma always greeted me when I came to her house. She lived in San Diego. I remember going to her funeral, it made me cry. It was a pretty big place. It had a t.v. for the kids. And my cousins were there. I love when they come. They are so comforting. But they make me feel small.

The seats at the funeral were comfortable. My poppy is really depressed. But I think that my grandma is enjoying herself in heaven. It's like she will burst into flowers and feel much better. Taking her time she will kiss the little child angels. She will dance with many men at a grand ball, wearing the most prettiest flower dress. It is brown, light brown. My grandma is having the greatest time, even if she does miss me. Someday I will be in heaven too.

I remember when I went in her computer room and listened to headsets when she was on the phone. In the headsets you could hear her talking on the phone. Her computer had a haunted house on it. At her house she has a pool and a jacuzzi. The pool is three feet to eight and a half.

Poppy does not let us play with a lot of his toys because he is depressed, I feel sorry for him. I remember when my grandma went out very early to jog. I remember when she used to bring me and my brother to the park. There was even a river there.

I miss my grandma. I wish she was alive again. I remember those good times when grandma took me everywhere. My grandma had black short hair. She was beautiful, and she wore a beautiful robe.

My grandma gives me Spider magazines. They come in almost everyday, even though she is not alive. She gives my brother Ladybug magazines. My grandma loves children, she adores them.

My grandma's house has carpeting. A couch in her house folds up. She has two beautiful statues above her fireplace. She has two cats, one named Bogart the other named Whiskers. She never got mad at me or my brother. When we spread my grandma's ashes it was like spreading magic into the sea. Grandmas are important because they treat you with love.

~ ~ ~

October 6, 1996. My mother came to me in a dream last night. As I sat on the bed next to her dying body, she wheezed slowly in and out. There was no one else in the room. It was dimly lit and completely quiet, except for the sound of her troubled breath. She abruptly took one long last breath and then there was silence.

I reached out to touch her, but she did not move. Her hands were cold. Suddenly, without warning she reached for me. The unexpected movement frightened me. She began to smile and then laughed aloud as if to allay my fears. "Don't be frightened," she said, "I just want you to tell Cathy not to worry. It's O.K. that she wasn't there."

At first I wasn't sure what she meant. I looked at her and asked, "Mama, are you really here?"

"Yes I am really here. Don't you believe me? Do you want me to write it down for you?"

"Would you? Could you really write it down for me?"

"Yes you silly girl, go and get me an ink pen."

I awoke and rose from my bed in the middle of the night. I felt my mother's presence near the desk, which was in the corner of my bedroom. I walked towards the living room to get a pen and pad and carefully placed them on my desk. I quickly returned to my bed fearing what might happen next, grateful that Nicole and Christopher were there to cuddle.

I awoke and rose the next morning and anxiously approached the desk. Even though I had been dreaming the night before, I had actually arisen and placed a pad and pen on the desk. I cautiously picked up the pad. I half expected to see words on that pad, words that Mama had written in the middle of the night, words confirming that she had been there and that she was here to stay. The print at the top of the pad read, "From the desk of Terri Austin." The rest of the page was blank. I held the pad up to the light see if there might be a visible imprint. A blank page starred back at me. I thought about how silly I must look and then proceeded to get dressed.

Later that morning, my sister Cathy called. As usual, her timing was uncanny. I suddenly realized what the dream meant. My mother wanted Cathy not to worry about missing her dying breath. That had to be the meaning, otherwise why would she have come to me on her death bed. I recanted the dream to Cathy in as much detail as possible. There was silence on the other end of the phone. It was difficult for us to talk about my mother.

"Did she say anything else?" she asked hesitantly.

"No, but she was adamant about giving you the message." I hung up the phone hoping the message helped.

October 12, 1996. My mind wandered off as I fell asleep. I dreamt that Mama was with me. She was talking to me and holding my hand as others looked at me in disbelief, shaking their heads saying that she was not really there with me. All except my stepsister Kathy, who not only believed Mama was walking and talking to me, but also wanted to know what Mama thought about organized religions.

Mama gave me and Kathy a big smile and told us that all religions were the same. "There is a God," she said, "a great God who is there for everyone. He is neither black nor white, neither male nor female. He exists everywhere, on heaven and on earth, inside of you and inside of me. He just is." Mama was so confident in her conviction, as if she had been in the presence of God.

It has been just over a year since my mother passed. Everyone said that the pain would pass, but I have not found that to be the case. Not a day goes by that I don't think about her. It's the little things. The things we take for granted, like children playing or sunsets. It's every little thing.

16

Saving the Best for Last

April 1997. Mama would have loved him. In many respects, I truly believe that she sent him to me. I was formally introduced to Dr. Ben Chiles at the 40th birthday party for my best friend Theresa. The party was organized by Theresa's husband, Vernon. Vernon's father was Ben's godfather and his dad's best friend. Ben was invited to the party because, like me, he was considered family.

Both sides of the family attended the party, all of Theresa's relatives and all of Vernon' relatives. Their friends from high school, college and law school were there. Even childhood friends from their respective neighborhoods attended the party.

The surprise celebration was held at a colossal banquet hall in southern New Jersey. Vernon hired a disc jockey who played hits from the 70's and 80's including *Celebration* by Kool and the Gang, *That's the Way of the World* by Earth, Wind and Fire and *My Girl* by the Temptations. The nostalgic music inspired us to our feet and conjured up images of the good ole days when boys made butterflies flutter in your stomach during dark basement parties or sent chills up your spine from across the stacks of books in the school library. People were dancing and singing to the oldies but goodies, like it was just yesterday, singing the parts known, humming the parts forgotten.

My escort to the party was a really nice guy who I had been dating for a couple of months despite the lack of chemistry between us. I continued dating him thinking that the sparks would eventually ignite. They never did.

My date and I sat at a table with many of my friends from law school. We drank spiked punch and ate plates full of Southern style food. The food made me feel right at home. I had not eaten all day and the smell of the food was making my stomach growl. I filled my plate with spicy barbecue chicken, collard greens, mashed potatoes and corn bread. I picked around at the plate, avoiding any food I could not eat with a fork and knife. I desperately wanted to grab the juicy fat chicken thigh in the middle of the plate and suck the rest of the meat off of the bone, but my table manners wouldn't allow me to do so in public.

Having satisfied my initial hunger pangs, I was ready to mix and mingle. I rose alone from the table, telling my date that I'd be right back. I was wearing a knee length black silky skirt with a side slit and a tight cream colored sweater showing off my curves, which fortunately were still in all the right places. I felt the eyes from my table follow my hips across the dance floor. The extra attention did not bother me.

I spotted my best friend Theresa standing on the other side of the dance floor, talking to some friends. She saw me approaching and waved her hand back and forth in the air as if to say, "Come on girl, let's paaaaarty!" I accommodated and shook my hips back and forth to the music in synch with the movement of her hips. When we stopped dancing and clowning around, Ben approached us.

He was 6' 4", handsome and at the age of 32, much younger than me and Theresa. In fact, Theresa introduced him as "little Bennie." He was entering the last year of his neurosurgical residency program at NYU. I remember thinking, wow, handsome and smart. I also remember thinking that he was too young for a 40 year old single mother of two. The introduction lasted only a minute, then my date rushed in and swept me away to the dance floor, very much aware of another man encroaching upon his territory.

This meeting was not actually my first encounter with Ben. I later learned that this was, in fact, our second encounter. Ben saw me for the first time in August 1982, at Theresa's wedding. He was 17 years old, barely a high school graduate. I was nearly 25. He saw me standing next to Theresa dressed in a long pink gown waiting in line with the rest of her bridesmaids to accompany her back down the aisle. Years after we were married, Ben told me that he decided right then and there, at Theresa's wedding, that we would spend our lives together. It was a force greater than the two of us. Chemistry. Nature's way of preserving the species. The will of our future daughter Amanda creating her path to us.

July 4, 1997. We were destined to meet for a third time. This time, we would not be separated. I was in the lobby of a building overlooking the East River, headed to the apartment of a mutual acquaintance who was giving a Fourth of July party. Ben walked up to me and introduced himself. I told him that I thought he looked familiar. He stood a foot over me smiling, knowing full well where we had met, though he led me on, pretending not to remember. As we stood beneath the fireworks, I could not deny the attraction. Ben made sure that before the evening concluded, he got my phone number. He would not let me slip away this time. The rest, as they say, is history.

October 25, 1997. Three months after we began dating and on my fortieth birthday, Ben asked me to marry him. I kept thinking to myself that Mama would have loved him. Ben said that he wished he could have met her. He said that she must have been a very special lady. I am convinced that she was present on the night he proposed.

On that brisk October evening, Ben took me to one of the most romantic restaurants in all of New York City, called One if By Land, Two if by Sea. The restaurant is located in an 18th century carriage house in the heart of Greenwich Village. Folklore suggests that the tunnels underneath the building were used to smuggle contraband during the Revolutionary War and were part of the Underground Railroad during the American Civil War. Hence, the owners of the restaurant appropriately named the restaurant, One if By Land, Two if by Sea, the phrase for signaling potential peril.

The restaurant had exposed brick walls, bright gold chandeliers and huge stone fireplaces. The lavish décor included extravagant floral arrangements, dramatic artwork and enormous mirrors draping the walls.

I had heard a great deal about the restaurant from friends and colleagues who predicted that a proposal was forthcoming. I sensed it was coming too, because of the tension surrounding the arrangements. "Make sure you're not late," he told me. "I want you to be there on time."

There was a pianist on the main floor whose melodic sounds greeted us as we entered. When we arrived at our table, there were two long stem yellow roses in a small vase in the middle of the table. I thought it was an interesting coincidence that my mother's favorite flower garnished our table. As we settled into dinner, Ben told me how lucky he felt to share his world with me and my two children. Then, just as he took out the ring and began his proposal, the pianist began to play, *Wind Beneath My Wings* by Bette Midler. It was my mother's favorite song. She once told me that this particular song reminded her of our relationship. "That's funny," I told her. "Me too."

That's when I realized it. These events were not mere coincidences. First the yellow roses, then the song. This was my mother's way of signifying that she was happy for me. I began to sob uncontrollably in the middle of the proposal. At first, Ben thought that I was simply overwhelmed by the proposal. But I could not stop crying. I tried to explain, but it was difficult for him to understand. He waited patiently until I regained enough composure to say "yes" to his proposal. I left the restaurant holding his hand knowing that my mother was with me, knowing that I had made the right decision.

A year and a half later, Ben and I were blessed with a beautiful, bright baby girl. We named her Amanda. We call her our miracle baby because at the age of 42, conception and childbirth were difficult at best. I trust that Nicole and Christopher and Amanda will all grow up to be strong, loving and compassionate, just like their grandmother.

If I had my druthers.

Afterword

My mother experienced many difficult times, but with each trial and tribulation, she emerged stronger and wiser. Though it all, she managed to provide us with food, clothing, shelter and enough love to nurture 20 families. These are quotes from a few people whose lives she touched and changed forever.

My Sister Cathy

Mama had to select a name for herself at one of her NTL conferences one year. She asked us to pick it for her. We chose "Rainbow," which she proudly displayed on her ID badge. She told me that one person at the conference commented that rainbows were just illusions and not real at all. She said it made her think about the name, but the more she thought about it, the more she liked it.

Brother Ben

I guess being raised around mostly women has had an impact on me. I have probably survived because of "HPM."

HPM stands for Head Preserving Maneuvers. As a man who has a strong, sword wielding woman, you must learn to implement Head Preserving Maneuvers. There are number of them. For instance, you may have to tell your strong, sword wielding woman, 'You are right, I am wrong, I am sorry.' Or, you might say, 'If you are happy, I am happy.'

It is also important to have a head basket readily available because if your strong, sword wielding woman decides to wield her sword, the head will roll and the basket will enable you to catch and keep the rolling head. That way, once the wielding ceases, at least you will still have your head. Sometimes she may feel it is necessary to cut off more than just the head, then, of course, you will need more than a HPM...

Aunt Adrienne

The thing I remember most about your mother was the way she made decisions. She may not always have made the right decisions, but she made them just the same. She recognized when circumstances were not right or when she was not happy. When she realized something was wrong, she took action to improve the situation. So many people can't do that. Most people are afraid of change. Not your mother. She was not afraid of anything, not even the prospect of being alone. I was always impressed by her ability to make a change.

The first time she surprised us all was when she announced that she was going to enter and win that beauty contest to pay for school. We supported her, but no one really thought she would do it. She shocked us again when she decided to leave your dad. We had no idea that was coming. She made decisions as though she understood life was short and there was no time to waste in an unhappy situation. I think by the time she realized the situation with Larry was not good, it was too late. She did not have the energy to make a change. He killed her spirit. You cannot survive without your spirit.

One of my first memories of your mother was that she loved to swim. Of course, we did not have a swimming pool, but that didn't stop your mother. There was a swimming pool at the park out in Insley where we went to school. Insley was in another neighborhood and we had to take a trolley car to get there. The first time she came back from swimming at Insley Park her skin was a golden red tan. Her normal skin tone was olive colored which looked so beautiful when it was tanned. Your mother was so beautiful.

Cousin Ari

Auntie La La always strove to be a better person. She pursued her career with so much passion and determination. Each time she attained one level she reached for higher ground. I marveled at her view of the world. She was very understanding. She would tell you to know yourself, always know yourself first. You know she was very progressive for her time. She was a risk taker.

The earliest image I have of her was when she posed on a stage, for a fashion show or a beauty contest, or something like that. I remember a picture of her posing on that stage. Remember?

My last memory was praying that she would have the strength to put her affairs in order before she passed. The first time she called to tell me and Mom about the cancer, she didn't sound very good. When she called back, she sounded a little better, but we were still very worried. At first we thought all of our prayers had been answered. But then it got worse.

My fondest memory of Auntie La La was in August of 1990 when I came to San Diego to visit her. She wanted to help me prepare my body and mind for the surgery to remove my fibroids. She took me to a natural hot springs spa right outside of San Diego. We were completely pampered with healthy food, mud baths and massages. When I left I felt like mush, in a good way. She was always very health oriented. That's why this whole thing is so hard to understand.

Cousin Michael

My fondest memory of Auntie La La was when you all came to visit Birmingham shortly after she and Bob were divorced. She had just moved from a big house in Houston to a small apartment in Philadelphia. I knew that she did not have a stereo system to listen to her music. Even though I didn't have much money of my own, I decided to spend it on a stereo system for her. I just felt like she could use something good right about then, something that would uplift her spirits.

So I gave her the stereo. Boy, you would have thought that I had just given her the world. You don't know how much that meant to her. The gratitude in her face was incredible. She kept telling me, "Michael, this means so much to me. It means so much to me." Really it was a small gesture, but she made me feel like a king, like I had done something really special, something really great.

Jackie (Wife of Cousin Michael)

I only met her once. It was at Ari's wedding on September 3, 1994. Michael introduced her to me. I remember hearing about her and looking forward to meeting her. I had on high heel shoes and was wearing something short. She said, "Girl, you must be a Fouther. Look at those legs. Michael, she looks like our family." Michael had this huge grin on his face, like he had just let the cat out of the bag. That was the last time I saw her.

My Girlfriend Theresa

I remember the very first time I met your mother. You and she came to our first apartment in Chatham, New Jersey. It was in October of 1982, around your birthday. We had recently graduated from law school and Vernon and I had just gotten married that May.

The apartment was small but seemed larger because we had no furniture. We never did furnish that apartment. You and your mom came for dinner to celebrate your birthday. That was back just after law school when we had time for each other, before you got married and before I started having babies. Life was much simpler then.

We were drinking wine, eating spaghetti and playing Luther Vandross on that little component stereo we had. We laughed and joked late into the night. At some point during the evening your mother realized that she had misplaced her thyroid medicine. Vernon called his dad and Doc got a prescription for her. She was so grateful to Vernon and Doc for doing her that favor. It was really nothing, but your mom made us feel like we had moved the world for her.

The thing I remember most about Amanda was her laughter and the way her smile lit up her entire face. Her smile and her laughter were contagious.

My Son Christopher

January 6th 2000

Dear Dah,

I really miss you. I chose to write about you because you are my mom's mom. I love you as much as my mom. Do you celebrate Christmas in heaven? I did. I love you. Is god a boy or girl? Is god black, white or brown? Does god have blond hair? Is Martin Luther King up there? I wish you were down here.

Love,

Chris

My Daughter Nicole

Dah was a wonderful person. She was never alone because she always had us around her. And she was very well known. I liked it when we talked to each other on those headphones in her office. She was a kind lovable grandmother. And I loved her very, very much, and I always will. It will be a long time till I see her, but I will never forget her. (Interview conducted shortly after my mother's death on July 23, 1995.)

978-0-595-39227-8
0-595-39227-X

Printed in the United States
51287LVS00003B/205-237